HOT SHOT TOTTENHAM

GARETH
DACE

HOT
SHOT

SPURS IN
THE 80s

TOTTENHAM

HODDLE, HUMMEL
AND HAZARDS

pitch

First published by Pitch Publishing, 2025

1

Pitch Publishing
9 Donnington Park,
85 Birdham Road,
Chichester, West Sussex,
PO20 7AJ
www.pitchpublishing.co.uk
info@pitchpublishing.co.uk

A CIP catalogue record is available for this book
from the British Library.

ISBN 978 1 83680 190 0

Typesetting and origination by Pitch Publishing

MIX
Paper | Supporting
responsible forestry
FSC® C016779

Printed and bound on FSC® certified paper in line with
our continuing commitment to ethical business practices,
sustainability and the environment.

Printed and bound in India by Replika Press Pvt. Ltd.

CONTENTS

PROLOGUE

IN 1961 Tottenham Hotspur completed an historic double, becoming the first English club in the 20th century to win the Football League championship and the FA Cup in the same season. That Spurs team, managed by Bill Nicholson, were not only the best team in the country but also the most stylish, playing with the swagger and flamboyance associated with the club since its founding.

That double team has become the high watermark for everything the club is about. Captain Danny Blanchflower famously explained that 'the game is about glory'. It wasn't merely about winning but doing it in style.

The FA Cup was retained the following year, by which time Spurs had completed the audacious signing of Jimmy Greaves, who went to embody the glamour and style of the club.

Spurs followed up domestic dominance with success on the continent. Cheated out of the 1962 European Cup semi-final against Benfica, they went on to become the first British club to win a European club competition by beating Atlético Madrid 5-1 in the 1963 European Cup Winners' Cup.

More FA Cup success followed in 1967 but the team was undergoing major transformation. As the 70s arrived, a second iconic Nicholson team that included Jennings, Mullery, Gilzean, Chivers and a young Steve Perryman emerged. Always falling slightly short in the league, Spurs established themselves as a 'cup team' and more silverware followed – the newly established Football League Cup in 1971 and 1973 sandwiched the 1972 UEFA Cup success in European football's new tertiary competition.

Football was changing, though. Defensive and cynical tactics became mainstream and provided a blueprint for success for many. The 1970 FA Cup Final replay between Chelsea and Leeds resembled a battle scene and shamed English football. League titles were won by the most disciplined teams, not the most entertaining. The FA Cup continued to capture the imagination, though the famous trophy evaded Spurs throughout the 70s.

The abolition of the maximum wage in 1961 gave players, and not owners, the upper hand. It changed the dynamic in transfer and contract negotiations. The Spurs board and chairman Sidney Wale refused to pay the high wages being demanded and wouldn't entertain the underhand tactics used by others to attract the best talent.

When Spurs played Feyenoord in the 1974 UEFA Cup Final, the second leg in Rotterdam was marred by unsavoury scenes of hooliganism. The vast majority of Spurs fans were victims but some had instigated the ugly scenes. When Nicholson himself came out to address them at half-time, he was distraught to be totally ignored.

Spurs lost over two legs – the first time they'd ever lost a major final – and four games into the new season, Nicholson resigned, feeling that football and society had moved on without him. It was widely assumed and hoped that his successor would be Danny Blanchflower but the board went leftfield by appointing the Hull manager and former Arsenal captain Terry Neill in one of the most baffling managerial appointments in the club's history. Neill did at least make a sound decision when he chose the unknown Newcastle first-team coach Keith Burkinshaw as his assistant.

Neill inherited an ageing side that was in desperate need of a rebuild. They survived relegation in 1975 and rallied the following year, helped by the emergence of teenage sensation Glenn Hoddle. Neill left that summer to join Arsenal and Burkinshaw was promoted to manager. His first season was an unmitigated disaster. Spurs were relegated and would play in the second tier for the first time since 1950.

It is almost unthinkable today that a Spurs manager could survive relegation but the board kept faith with Burkinshaw and Spurs returned to the top division at the first time of asking. Determined to make their way back towards the top of English football, they scooped the world with the stunning double acquisition of Argentine World Cup winners Ossie Ardiles and Ricky Villa in the summer of 1978. It was a reminder that Spurs wanted to do things in style. To Dare Is To Do.

In Perryman, Hoddle, Villa and Ardiles, Burkinshaw had the genesis of the great team that would emerge but, as the 70s closed, Spurs were in a state of transition. They finished that first season back in Division One in mid-table but a number of talented youngsters were knocking on the door of the first team. Burkinshaw also insisted on bringing Bill Nicholson back to the club in a scouting capacity. Nicholson had previously been in exile, working for West Ham, since leaving Spurs.

Burkinshaw had insisted on the creation of a Spurs under-15s team as a transition from schoolboy training into the apprentices who made up the youth team. Aided by a coaching team of Peter Shreeve, Robbie Stepney and double-winning left-back Ron Henry, Burkinshaw and Spurs would soon the reap the rewards for the next decade.

To set the scene as the 80s approached, it's important to provide the wider context of the archaic state that English football was in. The disgraceful scenes in the stands in Rotterdam in 1974 became more widespread. Far from being an outlier, hooliganism became rife. If the football establishment didn't trust supporters, then it was equally true that match-going fans couldn't trust the facilities they'd experience upon arriving at most grounds. Many hadn't seen a lick of paint in more than half a century and some were literally falling apart. It was a tragedy waiting to happen – and tragedies did happen.

Beyond the FA Cup Final, there was little appetite among clubs for football to be televised. Club directors were wary of live football, believing it would drive crowds, and revenue, away from stadiums.

The 80s were to prove to be as transformative for football as they were for society. The story of how football changed is told through the prism of Tottenham Hotspur in this book, which aims to highlight a decade of transformation as football emerged from the dark ages into the revolutionary 90s.

You may have read my first book, *Is Gascoigne Going To Have a Crack?*, which tells the story of the 90s. The 90s was a decade I recall vividly but, having only been born in 1981, the 80s have always been a curiosity for me.

My motivation for researching and writing about the 80s was to establish the genesis of the neurotic 90s. I'd grown up on stories of the great Spurs teams of the early 80s but wanted to understand how they'd gone from a team that perennially won cups and challenged for league titles to becoming also-rans living in the shadow of Arsenal by the time my obsession with the club began in 1988.

In this book, you'll read about all the players, managers and owners who played their part in a transformative decade for the club and for English football. You'll hear first-hand accounts from several players, supporters and journalists who were there. The book runs through the decade, season-by-season, and I start each season by giving you the 'average' starting XI. This isn't an exact science – it shows which player appeared the most times in each position, usually in a 4-4-2 formation but with the obvious exception of 86/87.

I hope that you will enjoy reading this book as much as I enjoyed researching and writing it. The only regret I felt was that I hadn't been born ten years earlier so that I could have lived through this incredible decade myself!

79/80 – THE EMERGENCE
OF A GHOD

DAINES

PERRYMAN   MILLER   McALLISTER   HUGHTON

YORATH

HODDLE   ARDILES

VILLA

ARMSTRONG   JONES

THE PREVIOUS season had its ups and downs but, having returned to the First Division after a one-year hiatus, Spurs had consolidated in mid-table and went into the 1979 off-season hopeful – but not expectant – that better times were coming. Spurs fan Paul Malshinger sets the scene:

> After the euphoria of Ardiles and Villa in 1978, it all went very flat. That first season had been disappointing and we hoped that 79/80 would see more signings of that calibre – but we didn't! Other than the Argentines, Hoddle and Perryman, our squad was short on quality, even though we had a few good youngsters about. The likes of Pratt and Naylor were coming to the end of their careers and we had not successfully replaced Pat Jennings.

Heavy defeats in the first half of 78/79 against Liverpool and Arsenal encouraged Burkinshaw to turn to the exceptional talent coming through the youth team, nurtured by Peter Shreeve.

The best example was defender Paul 'Maxi' Miller, who was given his debut at Arsenal in April 1979. Though Spurs narrowly lost 1-0, Miller impressed and kept his place for the remainder of the season. Mark Falco and Stuart Beavon had also made their first-team debuts. Terry Gibson had signed as an apprentice in the summer of 1979. He and his peers benefitted from Keith Burkinshaw's insistence on creating an under-15s team, as Terry explains:

> By the mid-70s, there was no youth system as such. You signed at 14 as a 'schoolboy', which meant training twice a week at the ball court at White Hart Lane with coaches Ron Henry and Robbie Stepney. There was no games programme until Keith decided the under-15s should play matches on Sunday mornings at the training ground. Peter Shreeve was the manager but Keith was always there watching and would give input to team talks. He knew us all by first name and it's no surprise that so many of us got into the first team.

As for the first team, after the customary post-season international tour – Spurs travelled to Kuwait, Malaysia, Japan and, finally, Bermuda between mid-May and early June – summer saw no new immediate arrivals.

Appearing frequently was Tony Galvin, who had enjoyed a dramatic rise to prominence. The Yorkshire-born Irishman had been playing non-league football for Goole Town while also on a teacher training programme (he had already completed a degree in Russian Studies). Bill Nicholson, by now the club's chief scout, had watched Galvin and recommended that Keith Burkinshaw sign the 21-year-old in the summer of 1978.

Galvin spent much of the 78/79 season in the reserves and was encouraged, by Burkinshaw, to complete his teacher training, so spent his weekdays in Nottingham, returning to London at the weekend to play in reserve-team games, also making one appearance for the first team. With his course completed, Galvin joined the first-team squad on a full-time basis in the summer of 1979.

Galvin was a winger and added to the abundance of creative players who could make goals. He may not have possessed the flair or natural skill of Hoddle, Ardiles or Villa but his energy and hard work provided a balance in midfield.

The problem for Spurs hadn't been lack of creativity. It was a failure to take the chances created. In 78/79, only Peter Taylor, a winger, had hit double figures in the league. Gerry Armstrong (1), Chris Jones (five), Colin Lee (seven) and Ian Moores (0) scored just 13 goals between them. The 18-year-old Mark Falco had scored on his debut at the end of the season but wasn't yet considered a senior player.

Spurs' first acquisition of the summer was 29-year-old Terry Yorath, the captain of Wales, from Coventry and he brought leadership qualities to strengthen the starting XI.

Aside from Yorath, the team for the opening day of the season at home to Middlesbrough was virtually identical to that which finished the previous season, with Colin Lee still playing out of his natural position as right-back. John Lacy, Perryman and Gordon Smith made up the rest of the defence. John Pratt and Yorath provided the balance for the creative trio of Ardiles, Hoddle and Villa in midfield, with Falco selected for just his second start as a lone striker. Chris Jones was the substitute.

Barry Daines was selected in goal, despite the fact that Milija Aleksic had started in each of the pre-season matches. This continued a pattern, since Pat Jennings had left in 1977, of never quite knowing who was Spurs' best goalkeeper. Mark Kendall had been selected most frequently the previous season, with 23 league appearances, while Daines – long-term understudy to Jennings – had started the season before featuring just twice after October. Aleksic ended the season as first-choice custodian.

It proved to be a hugely disappointing start to the season, as Middlesbrough won 3-1 at White Hart Lane, with Hoddle's late consolation the only moment of joy for the home crowd.

The mood didn't improve; Spurs were thumped 4-0 at Norwich and then lost 3-1 at Stoke, where the Potters' quick forward, Garth Crooks, impressed with two goals.

The League Cup, the last trophy Spurs had won back in 1973, paired Spurs with Manchester United in the second round, with the first leg taking place at White Hart Lane on 29 August. Spurs had met United in the FA Cup quarter-finals the previous season and were knocked out following a 2-0 replay defeat at Old Trafford.

In many ways, United and Spurs were kindred spirits. Both were synonymous with playing attractive football and had done so successfully, winning league championships, cup competitions and being victorious in Europe during the 60s. Both clubs went into decline during the 70s, each suffering the ignominy of relegation before coming straight back up.

By the end of the 70s, United had established themselves as 'cup specialists' – they may only have won one of the three FA Cup Finals they appeared in between 1976 and 1979 but had used those experiences to build a team that was expected to finally challenge Liverpool for the league title.

Under the lights at White Hart Lane, Burkinshaw brought Paul Miller back for the first time that season and, due to injuries in the full-back position, selected Chris Hughton, who had graduated through the club's youth system. Hughton, a right-footer, would play on the left side. He had joined Spurs as a 13-year-old and only turned professional in the summer of 1979, having completed an apprenticeship as a lift engineer.

Spurs secured their first win of the season, courtesy of a 2-1 victory in which the much-maligned John Pratt scored early and then Hoddle added a memorable second. Yorath played a quick free kick forwards to Hoddle, who played an instinctive one-two with Ardiles on the edge of the area. This element alone spoke volumes of the chemistry which had developed between the two. Ardiles's lay-off presented an opportunity for Hoddle, who duly obliged with a sublime strike. With both feet off the ground, his volley cannoned off the stanchion.

Sadly, the goal counted for little in the context of the tie when United pulled one back – a valuable away goal. United would go on to win the second leg 3-1, knocking Spurs out of the League Cup.

In between the cup ties, Spurs did finally record their first league victory of the season with a 2-1 win against Manchester City. Hughton and Miller retained their places in the starting XI but it was Hoddle, again, who earned the plaudits, scoring one of the goals. One win became two the following weekend when Brighton were beaten, Gerry Armstrong scoring his first goal in more than a year. The game was a memorable one for Peter Southey, another young full-back who made what turned out to be his only first-team appearance.

Southey's story is the most tragic of the decade. He played the rest of the season in the reserves but during the following summer's pre-season, he struggled during cross-country runs. Encouraged to seek medical advice, blood tests revealed that he had leukaemia and he sadly passed away in December 1983.

September began with a heavy 5-2 defeat at Southampton but Spurs then embarked on a nine-game unbeaten streak that included four consecutive league wins. In one of the most incident-packed games of the decade, Spurs won 2-1 at Leeds, despite having to replace injured goalkeeper Barry Daines in the 13th minute, with Hoddle taking over between the sticks.

It wasn't the first time an outfield player had 'donned' the green jersey for Spurs mid-game but the last known incident occurred in 1937 when Les Howe replaced Jack Hall in goal. Hoddle recalls in his 2021 book *Playmaker* that when it became clear Daines couldn't continue, Steve Perryman and Don McAllister were holding an inquest to decide who should play in goal. Hoddle, one of the tallest players, was asked if he fancied it. In his youthful naivety, he replied that he used to play in goal 'over the park'. Instantly regretting it, Hoddle was thrown the gloves and goalkeeper's jersey. Hoddle wrote:

> I had no idea what I was doing. Although I loved going in goal, I had no idea where to stand in an actual game. I was like a cat on a hot tin roof. It was total panic.

By half-time, the score was 1-1 but Spurs were now also down to ten men after Paul Miller was sent off.

Hoddle was able to seek advice from assistant manager Pat Welton – a former professional goalkeeper – at half-time, with Welton lecturing him about positioning and how to organise the defence. After the break, not only did the Spurs defence protect Hoddle and avoid conceding, they also managed to score the decisive goal through Chris Jones.

Three further wins followed the heroics in West Yorkshire. The third of those wins – 1-0 against reigning European champions Nottingham Forest – was decided by another exquisite goal from Hoddle. Aleksic's long kick was headed on by Chris Jones to Gerry Armstrong, who, in turn, nodded the ball into the path of Hoddle. What happened next lives long in the memory for all of the 49,038 who were honoured to have witnessed it live. The ball dropped just inside the right corner of the Forest penalty area and Hoddle acrobatically thumped a volley past Peter Shilton in front of the Park Lane End.

The ball hadn't touched the floor but Hoddle's technique to strike a moving ball in mid-air made the headlines on that weekend's TV highlights packages and helped to alert the nation about this precocious talent. The goal was scored from almost the same blade of grass that he'd scored the incredible goal against Manchester United in the League Cup just eight weeks prior.

Spurs were momentarily up into fifth going into a tough run of fixtures against Liverpool, Everton and Manchester United. With Spurs still seeking a first win at Anfield since way back in 1912, the year the Titanic sank, Liverpool were too strong for them and won by the narrow margin of 2-1. A week later, Spurs returned to Merseyside, drawing 1-1 with Everton.

Manchester United came back to White Hart Lane on 1 December. Hoddle scored again but United maintained their position at the top of Division One with a 2-1 victory.

It was a great period for Hoddle. He'd finally been given a long-awaited full England debut in the Euro 1980 qualifier against Bulgaria at Wembley in November. His wait was extended by an additional 24 hours when the game was postponed due to heavy fog. When it took place the following evening, Hoddle didn't disappoint, scoring a sumptuous goal as England won 2-0.

Hoddle became the first Spurs player since Martin Peters, in 1974, to represent England and the lack of full internationals reflected the turmoil Spurs had suffered on the field during the mid-70s. Now, Hoddle being selected for England symbolised the rebirth of Spurs as a serious club in English football.

For anyone of a Spurs persuasion, it was baffling that Hoddle had to wait so long before making his full debut. There was something of a clamour in the press for his inclusion but he had also developed an unfair reputation, particularly among northern club supporters, for being something of a luxury player – or a 'southern softie' – which earned him the nickname 'Glenda'.

Despite his goal and impressive performance against Bulgaria, Hoddle lost his place to Terry McDermott for the next match. It was a sign of things to come for Hoddle's England career.

Back in Spurs' lilywhite, Hoddle scored twice at Bristol City in a 3-1 win, with Miller netting his first-ever goal for the club, but it would be the last victory before a run of three successive defeats over Christmas – the last of these coming away at Arsenal on Boxing Day. It was a fourth successive north London derby defeat – the first time since 1953 that either club had enjoyed such a prolonged spell of success over the other.

Spurs' final game of the 70s was a home match against Stoke City at White Hart Lane on 29 December. John Pratt scored the only goal of the game but the afternoon was most memorable for young striker Terry Gibson, who made his senior debut. Born just around the north circular in Walthamstow, Gibson had only turned 17 the week beforehand.

Gibson recalls the circumstances around his debut:

I'd only signed as an apprentice that summer and had been playing in the youth team and reserves but I remember being asked to train with the first team the day before. I had no expectation of being named in the first-team squad until

Keith called me into his office back at White Hart Lane and told me he was thinking of playing me. Only three months ago I'd been on the terrace myself. It was really surreal because Steve Perryman, my hero, then walked in and Keith asked him whether he thought I was ready!

On the day of the game, I arrived at the stadium and it wasn't until I sheepishly walked into the changing room to see my boots laid out and my name against the No.9 on the team sheet. I was excited rather than nervous. This was all my dreams coming true! Keith told me he wanted me to be 'spiky' – this was an instruction I'd never been given before. It stuck with me and I was far more provocative than I'd ever been as a youth-team player. I committed a horrendous challenge on their keeper early on. It would definitely be a red card nowadays but I got my comeuppance when their centre-half, Mike Doyle, stamped all over me in the aftermath. It was a real battle but I think it helped endear me to the crowd – many of whom I'd been standing alongside months earlier!

I finished the game with a ripped shirt. I used the image on the front of my autobiography, *Giant Killer*. When I got back to the dressing room, I asked Jonny Wallis whether I could keep it. He told me in no uncertain terms that I couldn't, as it would be needed for the next game. A few days later, he threw it at me and said that the rip was too big to fix. They didn't change shirts from season to season back then, let alone game by game, so I'd never have been allowed to keep it otherwise. It's in a frame on my wall now.

One of the final acts of the 70s was for Spurs to be handed another tough FA Cup draw, with Manchester United once again pulled out as their opponents. The tie at White Hart Lane on 5 January was Spurs' first game of the new decade. Ardiles gave Spurs a second-half lead but United were quickly level through a Sammy McIlroy penalty. No further goals were scored, meaning a replay at Old Trafford four days later.

United were favourites to progress, as they were enjoying a great league season, sitting second behind Liverpool. They had won 11 of their 13 home games and hadn't lost at Old Trafford all season. It was the ninth occasion that the two teams had met in little over a year, with Spurs having won just once.

With an hour played, the game remained goalless, with the home side having created marginally the better chances but finding Milija Aleksic in good form. A deep cross from United's right saw Aleksic come out bravely but, in an era where it was still game for forwards to crash into goalkeepers, Joe Jordan (who would join Spurs as an assistant coach in 2008) clattered into Aleksic.

It soon became apparent that the Spurs goalkeeper was in significant pain and would not be able to continue. After a seven-minute delay, he was carried off the pitch on a stretcher.

This was the second time in three months that Spurs' goalkeeper had had to be replaced. It was still well over a decade before teams were allowed a substitute goalkeeper. Just as he had at Elland Road, Hoddle took the gloves and played in goal. The Spurs defence, marshalled by Perryman, managed to protect the stand-in goalkeeper.

Hoddle wrote in *Playmaker*: 'My nerves were on edge when they won a corner. "Hod, you know where this is going," Ray Wilkins said as he ran across to take it … United were trying to crowd me. Joe [Jordan] was in the six-yard box and Gordon McQueen, their big centre-back, was nearby. "Joe!" Gordon barked. "Do you want me to do him or are you okay? You've done the other one."'

Indeed, the corner was lofted high into the six-yard box and McQueen threw himself, elbows flying, towards Hoddle and loosely in the direction of the ball. Somehow, he failed to make contact with either and Spurs, and Hoddle, survived. Though he had to do so by often standing outside his penalty area as missiles, including a snooker ball, were thrown at him from the Stretford End crowd!

With no goals scored by the time the final whistle blew, it meant extra time. With just four minutes remaining of extra time and the prospect of a second replay looming, Spurs finally got the reward they deserved. Villa retrieved the ball on the left-hand side of the penalty area, looked up and spotted his fellow Argentine, Ardiles, free on the edge of the penalty area. Ardiles described in his autobiography, *Ossie's Dream*, what would become the winning goal and one that would go down in Spurs' folklore:

> I'm positioned just to his [Villa's] right, so Ricky gives me the ball and I trap it. I have a fraction of a second to decide what to do with it. I just haven't got the energy to whack it, so I decide to try to aim at an angle, to slot it in at the edge of the goal. Pum! In it went.

Ardiles barely had the energy to celebrate the goal in front of more than 3,000 delirious travelling fans. It was not over yet, though. Spurs still had a few minutes to see out. But, despite having not won an FA Cup tie away at a Division One opponent since 1972, Spurs managed the final stages expertly, with Ardiles and Yorath, in particular, doing well to run down the final seconds.

Hoddle kept a remarkable clean sheet, though the collateral of this bizarre occurrence was that Aleksic had lost five teeth and suffered a fractured cheekbone. His place would go to Barry Daines, who remained as first-choice custodian for the remainder of the season.

Steve Perryman explains the significance of this victory:

> We'd always been associated with entertaining football but this was as much about digging in, working incredibly hard and getting over the line. It was our first really big result against top opposition since we'd returned to Division One but the fixture attracted a lot of media attention and was featured on that night's *Sportsnight* [on BBC], which was still something of a novelty. I've no doubt that prospective players would have watched that and taken notice.

Terry Gibson started both cup ties against United:

To make my home debut against Stoke was one thing but to then be thrust into two intense cup games against Manchester United was incredible. I'd played at Old Trafford in the youth cup but this was with a crowd of over 50,000. I was really struggling with cramp but just kept running for 120 minutes. It was a great victory and one that set us up nicely for the cup runs in the years to come.

We stayed in Manchester for the rest of the week, as we were playing City on the Saturday. We all went to see Milija in hospital. He was in real agony but the worse thing was that everyone assumed it was his jaw. He still couldn't open his mouth to speak and kept pointing at his knee. No-one realised that he'd ruptured his cruciate ligament and he was trying to tell us.

The replay at Old Trafford proved to be Gibson's last first-team appearance until March 1982.

It was a really frustrating time for me. I was 13th man for that Man City game but just didn't feature after that. No one spoke to me and I just ended up back in the youth team. In May 1981, I was given the chance to go on loan to GAIS Gothenburg, as they played a summer league. I even missed the FA Cup replay, as I couldn't find it on TV in Sweden!

Spurs' reward was a fourth-round trip to third-tier Swindon. It was the first time Spurs had faced the Wiltshire outfit since an FA Cup tie in 1910 that Swindon had won 3-2.

Swindon were a formidable cup outfit, despite their Division Three status. In the League Cup, they had already knocked out Arsenal and Stoke and, going into the FA Cup match with Spurs, had beaten Wolves, another Division One side, 2-1 in the semi-final first leg. 'Cup fever' engulfed Swindon and the County Ground was sold out, with the terraces bursting at the seams.

In team news, the suspended Don McAllister was replaced by Naylor, who made his first appearance in nine months. He had made his Spurs debut in 1969 and only Perryman and Pratt had been at Spurs for longer.

The home side shaded the first-half chances but Spurs grew into the game in the second half. In a game played against a backdrop of black smoke from a fire in a building just behind the stadium, Spurs had the better chances after the break but Chris Jones couldn't find the target from two decent opportunities. As a result, the game ended goalless and the two teams reconvened in north London.

Spurs were given an almighty scare when Swindon deservedly scored in the second half. There was obvious anxiety in the crowd as the game progressed and substitute Peter Taylor's name was chanted in expectation that the former England winger, who had missed much of the past nine months through injury, would be introduced. When he was brought on it was, to the dismay of the home crowd, for Chris Jones and not Gerry Armstrong, who'd had a particularly difficult evening up until that point. Having not scored in 11 games since the win at Leeds in October, Armstrong would go on to enjoy one of his best nights as a Spurs player.

With only seven minutes remaining, Armstrong volleyed Spurs level but the finale was yet to come. Four minutes later, Taylor's free kick was glanced in by Armstrong, giving Spurs what had felt an unlikely last-gasp victory. By his own admission, Armstrong hadn't played well on the night.

Between them, Armstrong and usual strike partner Jones had scored just 12 goals in 49 games. Falco, who had been selected at the start of the season, had been injured since August and Gibson, at just 17, was still raw potential. Spurs' profligacy in front of goal, especially with such a creative midfield, was palpable and hadn't gone unnoticed by Keith Burkinshaw.

The fifth round paired Spurs with Birmingham of Division Two. Just like Swindon, Birmingham had enjoyed an enviable cup campaign, having knocked out two Division One sides – Middlesbrough and Southampton – to reach the last 16 of the FA Cup. A crowd just shy of 50,000 – considerably more than

Spurs were attracting for league games – filled White Hart Lane to see Hoddle score twice in a 3-1 victory.

The win saw Spurs into the quarter-finals for a second successive season but, once again, they were given the most difficult draw possible, with Liverpool pulled out of the velvet bag. At least the tie would be at White Hart Lane.

League form was mixed, though there was an enjoyable game at home to Coventry in the final week of February. Spurs won 4-3, with Hoddle (who else?) stealing the headlines with what proved to be his only Spurs hat-trick. Tottenham led 2-0 inside 20 minutes, only for Coventry to score twice in the space of 90 seconds before half-time. With the game looking to be heading to a 2-2 draw, Hoddle completed his hat-trick from the penalty spot – only for the visitors to equalise immediately. However, just 60 seconds later, Falco scored his first goal of the season and only his second for the club.

The FA Cup game against Liverpool was season-defining for Spurs but they were knocked out by one of the greatest opposition goals scored at White Hart Lane. Terry McDermott, who was keeping Hoddle out of the England team, teed up a volley for himself from outside the penalty area. His shot had dip and swerve and sailed past Barry Daines. It was in front of the Park Lane End, the same end at which Hoddle had scored his superb efforts against Manchester United and Nottingham Forest earlier that season. Spurs played well but found Liverpool and England goalkeeper Ray Clemence in inspired form.

McDermott's goal proved to be decisive and, so, Spurs' interest in the FA Cup ended at the quarter-final stage.

Feeling sorry for themselves, Spurs were thumped 4-0 at Nottingham Forest the following midweek. Miller was sent off for the second time that season and all four goals were scored within a 14-minute spell in the second half.

Spurs' inability to score cost them further points when a third successive game without a goal – a 0-0 draw with Crystal Palace – drew frustration from the home crowd. Chris Jones finally broke Spurs' 369-minute blank with a goal at Bolton, though it didn't prevent a 2-1 defeat.

The team was set up around the midfield qualities of Hoddle, Villa and Ardiles. While virtually every Division One side played an orthodox 4-4-2, Spurs occasionally played with only one striker but their diamond-shaped midfield – with Villa at the head and Hoddle and Ardiles nominally on either side – was fluid.

March had been miserable but it did end well with an unexpected 2-0 home victory against Liverpool – three weeks after the cup defeat. Liverpool would go on to record back-to-back league championships and it was further evidence that this was a Spurs team in progress, as Steve Perryman recalls:

> We could feel that something was happening. Earlier in the season, the win at Manchester United proved that we could beat the best teams, even in the most challenging of circumstances. We'd learned some lessons from that FA Cup defeat to Liverpool and were able to correct them for the league game. To beat them gave us greater encouragement that we could compete with anyone on our day.

After Hoddle scored Spurs' first against Liverpool, John Pratt found the net for what proved to be his final goal in lilywhite. A stalwart of the Spurs team since his debut in 1970, Pratt had often been unpopular with sections of the home crowd but nobody could doubt his commitment to the cause. He would go on to make five more appearances before departing for Portland Timbers in the NASL.

Lifelong fan and contemporary Spurs blogger Alan Fisher, who also co-wrote *A People's History of Tottenham Hotspur*, summarises the way many Spurs fans felt about Pratt:

> I'm grateful for this opportunity to make a public apology to John Pratt. In 1973, I went up to Derby to watch Spurs draw 1-1 in the cup. On a mudheap of a pitch, in the second half Pratt sprinted 35 yards from the edge of his box to close down the opposing winger. Right in front of me, he missed the tackle and I shouted with the full force of

teenage desperation, 'Get up John!' He gave me such a look, a mixture of incredulity and contempt.

So, John, I'm sorry. You had run your heart out for the team and all I could do was moan. A reaction which was wrong, yet it says something about his relationship with the fans. Supposedly, before his first game at Old Trafford, John asked Bill Nicholson what to expect. He replied, 'It would be like playing at Spurs, except 55,000 people will hate you, whereas at Spurs it's only 45,000'. There's so often been a Spurs scapegoat in the stands – I hate to admit it – and John took the brunt of it.

Every side needs an unsung hero, a player committed to the cause and who works hard, without whom the team would be diminished. That sums up John Pratt and we should be eternally grateful. What he lacked in finesse on the ball, he made up for in blood, sweat and toil, all for the sake of the team, without getting the credit he deserved. The players knew. His contemporaries, like Glenn Hoddle and Steve Perryman, understood that his graft gave them the space and time to play. His career at Spurs, his only British club, spanned 15 years and he held his post under Billy Nick and Keith Burkinshaw, mostly as a midfielder but he played in every outfield position at one time or another. Not known for his goalscoring, I remember a couple of long-range blasters against Wolves and Liverpool.

He sat behind us at Wembley for a cup semi-final a few years back, complaining about people standing in front of him. His knees had gone and he had to sit. That's the pain dedication brings. Cheers John.

Another player on his way out was Terry Naylor, who played the last of his 306 Spurs appearances in the defeat to Ipswich at the start of April. Having made his debut in March 1970 – alongside such contemporaries as Jennings, Mullery, Knowles and Chivers – he, Perryman and Pratt appeared in each calendar year of the 70s. Naylor was awarded a testimonial at the end of the month, with Crystal Palace providing the opposition. Phil

Beal, Chivers and Joe Kinnear all returned to play. Naylor joined Charlton the next season.

The impending departures of Pratt and Naylor signified the changing of the guard from the Nicholson era. It left Daines and Perryman as the only squad members who had played under Nicholson. With just weeks of the season remaining, Keith Burkinshaw was keen to turn to youth again and gave young midfield protégé Micky Hazard the opportunity to make his first-team bow.

It was yet another youth team player making their way into the first team. It meant that Falco, Gibson, Hoddle, Hughton, Miller and Southey had all been selected in the first team – a tremendous vindication for Peter Shreeve and Ron Henry, who worked with the youth team and prepared them for first-team football. While the others listed were all London-born or bred, Hazard hailed from the north-east.

Hazard had been spotted playing schoolboy football in his native Sunderland and was first invited to train with Spurs' youth team as a 12-year-old, eventually being put up in digs near White Hart Lane. Hazard shared, on the official club podcast *Off The Shelf,* how he was incredibly homesick and on six occasions escaped his accommodation to return home. However, with support from the club, he overcame his concerns and signed professionally. Hazard was a very skilful midfielder who, despite his diminutive frame, could control youth team games from midfield. He idolised Hoddle, just a few years his senior, and was honoured to read in an interview with *Shoot!* magazine that Hoddle listed Hazard as the 'best up-and-coming star'.

Having trained regularly with the first team, Hazard was earmarked to make his debut at Old Trafford in April 1980. However, in the final training session of the week, held in the ball court at White Hart Lane, Hazard developed a blister on his toe. Reluctant to tell the physio in case he was deemed unfit to play, Hazard tried to deal with the injury himself but ended up causing an infection, making it impossible to walk or to hide it from the physio and manager!

Hazard believes fate played its part. Spurs were beaten 4-1 at Old Trafford, with Pratt in midfield. Instead, Hazard had to wait a further week to make his debut – a home game against Everton. If he had been part of a team that suffered a heavy loss, he may not have been given another opportunity.

Never one to feel nerves, Hazard has said that any tension he felt was purely because of who he sat alongside in the changing room:

> I looked to my right and there's Glenn Hoddle. Then I turned to my left and it's Ossie Ardiles. I was thinking to myself, 'What the heck do they need me for?'

Hazard played his part in a 3-0 victory and fondly remembers the reaction of John Pratt, who he'd effectively replaced. Hazard described how Pratt came up to him before the game to congratulate him and wish him well. After the game, Pratt was among the first to tell him how well he'd played. That humility shown by Pratt has never left Hazard.

The win against Everton proved to be Spurs' final one of the season – home draws with Wolves and Bristol City and defeat at Aston Villa meant they finished 14th, three places lower and with one point less than the previous season but this was a team which had a youthful core and potential and it would go on to serve the club extremely well over the coming years.

The defensive unit was beginning to take shape. Perryman and Hughton offered natural balance in the full-back positions and, in the centre, Miller established himself as first choice alongside McAllister.

Of the current squad there was no doubt that Hoddle was the star and he won the PFA young player of the season award, as well as being named, for the first time as a Division One player, in the team of the season. His season's haul of 22 goals in all competitions proved to be the best in his career and those goals were essential in keeping Spurs away from the relegation zone.

Hoddle also made the England squad that travelled to Euro 80 in Italy, though he was only selected once in three games as England went out at the group stage.

Spurs fan Jill Lewis remembers Hoddle at this stage of his career:

> At the end of the 78/79 season, I remember saying to my father that I could see Hoddle scoring a lot of goals next year and, sure enough, he did! We could all see he was a special talent when he broke through but the instant understanding he had with Ossie and Ricky took him and the team up a level. I've been watching football for nearly 60 years. From the stand, you can see the passes that the players should make. Hoddle was different – he could see and make a game-changing pass that nobody else would have spotted, even from on high! Hoddle gave us a real sense of pride; he helped us to play football the right way, especially at a time when most other teams didn't – and that included England. After his first appearance for England, when he scored in the best England debut I've seen, Ron Greenwood then inexplicably told the press that he shouldn't expect to start regularly!

Alarmingly, Hoddle only had one year left on his contract and was attracting interest domestically and from across the continent. It was vital for both Hoddle and Spurs that the team could evolve to challenge for trophies. In Hoddle, Ardiles and Villa, Spurs had the most technically gifted midfield in the league. To take those next steps, it was essential that the board backed the manager – specifically to bring at least one new striker to the club.

Burkinshaw's attention had been drawn to the Scottish Premier Division where Aberdeen, under the management of a certain Alex Ferguson, were about to end 15 years of dominance by the 'Auld Firm'. The Dons' attack had been spearheaded by 23-year-old Steve Archibald, who had scored 22 goals and had also made his international debut, with a goal, for Scotland against Portugal in March.

Since the Victorian era, the best club sides in England had included Scottish internationals. The Spurs double team contained Bill Brown, Dave Mackay and John White and later in the 60s, Alan Gilzean was dubbed the 'King of White Hart Lane'. By the time the 1980s dawned, nothing had changed in this regard, with all the best club sides featuring a number of Scots. Liverpool had Dalglish, Souness and Hansen, Manchester United had Jordan and McQueen and Nottingham Forest had Gemmill and Robertson.

Archibald had been courted by Terry Venables at QPR. He discussed on *The Spurs Show* podcast in December 2019 how he was initially drawn towards a move to west London, knowing little of the history of both clubs. It was a team-mate, Ian Scanlon, who had previously played in England for Notts County and recognised the size and potential of the club, who implored Archibald to sign for Spurs.

Archibald had arrived in professional football relatively late. Prior to joining Aberdeen in 1977, he had been playing for Clyde on a part-time basis while running his own business, selling high-end motors. The maturity that comes from running a business in your early 20s no doubt aided the player's personal development, making such a move more achievable.

A transfer for around £750,000 – a new club record – was done between the two clubs immediately following the end of the season. Ferguson described the deal as the most 'painful experience of his football career'. It would not be the last time he'd trade centre-forwards with Tottenham Hotspur!

Mike Leigh, co-host of *The Spurs Show*, was, like many other Tottenham fans, not overly familiar with Archibald.

In England, you'd rarely hear much about Scottish league football but news of this Aberdeen team that had just taken the title away from the Auld Firm stronghold captured the imagination. It was so clear to us as fans that the team desperately needed two centre-forwards. We'd seen Archibald's name mentioned, so his signing was quite exciting, even if we hadn't seen him play. We hoped there was another forward to follow.

Archibald's signing may have dominated the back-page headlines but, around the same time, Spurs also completed another incoming transfer that would have a hugely important positive impact on the make-up of the team in the coming years.

Following the acquisition of Tony Galvin two years previously, Bill Nicholson pulled another non-league rabbit out of the hat when 19-year-old midfielder Graham Roberts joined the club from Weymouth. This outcome relied more on fate than perhaps any other deal in the club's modern history.

Having engaged in conversation with a non-league football anorak after a fruitless scouting mission in Swindon, Nicholson was encouraged to go and watch Weymouth, who it was suggested had two outstanding players – one of whom was young midfielder Graham Roberts. Nicholson took the advice and watched Roberts put in a commanding display, scoring twice. He recommended his signing to Burkinshaw.

Spurs had to fight off advances from West Brom, whose manager, Ron Atkinson, thought he had already agreed a deal. Such was the faith that Burkinshaw had in Nicholson's talent-spotting that his first question to Roberts, having signed him on a deal worth £20 per week (considerably less than Roberts was earning between his Weymouth salary and his full-time job), was: 'What position do you play?'

Roberts first appeared for Spurs in the post-season two-game tour to Austria. The shape of a formidable Spurs team was beginning to take shape.

League position	14th
Average league attendance	32,014
Most appearances	Hoddle (49)
Top goalscorer	Hoddle (22)
League winners	Liverpool
FA Cup winners	West Ham
League Cup winners	Wolves

80/81 – SPURS ARE ON
THEIR WAY TO WEMBLEY

DAINES
PERRYMAN MILLER LACY HUGHTON
ROBERTS
HODDLE ARDILES
VILLA
ARCHIBALD CROOKS

SUMMER 1980 saw many changes that would have significant impact on and off the field at White Hart Lane.

Largely unknown by any supporters, apart from those eagle-eyed enough to study the list of club directors in the matchday programme, Arthur Richardson replaced Sidney Wale as chairman. It was something of a coup following a boardroom split caused by disagreements over the level of funding the club required to rebuild the old West Stand.

Never held in the same regard as the iconic East Stand that sat opposite, the West Stand, built in 1908, hosted the directors' box and the most expensive seats in the ground. It was a safety concern owing to the large amount of wood within its structure and the Richardson faction in the boardroom were also attracted to a new stand that could incorporate executive boxes. The directors at Arsenal had wanted to do likewise but were denied planning permission as the East and West Stands at Highbury were listed buildings. Thus, White Hart Lane could become the only venue in London able to offer corporate hospitality.

The club had commissioned an architect, who created the blueprint for a futuristic design featuring 72 corporate boxes, and designs were first shared in the matchday programme at the back end of the previous season.

The cost of the build was forecast to be around £3.5m, which would require significant borrowing from the bank. The scale of the proposed expenditure caused a disagreement in the boardroom.

Wale's father, Fred, had first joined the board in 1944, becoming chairman in 1957. Sidney took over from him in 1969. The Wales had always backed Bill Nicholson generously, which included paying £99,999 to AC Milan to bring Jimmy Greaves back to London in 1961 and then, in 1970, making Martin Peters the country's first £200,000 player when he arrived from West Ham.

Since Nicholson left, the board had seemed less inclined to keep up with the ambition shown in the transfer market by Liverpool, Manchester United and even Nottingham Forest. Wale was understandably concerned about the impact of a huge capital expenditure, especially with interest rates raised by the government to a record high of 17 per cent in late 1979 in a bid to tackle inflation. The Mears family, who had owned Chelsea for most of the 20th century, had lost control of the club due to the spiralling costs of their East Stand rebuild in the mid-70s.

While boardroom matters would have meant little to most fans and players, pre-season was a source of optimism for what may happen on the pitch.

Spurs' pre-season schedule began with a 1-1 draw at Southend, with Archibald scoring his first goal in lilywhite – but he wasn't the only new striker in the starting XI.

Also arriving at White Hart Lane that summer was Garth Crooks, for a fee of around £600,000. Crooks had scored 14 goals, including two against Spurs, the previous season despite being part of a struggling Stoke team that only narrowly avoided relegation. Crooks had been capped by England at Under-21 level, where he had played alongside Hoddle. Crooks's most noticeable physical attribute was his pace and Archibald, likewise, was quick and willing to run in behind defences – a quality Spurs had previously lacked in attack.

With changes afoot in the playing squad, there was also a change in the dugout. Peter Shreeve, who had been with the club since 1974, initially as a youth team coach, was promoted to the role of assistant manager. It was a shrewd move, with so many of the young players Shreeve had nurtured now playing prominent roles in the first-team squad.

Shreeve was very popular, particularly among the young players who had worked with him in the youth team and reserves. He was a fantastic foil for Burkinshaw and the pair worked very well together. Shreeve was a great coach but also had the personal touch and the ability to make even the most seasoned international laugh, especially when he'd join in training sessions and demand the ball, always claiming that he 'had a plan'.

For the second summer in a row, Spurs' results were underwhelming. Archibald and Crooks initially struggled in the team structure. During pre-season matches and training, both raised concerns about the way the team was set up. Essentially, it was an attack built around the midfield, principally Hoddle, Ardiles and Villa. Archibald and Crooks both wanted the ball played behind the defence to run on to but the star midfielders had become accustomed to keeping it among themselves.

Crooks told *The Spurs Show* podcast how, in a training game, the new strikers agreed that the next time Crooks received the ball, instead of passing back to Hoddle, he'd look for Archibald. When this happened, there was a look of bemusement on Hoddle's face and he turned to Keith Burkinshaw to question what was happening! Before long, though, the midfield trio began to recognise their new strikers' strengths and Hoddle, in particular, mastered the ability to play a forward pass with exactly the right degree of backspin to set either away without them having to break stride.

Spurs only won one of six pre-season fixtures but, by the time the season opened, Archibald and Crooks had begun to understand each other's game and, crucially, had started to win the approval of the star-studded midfielders playing behind them.

It wasn't just who was wearing the shirt that was different. Another notable change over the summer was a new kit manufactured by French company Le Coq Sportif, which replaced Admiral. The silky shirt has since become iconic through the success that it is associated with and the silky style of play that matched it!

Steffan Chirazi, co-host of *The Game Is About Glory* podcast, discusses the new kit and what it meant to be a Spurs fan:

First off, it felt incredible to be able to buy such a gorgeous, sexy piece of kit. The club shop was on the corner of the High Road and Park Lane, across from The Corner Pin, and it was (as you'd imagine) a fraction of the size of today's megastore. I still remember seeing a whole row of them on display and feeling a surge of excitement as I got near the front to buy mine.

It's simply the greatest Spurs shirt in history for me. So sleek, so sophisticated and utterly timeless, it felt modern, yet classic. The silky sheen, the cockerel dead-centre and Le Coq Sportif's design intelligence in placing their logo on the sleeves. When paired with that gorgeous shade of deep, rich navy blue shorts (which sat no further down than mid-thigh), that kit was just an incredible affair. And, somehow, it projected the progressiveness of Tottenham Hotspur for me. We felt like a far more socially progressive club than others and it felt to me that we were firmly an Anti-Nazi League club and fanbase at a time when the National Front was associating with the Chelseas and West Hams. Their kits seemed clunky and drab, whereas this utterly sexy and sophisticated affair felt like the progressive future!

Despite only appearing twice the previous season, Mark Kendall started the season in goal. Chris Hughton was now established as full-back and was capable of playing on either flank. He had kept his place ever since being given his debut in August 1979. Gordon Smith started at left-back, with Lacy preferred over Miller (who had appeared in five of the six pre-season fixtures) to partner Perryman. Hoddle, Villa and Ardiles resumed creative duties in midfield, with Terry Yorath providing balance.

Spurs' first opponents were Nottingham Forest, who travelled to White Hart Lane on a hot August Saturday for their first competitive game since beating Hamburger SV in late May to retain the European Cup.

Three months may have passed since their European final exertions but Clough's team were well off the pace and succumbed to a highly energetic Spurs display. Archibald failed to take three first-half chances but his new partner, Crooks, immediately endeared himself to the fans when he coolly slotted home to give Spurs a decisive second goal after Hoddle had opened the scoring from the penalty spot.

It wasn't just Crooks and Archibald who made their debuts at White Hart Lane that day. Over the summer, the club had appointed a new stadium announcer, Willie Morgan, who was to become the voice of White Hart Lane for the next 15 years:

The club assistant secretary, Peter Day, had sent me a pair of tickets for a match, so that I could bring a famous DJ from BBC Radio 1 for a match. By means of a thank you, I invited Peter to lunch the following week. During the lunch, I mentioned I wasn't terribly impressed with the incumbent stadium announcer/DJ and Peter surprised me by saying they were contemplating a change.

Initially, I tried to source a DJ for him at Radio 1 and Capital Radio but no one I spoke with was able to commit to working every matchday. I had experience on hospital radio and, as a long-standing fan since the 60s, I was very happy to take on the role. The opening home game of that season, against Nottingham Forest, was my first time announcing the teams and playing records before the game and at half-time.

My cue came after the bell rang to tell me the Spurs team were about to emerge from the steps on to the pitch [the push-button to sound the bell was on the wall at the bottom of the steps, and was always pushed by Steve Perryman].

I put on the music I had made to replace McNamara's Band and for the first time I announced 'Good Afternoon, this is Willie Morgan saying Welcome to White Hart Lane – the world famous home of the Spurs' and after my 15 years of saying that, it became something of a catchphrase.

That midweek, Spurs won 4-3 at Crystal Palace – Crooks scoring two more and Archibald opening his account. Crooks scored again in the next game, with Hoddle also on the scoresheet, but Brighton twice replied to draw 2-2. With five points from three games, Spurs were momentarily top of the table. It may have counted for little – newspapers rarely bothered to print a league table until well into September – but it was the first time since 1967 that Spurs had sat top of the First Division.

Top of the league and unbeaten in four, Spurs travelled across north London to meet Arsenal on the final weekend in August. It was now seven games against them since a Spurs win but the mood was buoyant in the camp that this might be the moment.

Spurs had the better of the first-half chances with Jennings denying Crooks on three occasions and Archibald failing to hit the target after Villa's shot had been parried out to him. Jennings was still yet to concede a goal to Spurs since crossing the north London divide, so it was ironic that Arsenal's two second-half goals came from mistakes from Mark Kendall. It proved decisive. Arsenal won the game 2-0 and Kendall never again played for Spurs.

Barry Daines came back for the next game, a 3-1 League Cup second-leg win over Orient (4-1 on aggregate) and kept his place until mid-December. Three successive 0-0 draws followed in the league before defeat at Leicester at the end of September meant Spurs were back in mid-table.

October followed in an equally inconsistent manner – three wins and two defeats, although Spurs did score 11 goals. By the beginning of November, Crooks (seven) and Archibald (nine) had already scored more goals than Armstrong and Chris Jones had managed throughout the whole of the previous season.

Co-host of *The Spurs Show* podcast, Theo Delaney, recalls that he immediately took to both players but reflects on the crowd's particular affection for Archibald:

My Dad and uncles worked in advertising, so I was particularly intrigued by the song that the crowd soon adopted: 'We'll take more care of you, Archibald.' It was to the tune of a British Airways advert that always seemed to be on at the time. I guess it just worked because of the number of syllables. Incongruously, Archibald showed little signs of vulnerability and didn't give any indications of wanting anyone to take care of him!

Gerry Armstrong and Peter Taylor played their final games for Spurs in the 3-0 defeat at Aston Villa. Both had been with Spurs through relegation and promotion. Taylor is perhaps more affectionately remembered. He joined Orient in November 1980 but would go on to make a name for himself as a coach, even leading the senior England team as caretaker manager in 2000.

Armstrong joined Graham Taylor's revolution at Watford but his career peaked at the 1982 World Cup when he stunned the host nation Spain by scoring the only goal in a shock Northern Ireland victory. Armstrong spent three seasons playing in Spain for Real Mallorca and his voice is well known as a Spanish football correspondent on Sky Sports.

November finally saw a north London derby success as Spurs beat Arsenal 1-0 in the League Cup fourth round, with Ardiles scoring the goal. Keith Burkinshaw described the team's performance as the best since becoming manager. However, interest in the competition would only last for one more round, West Ham knocking out Spurs at Upton Park.

Garth Crooks scored a hat-trick at home to Crystal Palace in mid-November but the game is more memorable for being the final time the old West Stand was in use. Work began immediately after the game. The shell of the stand remained intact throughout the rest of 1980 but by early 1981, spectators in the East Stand, and the TV cameras placed on that side of the ground, had clear views of London buses travelling up and down the High Road.

The club invited supporters to the Chanticleer restaurant (owned by the club as a function room on Paxton Road) to view an architect's model of the new stand in an attempt to drum up interest in the 72 corporate hospitality boxes that it was hoped would help fund the costs of the rebuild. A box, with capacity for eight people, was available for £10,000 per season, though the club wanted buyers to purchase for three years at a cost of £30,000, made as an up-front payment. Among those who attended the evening was Irving Scholar.

Scholar had first been taken to White Hart Lane in the 50s and instantly fell in love with the club. He was a dedicated fan, attending home and away games, and developed an encyclopaedic knowledge of the club. Away from football, he had become a millionaire in the 1970s through property and his business interests had taken him to Monaco, where he was domiciled, though he still attended games as a season ticket holder. His 1992 memoir *Behind Closed Doors*, co-written by Mihir Bose, tells Scholar's story of his infatuation with the club that he would become owner of in 1982.

At this point, he claims to have had no thoughts of anything other than ensuring he could retain his season ticket in the new West Stand and was intrigued to learn more about the facilities he could enjoy. Scholar knew a thing or two about construction projects and, having listened to Arthur Richardson's presentation, he became concerned at the finances presented and questioned the chairman in front of an audience.

He subsequently wrote to the chairman, offering his support, though never received a response. It was not the last Richardson would hear from Scholar.

On the pitch, Graham Roberts had shown patience, mostly playing in the reserves bar the occasional substitute appearance. Due to an injury to Miller, Roberts made his first start at Anfield on 6 December, playing in midfield. Archibald scored but Liverpool won 2-1.

December saw more goals – at both ends. Ipswich had the meanest defence in Division One, having conceded just 14 goals in 19 games before travelling to White Hart Lane, yet Spurs put five past Bobby Robson's team in an incredible 5-3 win on a windswept night in north London. That was followed by a hugely disappointing 4-1 defeat at Middlesbrough just before Christmas. On Boxing Day against Southampton, Garry Brooke, another product of the youth set-up, scored twice on his full debut. Crooks and Archibald both scored, too, but Spurs let a 4-2 lead slip to draw 4-4.

Brooke, who hailed from Bethnal Green, had made his debut as substitute against West Brom in November but he already had competitive first-team football experience, having been sent out on a six-month loan to GAIS of Göteborg in Sweden.

Just 24 hours later, Spurs travelled to Norwich City, making just one change from the team that had drawn with Southampton. Chris Hughton had suffered an injury (he would miss the next six weeks) and was replaced by Gary O'Reilly, who was making just his second appearance for the club. Milija Aleksic had replaced Daines in goal after the Ipswich game but his return to the first team was again ended by serious injury.

With Spurs 2-1 ahead, through a sumptuous Hoddle strike, the Spurs goalkeeper collided with Steve Perryman while defending a corner. He reinjured his knee and jaw and was carried off on a stretcher, just as he had been 11 months previously at Old Trafford. As was the case then, Hoddle took the gloves and jersey. This time, though, Spurs had already made their one permitted substitution, so they had to play on with ten men.

They would have recorded a victory had it not been for a terrible decision to award Norwich a penalty when the foul clearly took place a yard outside the area. Hoddle dived the right way but couldn't keep out Kevin Bond's penalty. The game ended in a 2-2 draw and Spurs finished 1980 in tenth position, having won nine, drawn eight and lost eight of their 25 league games. Tellingly, they were the top scorers in the league but only Crystal Palace, in bottom spot, had conceded more.

Such form made it unsustainable to challenge for the league title but Spurs had all the attributes to challenge for the FA Cup. It was now 14 years since the club's last FA Cup success, meaning a whole generation of fans were yet to see Spurs perform on English football's biggest stage. The omens were good. This was a year that ended in a one and Spurs had previously won the FA Cup in 1901, 1921 and 1961, while winning the league in 1951 and the League Cup in 1971.

The third-round draw sent Spurs across London to face Second Division QPR, who were managed by Terry Venables, who had been part of Spurs' 1967 FA Cup-winning team. Spurs were fortunate to leave Loftus Road with a draw but did win 3-1 back at White Hart Lane. Like Roberts, Galvin had had to bide his time; he was sub in the first game at Loftus Road but started in the replay for the first time that season and scored the first goal of the night.

The replay against QPR was the first of four successive home games. Three days later, Spurs beat Birmingham, with defender Georgio Mazzon making the first of seven first-team appearances. The following week, Spurs beat Arsenal in a league game for the first time since 1976. Archibald scored both goals and it meant that Jennings had finally conceded against Spurs (George Wood had played for Arsenal in the League Cup tie).

Back in the FA Cup, Third Division Hull were beaten 2-0 at White Hart Lane in a game that Spurs dominated, although they had to wait until the 83rd minute to break the deadlock.

Four days later, another FA Cup fourth-round tie took place at White Hart Lane. Non-league neighbours Enfield had enjoyed a high-profile FA Cup run, culminating in a 1-1 draw at Barnsley. With a huge crowd expected for the replay, the tie was switched five miles down the A10 from their Southbury Road home to White Hart Lane. A crowd of 35,244, including many Spurs fans, turned up but Barnsley's league class told in a 3-0 win.

The draw was opening up for Spurs. Drawn at home to Coventry in the fifth round, Spurs were emerging as bookies' favourites following the exits of Liverpool, Arsenal and Manchester United. Goals from Ardiles, Archibald and Hughton saw Spurs comfortably through to a quarter-final home tie against Exeter.

Meanwhile, the league campaign appeared to be an inconvenience. Spurs failed to win six successive games from the start of January until mid-March, keeping them outside of the top six positions.

The team was now starting to take shape, though. Roberts, Miller and Galvin had been ever-present throughout 1981, with Perryman showing his versatility by playing in a range of positions, though most commonly at right-back. Perryman's leadership was essential to the rapid development of the team. An injury to Hughton saw Don McAllister briefly come back into the team.

By this point in the season, the players were benefitting from the work of psychologists Chris Connolly and John Syer, whom Burkinshaw had asked to come and work with the squad at the start of the season. Mike Varney, the physiotherapist, had heard them speak at a conference and was impressed, encouraging the manager to invite them in to the support team. A brave move to introduce such a progressive intervention appeared to pay off.

One of the key techniques used was to work on players' communication, specifically in pairs and small groups, and most players speak positively about the impact. Steve Perryman wrote in his book *A Spur Forever*: 'They didn't know much about football but they knew about communication and how to ask questions. A lot of football chat is piss-taking. John and Chris just made that chat more useful. They gave Keith reports on how he held his meetings, who he encouraged to speak and who was less willing to speak.'

In the FA Cup quarter-final, Spurs faced Third Division Exeter, who had already beaten Leicester and Newcastle to progress to the last eight. It required both Miller and Roberts to score their first goals for the club to record a 2-0 win in torrential rain to progress to a first semi-final since 1967, with Wolves providing the opposition.

Mike Leigh felt that the stars might just be aligned:

Like my fellow generation of Spurs fans, we'd never seen us win the FA Cup. I had very vague memories of the 1973 League Cup but the FA Cup was huge – I'd say it was as big as winning the league from a fan's perspective. The draw had been kind to us and, one by one, the biggest teams were being knocked out. The semi-final draw was significant. Ipswich were a really strong side and Manchester City were something of a bogey team, so to avoid both of them and get Wolves felt a further sign that our name might be on the cup. The fact that the year ended in one and that it was the Chinese year of the rooster only added to the feeling that fate was with us for once!

The semi-final was a huge occasion. It was the first time I'd be able to watch Spurs play at a neutral venue.

The tie would be played at Hillsborough, which was the same venue Spurs had won at in their last two semi-final appearances. It was the first time Spurs had left London in the competition that season.

Back in the league, Spurs played their role in the race for the title, where Ipswich and Aston Villa were the surprise frontrunners. Ipswich, then top, beat Spurs comfortably 3-0 on a chastening afternoon in Suffolk, extending Spurs' run without a league win to six games. The following weekend, Aston Villa arrived in north London knowing that a win could send them top.

Significantly, Burkinshaw reshuffled his defence, partnering Roberts with Miller in the centre for the first time. The pair, who had obviously worked together in training but had not started a match together, complemented each other perfectly, providing the foundation for a 2-0 win in which the team's other great double act, Crooks and Archibald, scored the goals.

The fit-again Aleksic had been reinstated in goal following an injury to Daines against Ipswich. With little to choose between the two, Aleksic kept his place. It was unfortunate for

Daines, who had played in each round of the cup up until that point. He would ultimately be denied a cup final appearance and winner's medal.

Elsewhere, Villa returned from a three-month injury absence to appear as a sub in a 2-2 draw with Everton the week before the semi-final. A starting XI of Aleksic, Perryman, Roberts, Miller, Hughton, Villa, Ardiles, Hoddle, Galvin, Crooks and Archibald was put together for the first time at Hillsborough.

For Perryman, his selection was significant, as it was his 591st appearance for Spurs, surpassing Pat Jennings as the player with the most appearances for the club.

The scramble for tickets was unprecedented and the trains and roads to Sheffield were full of expectant Spurs fans. Spurs had been allocated the Leppings Lane End and anyone familiar with the tragedy that occurred eight years later may shudder at the next few paragraphs, as will those who were there watching Spurs in 1981.

On the pitch, Spurs, wearing an all-white kit to avoid a clash with Wolves' black shorts, got off to the perfect start. Galvin's sheer determination and quick feet enabled him to get to the byline, where his low cross was converted by Archibald after just four minutes. It was the Scot's 25th goal of the season.

Scored at the far end, the goal created a surge of fans from the back of the terrace. Supporters can be seen climbing up from the terracing into the top tier to avoid the crush that was ensuing. As the game progressed, fans can be seen scaling the fencing at the front of the terrace to sit around the perimeter of the pitch. By the grace of God, nobody died that day, though 38 people were treated for injuries, including broken arms and a broken leg. An inquiry found that worse scenes were only avoided because an off-duty police officer ordered the emergency gates to be opened. Tragically, lessons weren't learned. Eight years later, 97 football supporters (including one Spurs fan, Colin Sefton, who had attended with Liverpool-supporting friends) lost their lives at the same end.

Paul Malshinger was one of many thousands of Spurs fans in the Leppings Lane End that afternoon:

We had been allocated the Leppings Lane End but, with a larger following than Wolves, we should have been at the other end. There were no individual pens on the terraces then but a large fence was in situ, as it was at most other grounds at that time. We were in the ground quite early, as the two women with us were on the short side and wanted to be near the front. The terrace soon filled up and, with the usual pushing and shoving from people at the back trying to get forward, a real crush developed at the front. People just in front of us were being crushed on the fence and others were being lifted off the ground by the force of bodies pressing down. There were calls to the police officer standing by the gate in the fence to open it. He wouldn't. The calls and shouts got louder and more intense until, in the end, he relented and opened the gate. The fans that got out of the Leppings Lane End were escorted to sit on the pitchside, not only behind that goal but all the way along one side of the ground.

Whether or not he acted on his own or got authorisation from someone more senior, I don't know, but his actions, without doubt, prevented what could have been a dreadful disaster. Sadly, the football authorities failed to heed this warning as to what could potentially happen and we witnessed the terrible tragedy in the exact same place in 1989.

Tottenham's lead was short-lived as, within seven minutes, Kenny Hibbitt scored with a well-placed shot from the edge of the area. The match saw a contrast in styles. Wolves played very direct, while Spurs attempted to play through midfield. Spurs always looked the more fluent and were able to create space on the edge of the Wolves area. With eight minutes remaining in the first half, Ardiles was fouled inches outside the penalty area. The Wolves defenders were keen to point out that the foul hadn't occurred in the box but might as well not have bothered, as Hoddle casually curled in the free kick to put Spurs back ahead.

The moment created a bizarre consequence for then ten-year-old Daniel Wynne, who was sitting in the main stand at Hillsborough:

> The man sitting next to me gave me his cap when the ball went in. I wore it to the replay and then to the final and, to my utter amazement, the same man was sitting next to us at Wembley. He remembered me and was delighted to see me sporting that cap!

Spurs, kicking towards their fans in the second half, had chances to win the game but, as the match reached its conclusion, Wolves upped the pressure. With the game into the final minute and the Spurs fans audibly whistling to encourage referee Clive Thomas to blow for full time, the ball bounced around the edge of the Spurs area. Kenny Hibbitt got to the ball and, tracked by Hoddle, knocked it inside the area. Never renowned for his tackling, Hoddle clearly got good contact on the ball while lunging to knock the ball back to Aleksic but Clive Thomas believed he had seen otherwise and pointed to the spot. Despite the mass protests, only Archibald was booked.

Willie Carr scored and there was barely time for Spurs to kick off before the final whistle signalled the game was going to extra time. Archibald angrily volleyed the ball away and was lucky that referee Thomas showed leniency. Keith Burkinshaw had to push several players away from the referee. Extra time failed to produce a winner, with Hoddle going closest with a shot from range that was saved by Bradshaw.

Even Kenny Hibbitt admitted in his post-match interview that Hoddle had taken the ball in the incident leading to the penalty award. Burkinshaw banned his players from speaking to the media, concerned that they might talk themselves into trouble. In his post-retirement autobiography, *By the Book*, Thomas confessed that it was one of very few decisions in his career that he wished he'd had the opportunity to award differently!

Julie Welch was in the press box at Hillsborough reporting for *The Observer*:

There is a certain level of decorum expected when working in the press box, especially as the first female sports writer! I had to forcibly stop myself from jumping up in absolute disgust at the decision. It was so obviously a dive and should never have been a penalty. I have been watching Spurs for six decades and I still consider this to be one of the worst decisions to have gone against us. However, had the penalty not been awarded, we'd have been deprived of the wonderful night at Highbury that was to come!

A draw meant that there would be a replay four days later and it was decided that the game would be played across north London at Highbury! Mike Leigh was overjoyed at the prospect:

I still can't believe that the FA decided to play at Highbury. It was the equivalent of it being played at West Brom, so gave us such a huge logistical advantage and provided the opportunity to take over our biggest rivals' ground!

Burkinshaw was able to name an unchanged team for the replay. Villa had played 105 minutes following his return from injury and was available to play again. Conversely, Wolves' leading striker, Andy Gray, had sustained a hamstring injury and was absent.

As the designated 'home team', Spurs fans were given Arsenal's iconic North Bank and thousands savoured the opportunity to reach the FA Cup Final on enemy territory. Hoddle, who had supported Spurs since before joining the club's youth ranks, wrote in *Playmaker*: 'Either we reached Wembley by winning on Arsenal's turf or we crashed out by losing at the home of our greatest rivals. Yet, while that was on our minds at the start, it was great to see the ground packed with Tottenham fans.'

Spurs settled quickly into the game and scored in the 11th minute. Hoddle controlled a bouncing ball and lofted it into the Wolves penalty area. Crooks took advantage of some hesitation in the Wolves defence to head Spurs into the lead in front of the North Bank.

Wolves got back into the game and enjoyed their best spell across the two games. Hughton cleared off the line, Berry had a volley cannon back off the crossbar and Aleksic had to take evasive action, punching the ball clear from outside the penalty area to concede a free kick and a booking. However, Spurs rode the storm and, against the run of play, scored a beautiful second through the same combination that produced the first. Hoddle received the ball inside his own half and, with the outside of his left foot, played a beautifully weighted pass into the space behind the Wolves defence. Crooks read the pass and burst into the space, knocking the ball clear of the defenders and then, with his next touch, fired home a right-footed shot in front of the salivating Spurs crowd behind the goal.

If there were any nerves from the crowd, they didn't transfer to the players, who seemed to enjoy the second half even more so after Ricky Villa added a third. Drifting in from the right wing, the Argentine drilled a left-footed shot from 20 yards in off the post to give Spurs an unassailable 3-0 lead. Remarkably, it wouldn't even be the best goal he'd score in the FA Cup that season! Crooks and Archibald had chances to add further goals but the injustice of the late penalty at Hillsborough had dissipated as Spurs looked ahead to a place in the FA Cup Final at Wembley on 9 May.

For many fans, this night lives long in the memory as being among the greatest of their time following Spurs.

Paul Malshinger still has vivid memories of what he witnessed from his spot standing on the North Bank:

> That night, the 'Highbury Library' was the loudest it has ever been! It was particularly loud whenever Hibbitt got the ball and he was booed for his dive in the first game. I was near the front behind the goal when Crooks scored his second and, as he came to celebrate with the fans, he yelled out 'Perfect!'. Whether that was referring to his strike or the sublime ball into him from Hoddle, I don't know. Then Villa capped it off with a stunning strike into the top corner in the second half. A memorable night indeed.

With Burkinshaw now settled on his strongest XI, the remainder of the league season saw several changes to preserve fitness. McAllister, Smith, Hazard and Falco all appeared, with Roberts, Hoddle, Archibald and Villa rotated in and out of the team. Spurs didn't win any of the final five games, finishing the season in tenth and on 43 points.

The FA Cup Final was very much the showpiece event in the domestic football calendar and the 1981 final was the 100th in the competition's illustrious history. Spurs had won all five FA Cup Finals that they had previously appeared in and had also never lost at Wembley.

The build-up to the match began weeks in advance and a relatively new tradition had been set for teams to record an FA Cup Final song. Having not been to an FA Cup Final since 1967, many supporters, like Daniel Wynne, had a big day to look forward to:

> It may be a cliché but the FA Cup Final was the biggest day of the year in the football calendar, so, as a Spurs and football-mad kid, reaching the cup final in 81 was set to be the biggest day of my life and I could barely sleep in anticipation of it for weeks. Spurs hadn't reached an FA Cup Final since 1967, so for many of us, this was a first.
>
> I'd been brought up on stories of the great double team and, although it was only 20 years ago, it felt like a different lifetime. To go 14 years without winning the FA Cup seemed a very long time for Spurs and we'd suffered the mediocrity of the mid-70s, followed by relegation. We were desperate to enjoy *OUR* glory, glory era.

The club approached music producer and Spurs fan Bob England to ask one of his acts to write a song and he appropriately commissioned the cockney duo Chas & Dave. The pair had enjoyed a breakthrough in 1980 with their first top ten hit, 'Rabbit', but their Spurs credentials had first become clear the year before with the song 'Gertcha', which peaked at No.20 and contained the line 'Tottenham Hotspur couldn't get one in'.

They learned that there was a joke among the players about Ossie Ardiles having always 'dreamed' of playing at Wembley and that sowed the seeds for what would become an iconic anthem for all Spurs fans. In Willie Morgan, the club now had some inside expertise when it came to promoting a pop record:

> I was there at the recording for 'Ossie's Dream'. What many people won't know is that Ossie had proudly learned how to pronounce Tottenham properly by then, so he had to be convinced to say it 'Tottingham', as that's how Chas & Dave had written it and it was the USP of the record! Just as the recording was due to end, I enquired about a B-side, as I'd already re-written the words to 'Glory, Glory'. We got the players and Chas & Dave to record it there and then. It's the version that's still played prior to kick-off now! I made an arrangement in the studio control room with Chas & Dave's manager regarding the promotion and publishing of the disc.
>
> I was asked to arrange for the squad to perform 'Ossie's Dream' on *Top Of The Pops*.
>
> Unusually, the show on the Thursday was to be a live transmission (it was always pre-recorded on the Wednesday) and this clashed with Keith Burkinshaw's schedule. It took a lot of negotiation but we reached a compromise when the producer agreed to pre-record at the 4.15 dress rehearsal and then slot it into the programme. Only the people attending the live show that night would have known otherwise.

'Ossie's Dream' peaked at No.5 in the UK charts. No doubt aided by the now happy associations with the eventual cup final success, the song has gone down in Spurs folklore and the chorus is still enjoyed several generations later.

> 'Spurs are on their way to Wembley,
> Tottenham's gonna do it again,
> They can't stop 'em,
> The boys from Tottenham,
> The boys from White Hart Lane'

The night before the game, Ardiles and Villa appeared live on Argentinian TV to talk about the game but Hoddle felt subconsciously that all the media attention had affected the team's focus.

Such was the pomp and ceremony of the occasion that neither team was allowed to warm up on the pitch beforehand. Instead, the players were cooped up in the dressing room after going for their initial walk around on arrival. There was further disruption when it was discovered that the FA had misprinted the matchday squads and had allocated Perryman as No.5 and Villa as No.6. They were told that they'd have to play in those numbers.

Spurs went into the game as favourites but the match was billed as 'the footballers against the workers', reflecting the respective predominant qualities of each team.

As the first half progressed, it became clear that Manchester City were working harder than Spurs were playing football. Spurs had their moments but were off the pace. Villa, in particular, was having a poor game, misplacing passes and being beaten to 50-50s.

Just before the half-hour mark, City scored. Ranson crossed from the right and Tommy Hutchison reacted quickest to stoop and head the ball inside Aleksic's near post. It was the first time that Spurs had trailed in the FA Cup that season.

For Graham Roberts, the first half was as physically painful as it was mentally draining. In the final league game of the season at West Brom the week before, Roberts had left the pitch on a stretcher having been knocked unconscious but he declared himself fit for the cup final.

Having already got another bang to the head that drew blood, Roberts and Chris Hughton challenged for the same ball and Roberts came off the worst, suffering a nasty gash to his head and losing three teeth. The doctor recommended that he come off at half-time but Roberts was having none of it, sprinting out of the dressing room and on to the pitch before the doctor could make his point to Keith Burkinshaw!

The second half continued in much the same way. Spurs lacked their usual incisiveness and Villa was substituted, replaced by Garry Brooke, midway through the second half. Instead of sitting down on the Spurs bench, Villa trudged around the pitch perimeter back to the changing room and looked a broken man. He would later admit to Ardiles that it was his Latin temperament taken too far! The sad image of Villa walking back to the dressing room became iconic and featured heavily after the replay.

Within ten minutes of Villa's departure, his compatriot, Ardiles, sparked what appeared not to have been coming. He won the ball back just inside the City half and dribbled diagonally forwards before being fouled 20 yards from goal but just wide of the 'D'. Hoddle territory.

Ardiles rolled the ball to Perryman, who stopped it for Hoddle to run on to. His right-footed shot was curled around the outside of the four-man City wall and was heading towards Joe Corrigan's left-hand post. Corrigan had committed to diving to his left but, inexplicably, Tommy Hutchison had left the wall and now stood face-on to the coming ball. Instinctively, he glanced the shot with his right shoulder, from just a few yards away from where he'd scored in the first half, and back across the goal, completely wrong-footing Corrigan, who could only look on helplessly as the ball hit the centre of the net.

David Harris, a contributor to *The Spurs Show* podcast and the *Lads, It's Tottenham* YouTube channel, was among the crowd at Wembley:

> Even as a nine-year-old, I can remember the unmistakable feeling that this wasn't going well. Everything was off; the weather was miserable, City were outfighting us and when Villa took his slow disconsolate walk around the side of the pitch, I was coming to terms with the fact we might actually lose. My uncle, who was sat with me, always used to comment that he'd never seen me so sad. Then, out of nothing we equalised!
>
> I'm certain that Hutchison only did what he did because he'd seen Hoddle's free kick in the semi-final. I vividly remember my older cousin turning to me and kissing me on the face! That's what football does to you.

Obviously we didn't know it at the time but, looking back, I'm convinced that this goal was the pivotal moment for the club and for all the good things that followed.

Spurs were off the hook. The goal, officially credited as an own goal, seemed to give Spurs an energy boost but adrenalinee alone couldn't force another meaningful attack and the game went to extra time. Hoddle mentioned the palpable feeling of relief at having not lost a game in which Spurs appeared destined for defeat. For City, the late equaliser was a crushing blow. It led to an insipid extra-time period, with players from both sides suffering cramp. A replay was required and would take place just four days later.

Spurs had been consistently inconsistent throughout the season, as their final league position of tenth testified and as many supporters like Theo Delaney recall:

Spurs have often been labelled as 'inconsistent' and this is definitely true of this team. You never knew what you were going to get from game to game. We were dreadful in the first game, which meant you could expect us to be much better second time around and I think Man City knew that, too.

The whole squad recognised that they had simply not played well enough and this was rammed home by none other than Bill Nicholson, who gave them a roasting at the pre-arranged evening banquet.

Reflecting on why the performance had been so below-par, Hoddle told *The Spurs Show* in January 2018 that the players had had a really good team meeting on the Monday before the replay and had discussed how, instead of the usual collective team approach, many of them had got too caught up in the occasion and played as individuals.

All the talk immediately after the game was whether Villa should retain his place for the replay. He had irritated several of his team-mates by walking back to the changing room.

However, Burkinshaw had already made up his mind that the mercurial Argentine was going to start and told him in front of the rest of the team of his decision. It appeared to instantly galvanise Villa and his demeanour changed.

On the Monday evening, seven of the starting XI – Aleksic, Miller, Perryman, Ardiles, Villa, Archibald and Crooks – played in Barry Daines's testimonial at White Hart Lane against West Ham. The game had been arranged several months beforehand and, in other circumstances, Daines may well have just won an FA Cup Final winner's medal. It seemed emblematic of his Spurs career that this tribute to him should be sandwiched between the final and replay in neither of which he featured!

Steve Perryman, who signed his first professional contract in the same summer as Daines, explains the affection for him among the squad:

> People often describe me as a loyal servant but how could I ever have been anything but loyal when I was able to play in several brilliant teams that achieved successes over a 19-year period? For me, Barry was the most loyal of servants.
>
> He had the choice of joining Spurs or West Ham but he knew that if he had gone there, he'd have been fourth choice behind two England youth internationals and Bobby Ferguson, who, at the time, had been signed for a record fee for a goalkeeper. Instead, Barry ended up being understudy to Pat Jennings!
>
> Not only was Pat nearly always available but he was, of course, an absolute one-off in terms of what he could do. It was a sign of Barry's loyalty that his chance came about too late once Pat had left in 1976 and it was always going to be very hard for him to live up to Pat's level. On his day, Barry was brilliant – perhaps better than Milija but not quite as consistent.
>
> He was an incredibly honourable man and he made no fuss over his testimonial nor that the cup finals, that he wasn't going to involved in, dominated everyone's thoughts.

A crowd of 7,172 went to the testimonial, in which West Ham ran out 3-2 winners. Hazard and Gibson scored Spurs' goals. Daines left the club that summer, playing professionally in Hong Kong before returning to England and Mansfield Town.

The replay provided opportunities for more Spurs fans to buy tickets and go to Wembley. Theo Delaney was one of them:

> I was 15 and had been going to games at White Hart Lane for a few years but, as only a club member, hadn't got a sniff of a ticket for the first game. As per the cliché and Chas & Dave's lyrics, cup final day was next best to Christmas Day! I'd watched the first game at home, mostly in dread, as it was a drab game and Spurs hadn't played well at all. I went berserk when Hoddle scored.
>
> As the only London team, it was easier to get tickets. City fans, understandably, couldn't all travel back to Wembley four days later. I remember the sheer exhilaration at learning that my uncle had queued up and bought tickets for him, me and my younger, QPR-supporting brother. It was set up to be a special night.

Also unchanged, City started the game just as they had approached the original tie, on the front foot and combatively. Within three minutes, midfield henchman Gerry Gow committed a nasty challenge on Ardiles. City had the first chance, forcing a corner from which Hughton intervened, kicking the ball away from the post.

Within minutes, though, Spurs found their stride and Villa was noticeably more assured on the ball. Ardiles picked up possession on the left-hand side of the penalty area and glided infield. His shot from 20 yards cannoned favourably into the path of Archibald and, although he was thwarted by Corrigan, the ball landed for Villa, who slotted home from eight yards. He was on his redemption arc, though nobody would comprehend the journey he was still to go on that evening!

In the semi-final replay against Wolves, Spurs had taken an early lead and then been fortunate to weather the opposition storm. On this occasion, they weren't so lucky. Within three minutes, Steve MacKenzie scored one of the great FA Cup goals volleying in from 20 yards to silence the Spurs supporters.

It was shaping up to be quite a game – completely in contrast to the attritional and lethargic first meeting.

Just two minutes later, Hoddle hit the post from a free kick and the game continued at frenetic pace. In another repeat from the semi-final replay, Aleksic panicked and punched the ball clear from outside the penalty area, this time avoiding a booking. Villa became the dominant force in the game, twice forcing saves from Corrigan but there were no more goals before half-time.

The second half began with more end-to-end action. Spurs won a corner that had to be delayed when referee Keith Hackett noticed a wounded bird on the pitch, which the reserve official had to come on to remove! Hackett was equally alert minutes later when, at the other end, City winger Dave Bennett went down in the penalty area under the most minimal of contact from either Miller or Hughton. The penalty was given and Kevin Reeves duly converted it.

As on the Saturday, Spurs found themselves behind and looking to pull the proverbial rabbit out of the hat. The goal and sense of injustice seemed to rattle Spurs. Despite Spurs having most of the ball, both Galvin and Archibald found their way into referee Hackett's book for petulance.

With little over 20 minutes remaining, the ball appeared to bounce off the upper arm of City defender Tommy Caton following a deep corner from Hoddle. Hackett was well positioned but waved play on. As the fans protested, the ball was picked up by Villa on the left and he passed square to Hoddle some 30 yards from goal. For once, he had time to consider his options. City's defence naively charged towards him and Hoddle deftly clipped the ball, with backspin, into the path of Archibald, one of three Spurs players inside the area who had been played onside by a City defender.

As Archibald brought the ball down, Joe Corrigan, who had made several vital blocks already, came rushing towards him. The only other player who reacted quicker was Garth Crooks, who stabbed at the ball, sending it past Corrigan and into the corner of the goal. It was his 22nd goal of the season but undoubtedly the most important. With Hoddle, Ardiles and Villa now dictating the tempo, Spurs had the momentum.

Theo Delaney, who was sitting low down, close to the Wembley touchline, describes his emotions as the game unfolded:

> The big story going into the game was whether Villa would start again. So, when he scored the first goal early in the game, it felt like the headlines were already written. I'd watched most of the cup finals of the 70s, with many games finishing 1-0, so this might have been it. However, they then scored an unbelievable goal straight after and then, to our horror, went 2-1 ahead.
>
> When Crooks equalised, this was football at its most high-octane. The stakes were so high. Winning the FA Cup was bigger than the league at the time. So, with the game level with not long left, the tension inside the stadium was extreme.

The winning goal has gone down in Spurs and FA Cup folklore but the roles that Roberts and then Galvin played in winning the ball back on the edge of the Spurs penalty area and then breaking forward midway into City's half are often forgotten. Galvin passed the ball to Villa, who found himself in space 30 yards from goal, just left of centre but with several City defenders blocking his route to goal.

Interviewed in the 2024 book, *Go To War*, Villa told author Jon Spurling how, as a kid growing up in rural Roque Perez, he'd spend hours near his house practising what is known in Argentina as *gambeta* – the art of dribbling – by slaloming between a line of trees. The ability to dribble and feint with the ball under close control at speed had never left Villa and now it would mark his place in history.

Crooks was positioned ahead of Villa and the Argentine used him as a distraction to entice two City defenders towards him just inside the box, slaloming outside and then inside to manipulate the ball on to his right foot. Everything appeared to be happening in slow motion and Spurs fans and players willed him to take the shot. Garth Crooks, in the periphery of the TV footage, can be seen kicking an imaginary ball just as Villa strikes his shot.

Famously, BBC commentator John Motson expressed the thoughts of all watching: 'It's still Ricky Villa! What an incredible run. He's scored – what an amazing run!'

In just under 200 minutes across both games, Spurs had so far only led for three minutes. They now had about 15 minutes to see out. The team were now running on adrenaline and Burkinshaw refrained from using his one substitute, Brooke. For all their hard-working ethic, City now looked beaten.

The final action of this pulsating game was Archibald running the ball down towards the City corner flag. When the ball trickled out for a throw-in, Hackett blew for full time. A few fans got on to the pitch, one handing Ardiles a blue and white scarf. Crooks jumped for joy like a schoolboy and Villa just looked thoroughly drained. Hoddle broke down in tears; as a lifelong Spurs fan, the emotion overwhelmed him. His contract was due to expire that summer and his future was uncertain but, for now, it was just about the sheer joy of winning the FA Cup.

Theo Delaney was among the Spurs supporters barely able to believe the thrilling climax they had witnessed:

When Villa picked up the ball and started dribbling, I, like everyone else I've spoken to, including his team-mates, was screaming at him to 'lay it off' but he kept going for what felt like about ten minutes until he finally put it in. There was pandemonium around us. We knew it was a brilliant goal but, being quite low down, didn't comprehend just how good it was until I was able to watch it back. Had the game ended 1-0 after his first goal, that would have been a story after what had happened to him in the first game but this took it to a whole new level and ensured that he entered Spurs and FA Cup folklore.

Through talking to fans, not just Spurs fans, on my *Life Goals* podcast, it's amazing how many people list this as one of the best and most memorable they've ever witnessed.

Then, to see Steve Perryman, who we already recognised as an iconic symbol of the club, going up to lift the cup means that this night has to go down as my greatest football experience. Talking about it now makes me emotional!

Steve Perryman led the team up the famous 39 steps into the Royal Box and John Motson rightly highlighted his incredible leadership qualities that seemed to have such a unifying impact on the squad and club as a whole. Perryman had been to Wembley to see Spurs lift the FA Cup in 1967 and signed as an apprentice the following Monday. Here he was now, 14 years later, lifting the trophy aloft to bring Spurs back into the big time.

Perryman's role at the club should never be underplayed. He was more than just a captain who wore an armband and tossed a coin at the start of every game. His relationship with Burkinshaw and the rest of the squad played a huge role in its harmony and determination to succeed.

Captain and manager would spend hours on the phone every Sunday discussing the previous day's game and other team matters. Among the rest of the squad, Perryman was hugely respected and still today, some 40 years on, is revered. By lifting the cup, he joined a pantheon of great Spurs captains – Danny Blanchflower, Dave Mackay, Alan Mullery and Ron Burgess – to have led Spurs to trophy success.

Perryman felt that many lessons had been learned from the first game:

Having got the replay, we had to look at our approach. In the first game we were distracted. The Argentinian TV coverage highlighted how big the game was. We were a team that was always set up to entertain and went into that first game assuming we'd have the superior talent to win. City worked us out and reminded us that if you think more about the entertainment than the graft, then you risk being caught out, as we nearly were. Someone said to me in later years that they knew we'd win the replay after I'd made a very strong challenge on Gerry Gow. I've got no idea if that had any impact but we all took it upon ourselves to lay down the foundations before we let our football have the ultimate say.

While Villa has become immortalised because of his winning goal, many people, including Keith Burkinshaw, reckoned that Hoddle had been the best player on the pitch. Burkinshaw was particularly keen to highlight how hard he had worked in midfield – often an attribute not associated with Hoddle by the outside world. Hoddle, himself, considers the replay as one of his best performances in a Spurs shirt.

For Ardiles, his 'dream' had come true. He and Villa became the first overseas players to win the famous competition since Bert Trautmann in 1956. Ardiles even left his physical mark on the trophy. Holding the cup in a loose grip, he tossed it high in the air whilst jumping into the team bath, causing a significant dent to the rim. In the pictures taken over the next few days, teammates were careful to place their hands strategically over the dent!

Celebrations among players and fans ran through to the early hours of the morning. The players and staff returned to White Hart Lane for a function in the Chanticleer and were met by up to 70,000 fans waiting for them on the High Road. It is estimated that 250,000 fans attended the trophy parade to Tottenham Town Hall the following weekend. For the sixth time, Spurs were FA Cup winners, maintaining a proud record of winning every FA Cup Final they had appeared in.

There was something about this side; they seemed to be able to overcome adversity and possessed an inner strength and determination fostered by Burkinshaw and Perryman, who had endured relegation in 1977. Hoddle and Perryman were the only members of the team who had gone down (though Daines, McAllister and Smith were still on the books). It was a vindication for the patience shown by the board to stick with Keith Burkinshaw.

The team of 1981 were a group of players a fan could relate to and fall in love with. Mike Leigh explains why this team are remembered with particular affection:

> Of all the Spurs teams I've fallen in love with, the 81 team was the most endearing. You had the homegrown boys like Hughton, Miller, Brooke, Hoddle and, of course, Perryman, who knitted everything together. Then you had Roberts and Galvin, two boys plucked out of non-league who always seemed to have something to prove and that inner determination spurred them on. We obviously took to Crooks and Archibald instantly but it felt like they'd always been there. Ardiles and Villa were the icing on the cake – the Latin flair made Spurs unique. For one of the only times in my Spurs-supporting lifetime, it felt as if the management and board had recognised the same priorities as we, the fans had; i.e. that we needed a central defensive partnership and a new strikeforce. So, that helped create the feeling that this was 'our team'.

Spurs travelled to the Middle East for three post-season tour games but the big question was whether this success was the culmination of the rebuild under Burkinshaw or just the start of even better things to come?

League position	Tenth
Average league attendance	30,663
Most appearances	Perryman (57)
Top goalscorer	Archibald (25)
League winners	Aston Villa
FA Cup winners	Spurs
League Cup winners	Liverpool

81/82 – WE'RE GONNA DO IT LIKE WE DID LAST YEAR

CLEMENCE

PERRYMAN MILLER ROBERTS HUGHTON

ARDILES

HODDLE GALVIN

VILLA

ARCHIBALD CROOKS

IT WAS just three years since the incredible double signing of Ardiles and Villa in the summer of 1978, when Spurs had returned to the First Division, and now, having won the FA Cup, the club were on an upwards trajectory. The hurt of relegation felt like a lifetime ago.

In the summer of 1981, Barry Daines, Terry Yorath and Don McAllister all left the club. McAllister's role in the revival is often underplayed; it was his vital goal against Bolton during the business end of the Division Two campaign that contributed to Spurs being promoted at his old club's expense and set off a chain reaction that resulted in promotion, Hoddle staying, Ardiles and Villa arriving and, latterly, the FA Cup success in 1981.

For the first time since 1973/74, Spurs embarked on a European campaign, meaning they were competing on four fronts. Squad depth was needed, particularly in defence. Lacy had suffered a serious injury and missed most of the 1980/81 season, which had allowed Miller and Roberts to establish themselves as a partnership. However, they were still only 21 and 22 respectively. Also, Hughton, now approaching

100 first-team appearances, was also just 22. Additional experienced defenders would provide depth and competition for places.

Burkinshaw signed versatile defender Paul Price, a near ever-present for Luton over the previous three seasons. Price, born in England, was now a full Welsh international, playing under former Spurs defender Mike England.

Price played in all four official pre-season fixtures – two in Ireland, one at Norwich and, lastly, at Aberdeen. Garth Crooks didn't feature at all, having picked up an Achilles injury, but it did present an opportunity for Mark Falco to come back into the reckoning, having only played three times at the end of the 1980/81 season.

While the squad now had depth in defence, the goalkeeping issue had never really been resolved since Jennings left. In the three seasons since Spurs returned to the top flight, Daines had played 92 times, Aleksic 30 and Kendall 31.

The perfect opportunity arose when Ray Clemence made it known that, after 13 seasons with Liverpool – during which he had won 12 major honours and earned 56 England caps – he was ready for a new challenge. Clemence and Burkinshaw had actually played in the same Scunthorpe team as far back as April 1966 – Clemence as a 17-year-old goalkeeper and Burkinshaw in the latter part of his playing career as a defender.

A deal was done towards the end of August, with Clemence joining for £300,000. Speaking to Danny Kelly on talkSPORT's *My Sporting Life* in 2014, Clemence revealed that the timing felt right for him to move (Bruce Grobbelaar was establishing himself as his long-term successor) and that Spurs with whom there would be the opportunity to continue winning trophies, with the fact they were now in Europe adding to the appeal.

Aleksic remained at the club but Burkinshaw turned to the youth team to select his new No.2 goalkeeper. Tony Parks had joined the club as a 12-year-old in 1975 and had made his way into the reserve team, where he'd impressed. Parks still has very positive memories of his development:

Initially, I'd been at QPR for a year but really didn't enjoy it, so went back to grassroots football until Spurs picked me up as a 12-year-old. I was instantly impressed by the professionalism of the club. We were trained by Peter Shreeve and Ron Henry and every Tuesday and Thursday evening we'd use the ball courts at the stadium. There was no such thing as goalkeeping coaching, so I'd be there saving shots and taking crosses all night. Technique was always drilled into us. I was given an apprenticeship and spent my time in the youth team. Playing in the reserves was also a great experience, as home games tended to be on Saturday afternoons at White Hart Lane when the first team was away.

We all got a great grounding. The likes of Steve Perryman and John Pratt had worked under Bill Nicholson and they made sure everyone understood the standards that were expected, both on and off the field. We grew up with great respect for the senior players but the environment meant they were never on a pedestal.

As far as the goalkeeping situation was concerned, I was sorry to see Barry Daines leave. I got to know him well and he was an exceptional goalkeeper but maybe a bit unlucky because he had to follow Pat.

I was delighted when Clem signed for us and to know I was his understudy meant that I'd get to work with him and learn from him.

Having won the FA Cup and now having signed Ray Clemence, Spurs were an outside tip to challenge for the league title. The current champions were Aston Villa, who had won their first league title since 1910, narrowly pipping Ipswich. Liverpool had suffered a blip in the league, finishing fifth, but they had won a fourth European Cup.

There were two unfamiliar names joining Division One. Notts County were promoted to the top flight for the first time since 1925 and Swansea City completed their incredible journey from Division Four, having gained promotion three times in four years. West Ham also returned to the top flight after three seasons, providing Spurs with yet another London derby.

The Football League had decided to change the points structure that had been in place since the league's inception in 1888. From now on, a win would be rewarded with three points instead of two. This gave a greater incentive for teams to take more risks to try and win games.

Spurs returned to Wembley for the season's traditional curtain-raiser – the FA Charity Shield, played between the previous season's league champions and the FA Cup winners. It was Spurs' first appearance since 1967, when Pat Jennings famously scored from a long kick in a 3-3 draw with Manchester United. The fixture had, since 1974, been played at Wembley. Villa would be a good test of Spurs' credentials for the upcoming season.

It was Clemence's Spurs debut but he was in very familiar surroundings – it was the sixth time in eight seasons that he'd played in the Charity Shield and his 35th appearance at Wembley. However, his Spurs career got off to a terrible start when he dropped a routine cross, allowing Peter Withe to put Villa ahead. The deficit didn't last long. Falco, the only other change to the XI that had started the FA Cup Final, scored a wonderful goal with a shot on the turn from outside the area.

Within three minutes of the second half, Falco was at it again, converting from close range after a Galvin cross, but Spurs' lead was short-lived. Another high cross from the left deceived Clemence, who appeared to be caught by the elbow of Tony Morley, and Withe pounced for his second. Despite his errors, Clemence commanded his area and organised his defence in a far more vociferous manner than Aleksic had. The game ended in a draw and the shield was shared.

For the third time in seven seasons, the fixture 'computer' provided Spurs with an opening day clash with Middlesbrough – this time at Ayresome Park. Two years previously, Spurs had disappointingly lost 3-1 but this time the scores were reversed, with goals by Villa, Hoddle, with a beauty, and Falco giving Spurs their first-ever three-point league haul.

Expectations were high as Spurs returned to White Hart Lane for the first time since winning the FA Cup for a derby against West Ham. The Hammers hadn't won at Spurs since 1971 but inflicted Spurs' biggest home defeat since Arsenal had won 5-0 in 1978. Journeyman striker David Cross scored all four goals in a 4-0 rout. Three of the goals came from crosses and this was already becoming something of an issue for Spurs; the two goals conceded in the Charity Shield and the goal at Middlesbrough were also from crosses from wide positions. The fourth West Ham goal was even more calamitous – Clemence made a mess of his first save and then scrambled around his six-yard box in vain as Cross bundled the ball over the line.

Spurs' next match saw another home defeat in a re-run of the Charity Shield. Chris Jones made a rare start, with Crooks, Archibald and Galvin all unavailable. Jones hit the bar and all seemed well until Villa blitzed Spurs with three first-half goals – all created by crosses into the box! The first was an own goal from the largely forgotten Gordon Smith, who returned to the team due to an injury to Price. Villa (Ricky, that is) scored the goal of the game but it was a mere consolation.

The West Stand was now beginning to take shape, with the roof and seating rows assembled above and below the two rows of executive boxes. ITV's *The Big Match* featured the near-completed boxes within their highlights coverage of the game.

Daniel Wynne and his father had been West Stand season ticket holders since 1974. They had been relocated to the East Stand and Daniel was excited by the prospect of coming back to the new West Stand:

> The West Stand was always the side of the ground I wanted to watch games from. Ironically, later in life I became the club's in-house commentator and was located right at the top of the East Stand! But back in 1981, my excitement ahead of each home match was just as much about seeing what progress had been made on the new stand as it was about the match itself. You could see from the designs that it was going to be futuristic, with a cantilever roof

providing unobstructed views. The facilities on offer for non-hospitality supporters like my father and I were going to be significantly superior to anything we'd experienced before. I remember one game the ball being kicked up into the empty upper tier and thinking in my naïve youth that it might just end up where my new seat would be and that I'd get it when we moved in! There was a fresh feel to the stadium and that was mirrored by the team on the pitch. It felt like we were embracing the 80s!

In the same month, the club held the AGM for shareholders. Irving Scholar was asked to attend by a shareholding friend and challenged Arthur Richardson about the ongoing costs of the stand and the impact this would have on investment in the team. Richardson at first refused to recognise Scholar's right to ask a question as a proxy but, after some deliberation, the club solicitor advised that he was.

Scholar continued to push back against Richardson's assurances, which sparked others in attendance to challenge the state of the club's accounts. According to Scholar, this unsettled Richardson but also caused concern for Keith Burkinshaw, who was in attendance. After the meeting, Burkinshaw approached Scholar to confirm that funds were, indeed, limited.

On the pitch, back-to-back wins, without conceding, against Wolves and Everton were encouraging, though the big story in September was the return to European football, with a mouth-watering draw pairing Spurs with Ajax in the first round of the Cup Winners' Cup.

The Dutch giants weren't the force they had been a decade earlier, when they won three successive European Cups, but were still a formidable outfit and a big name. Bill Nicholson had famously claimed that 'Spurs were nothing without Europe' and it was ties like this that furthered the sense that Spurs were back in the big time.

Playing in all yellow in the first leg in Amsterdam, Spurs were majestic. Falco scored twice in the first half and Villa rounded off the scoring after the break. Ajax scored instantly from the restart but Spurs had a two-goal cushion to bring back to White Hart Lane.

The second leg at the end of September saw a comfortable 3-0 home victory. Spurs maintained a tradition set by Nicholson in the 60s by playing in all white. The goals were all scored in the second half – by Galvin, Falco and Ardiles – with Hoddle purring in midfield.

The game against Ajax was the first of 32 European fixtures Spurs played in the 80s. Many players have discussed how the more technical and sophisticated style of play adopted by most continental teams suited their own style of play. This first result against Ajax was a statement of intent for the way they would approach European football.

Domestically, Spurs seemed reluctant to shake off their 'inconsistent' tag, going down 2-1 at newly promoted Swansea City, but defeat in South Wales was followed up with six straight wins in all competitions without conceding a single goal. League wins against Manchester City, Nottingham Forest, Stoke and Sunderland pushed Spurs up into second, just a point behind shock leaders Swansea.

There was also a League Cup second-round first-leg victory over Manchester United, who had just purchased Bryan Robson for a British record transfer fee of £1.5m. Archibald scored the only goal of the game, though the win was marred by an injury to Falco, who had scored nine goals in 11 games that season. At least Crooks was back on the bench, ready to replace him.

Having beaten Ajax, Spurs were given an intriguing second-round tie against League of Ireland Cup winners Dundalk. The first leg took place in the Republic of Ireland, just ten miles from the border with Northern Ireland at the height of 'The Troubles'. A very heavy police presence and security was provided for the team – measures taken to the extent of police officers with dogs being stationed around the perimeter of the pitch.

Hoddle and Perryman have both written about the incredibly tense atmosphere which reached boiling point when, during the game, a loud PA Tannoy alerted everyone of 'an important announcement'. To the relief and, latterly, the amusement of the players, it wasn't to announce an emergency evacuation but merely to advise that 'Bovril will be served in the West Stand during half-time'!

A heavy pitch and a determined home side meant Spurs were given more of a game than they had faced against Ajax in the previous round. Crooks gave Spurs a first-half lead which was cancelled out after the break and the game ended in a draw.

Back in league action, Spurs lost at home to Brighton when a win would have put them top but they did finish off the job in the League Cup, by beating Manchester United in the return leg at Old Trafford. October was rounded off with a last-minute winner at Southampton. Graham Roberts opened the scoring with a goal against the club who had rejected him as a teenager but it was another youngster, Pat Corbett, who popped up to give Spurs a late winner on his debut. Corbett was a defender but, having replaced the injured Crooks, played as an emergency striker and was in the right place to pounce after Archibald's shot had been saved.

November saw Spurs progress in both the European Cup Winners' Cup – despatching Dundalk 1-0 at White Hart Lane – and Wrexham, of Division Two, were beaten in the League Cup, with goals from Hughton and Hoddle. The league championship still seemed an open race. Spurs were back up to third and only six points separated Manchester United, who were now top, and West Ham in sixth.

Both games against Dundalk seemed to take their physical toll. After the first leg, Spurs had lost to Brighton in the subsequent league game and they suffered the same fate when West Brom, fourth from bottom, won 2-1 at White Hart Lane. Due to West Brom's green and yellow kit, Ray Clemence was forced to wear a red jersey for the game, an unusual sight for any Spurs player. The winning goal was scored by Dutchman Martin Jol, who, almost 23 years to the day later, would become Spurs manager.

By the time of Spurs' next game, English football was on a high after the national team beat Hungary at Wembley to qualify for their first World Cup since 1970. Hoddle had missed the game through injury but recovered in time to face Manchester United for the third time that season. Spurs were again victorious, with goals from Hazard, Roberts and Archibald. The result pushed Spurs back up into second, only two points behind United and with two games in hand. Talk of a title challenge was now firmly on the cards.

While Spurs continued to entertain, the matchday environment was turning particularly unsavoury. The 1981/82 season had seen an upturn in arrests and ejections at football stadiums. At a time when Spurs' football was a huge draw, the overall experience of going to games put off many, including Simon Shroot, then a 14-year-old from north-west London for whom the game against Manchester United was his first:

I'd got into a routine of going to my friend, Michael's, house on a Sunday afternoon and we'd watch *Match of the Day*. Spurs were very much our team and, with a little bit of disposable cash and being allowed to do what I wanted to at a weekend, Michael and I decided we'd actually go and watch Spurs play live. Our journey across town from Wembley to White Hart Lane was one initially of excitement and anticipation at being able to see Hoddle, Crooks, Archibald in the flesh. But, as we got off the train at White Hart Lane, the reality of the occasion became apparent.

We made our way around to Worcester Avenue so that we could stand on The Shelf but arrived at the very moment that a sea of Manchester United fans' coaches had just pulled up and hundreds of their fans emerged on to the street like a pack of feral animals just released from a cage. Glass bottles and missiles flew over us, which then provoked several Spurs fans to retaliate. I was Jewish, so to then hear antisemitic shouts and songs from the United fans and the 'Y word' chanted back in defence only added to what was becoming a thoroughly unpleasant and shocking experience. We got inside the stadium for what I'm sure was an incredible view of a great match but all I can remember were the offensive songs, pent-up aggression and avoiding the urine that found its way along the concrete below us from all angles.

Maybe I was unlucky just to be in the wrong place at the wrong time but it put me off going to football. Spurs have continued to be 'my team' but I've never got over that first experience.

Simon was not the only supporter to be turned off attending matches during the period but for others, visiting White Hart Lane provided a sense of belonging, despite the ongoing risks. Marlene Peirce, then in her 30s, still attended regularly:

I knew there could be trouble outside the grounds but was always quite savvy, so knew how to avoid it. There were certain games that were a risk but it never stopped me going. I travelled down from Harlow in a group that included my husband, Steve. When we arrived outside the stadium, he'd go and meet up with his mates and I'd meet up with a group of other women I'd got to know. We'd queue up early to get into our same spot on The Shelf; quite low down but right on the halfway line.

If I heard any particularly bad language, I felt confident enough to turn around and tell them to stop and I knew I'd be backed up. I remember the peanut seller; he'd pass them down a long line to the recipient and eventually a handful of coins would come back the other way in payment. There was a real community feel on The Shelf. As a group of women, we always felt very safe and secure and part of something bigger.

Going to Spurs in the 80s was a huge part of my life. When The Shelf became seats, we all continued to sit together. We've been split up since the new stadium opened but I'm still in contact with many of the friends I made.

Aside from hooliganism, the other factor that could be guaranteed to wreak havoc on English football was bad weather.

In the week that followed, the North and West were battered by a weather system that caused Europe's biggest recorded tornado outbreak. A remarkable 104 recorded tornadoes hit parts of the country and, though they didn't cause much damage, they induced a cold snap that would have a profound impact on Spurs' title ambitions.

The weather held no responsibility for two disappointing results – a draw at Notts County and a defeat at home to Coventry – but a 0-0 draw in the snow at Elland Road on 12 December, one of only three games played in Division One that day, still meant that Spurs were within three points of Manchester United with a game in hand.

The weather had not had such a significant impact on the English football calendar since the big freeze of 1962. Back then, Spurs had been top in January before the inclement weather only allowed them to play once in six weeks. The eventual fixture backlog, compounded by an ultimately successful European Cup Winners' Cup campaign, cost a great Spurs team the opportunity to win the league for a second time in three years. Unbeknown to anyone leaving Elland Road that evening in 1981, history was about to repeat itself.

All of Spurs' remaining league games throughout the rest of December were postponed. Of 40 Division One matches scheduled between 12 and 28 December, only nine were played and most of those were at grounds, such as Everton and Manchester City, where an effective undersoil heating system had been installed.

One Spurs fan leaving Elland Road and heading back down the M1 to London had far more than weather on his mind. Since attending the AGM in September, Irving Scholar had become slightly obsessed with the predicament he saw his beloved club potentially falling into. While his friends were talking about the game at Leeds, the prospects for the rest of the season and plans for Christmas, Scholar was contemplating how he might be able to become more than just a supporter of the football club.

As recounted in his book, when the club formed as a company in 1898, 8,000 shares were offered to the public, of which just shy of 5,000 were actually taken. They were in the hands of somewhere between 500 and 600 individuals, many owning just one share gifted to them as a birthday or Christmas present. Some shares had travelled as far and wide as Australia and North America.

The largest individual shareholders were the members of the current board. Sidney Wale had stepped away since being replaced by Arthur Richardson in 1980 but still owned 734 shares, meaning he owned approximately 15 per cent of the company.

Around Christmastime, Scholar received a full list of shareholders, along with copies of the accounts and the articles of association (the rules of the company). Scholar painstakingly went through the list and wrote to all shareholders, offering them £250 per share for anyone owning between one and 20 shares, £150 to those with between 21 and 50 shares and £100 for anyone with 51 or more.

Scholar was delighted to receive several swift positive responses and began to accumulate a small number of shares but was then dismayed when he learnt that the articles of association gave the directors the right not to recognise the transfer of shares between individuals. There had been previous examples of supporters being blocked when trying to purchase shares. As far back as 1935, there had been a legal precedent set when a disgruntled supporter, Hubert Berry, had tested the waters by attempting to transfer a single share to a friend. The transfer was blocked by the directors (long before the Wales and Richardsons were on the board) and this was ratified in court.

Seeking legal guidance, Scholar was advised that the article in question (article 14) was still valid in law, though there might be a loophole whereby, although the transfer of shares may not be recognised, there was nothing preventing Scholar legally acquiring the shares. This galvanised Scholar, who believed he could continue to purchase shares and exert influence on the board. He didn't harbour any realistic ambitions of actually mounting a full takeover.

The cold snap that engulfed Britian through December finally gave way ahead of New Year, with a milder front bringing heavy rain instead. Spurs' first game since that draw at Leeds was the opening tie in their defence of the FA Cup and the third-round draw paired them with Arsenal at White Hart Lane for only the second meeting between the two clubs in the competition's history.

Supporters, who had suffered from football withdrawal symptoms, braved a torrential downpour to queue for tickets that 2 January morning and the game was, unsurprisingly, sold out. At the first match at White Hart Lane for almost a month, fans and the TV cameras from ITV were drawn to the development of the West Stand, where plastic blue seats had now been installed in the upper and lower tiers. The opening was now only weeks away.

The enforced break had at least provided time for Mark Falco to return following the Achilles injury he had picked up in October. Archibald was still unavailable and, with Crooks having missed the start of the season through injury, Falco remained the club's top scorer with nine goals.

The Tannoy system blasted out 'Ossie's Dream' immediately ahead of kick-off but the game could be remembered as 'Pat's nightmare'. The Arsenal goalkeeper endured perhaps the most miserable afternoon of his professional career. Crooks's speculative shot in the first half managed to creep underneath him for what proved to be the only goal of the game and Jennings's afternoon got worse when he pulled up with a thigh muscle tear.

Jennings was eventually helped to his feet but was clearly in a lot of pain and couldn't continue. He was led off the pitch, receiving a round of applause from both sets of fans. He remains, perhaps, the only player in north London who could generate such a positive response from across the great divide.

Arsenal ended the game with an outfield player in goal but couldn't recreate the heroics that Hoddle and Spurs had achieved at Old Trafford two years previously. Spurs saw out the game and progressed to the fourth round, where they would meet Leeds at White Hart Lane.

A second cold snap hit Britain again by the start of the following week. Only two league games were played the following weekend and half the Division One games, including Tottenham's, were postponed on 16 January. It now meant that five league games would have to be squeezed into a busy fixture list that was swollen by continued progress in both domestic cup competitions.

The West Stand was opened to the public for the first time (though the official opening was a few weeks away) for the League Cup quarter-final against Nottingham Forest on Monday, 18 January. Ardiles scored the only goal in a 1-0 win, though the game was also memorable for a three-times-taken penalty by Hoddle that was finally saved by Peter Shilton. In the FA Cup, a dogged Leeds team stifled Spurs until Burkinshaw replaced Falco with Hazard, who was involved in the game's only goal, scored by Crooks.

League action finally returned when Middlesbrough visited – Crooks again scoring in a 1-0 win. Spurs went into the game in 11th place, having played fewer games than everyone else in the division. The three points lifted them to eighth, seven points behind leaders Manchester United, who had played three games more.

The win over Forest put Spurs into the semi-finals of the League Cup, sponsored now by the National Dairy Council and now known as the Milk Cup – a sign of the growing commercialisation coming into English football. Appearing in the final four for the first time since 1976, Spurs were drawn against West Brom, who were fast becoming their bogey team, having won each of the past four league encounters.

Spurs travelled to The Hawthorns on 3 February for what turned out to be a particularly nasty encounter. Seven players were booked and Tony Galvin was sent off following an altercation with Martin Jol, who was also dismissed. There was far more action in the referee's notebook than there was goalmouth action and the game ended 0-0 amid a small number of West Brom fans running on to the field at full time to direct their anger at Spurs players and the referee.

Before the second leg, the following midweek, Spurs officially unveiled the new West Stand. Former FA and FIFA president Sir Stanley Rous conducted the opening ceremony and watched on in awe as Spurs put six past Wolves – Villa netting a hat-trick and Crooks, with a bullet header, also among the goals.

Spurs beat West Brom 1-0 in the Milk Cup second leg. Hazard made his first start since December and it was his goal that separated the teams, sending Spurs back to Wembley, where they would play Liverpool in March.

Against another familiar West Midlands opponent, Aston Villa, Spurs progressed to the FA Cup quarter-finals. The 1-0 win, courtesy of a Mark Falco header, marked a record-breaking ninth consecutive cup game without conceding a goal. Ray Clemence made a huge contribution in Spurs' defensive robustness. His organisation and leadership skills were as important as his actual goalkeeping, which was invariably immaculate.

Having now knocked out Arsenal and Aston Villa, Spurs were also pleased to see Liverpool and Ipswich eliminated at the fifth-round stage. Liverpool were beaten 2-0 at second-tier Chelsea. It meant that Spurs were installed as favourites to retain the trophy – a feat no club had achieved since Bill Nicholson's team had won it back-to-back in 1961 and 1962. Spurs were the highest-placed league team in a final eight which included fellow First Division outfits West Brom and Coventry, plus five lower-division sides; three from London, in Chelsea, Crystal Palace and QPR, along with Leicester and Shrewsbury.

With four London clubs involved, the Metropolitan Police would have been listening with some dread when Crystal Palace drew QPR, leaving just Chelsea and Spurs to come out of the bag for a game scheduled for Stamford Bridge on 6 March.

Spurs' continued participation in the cups only put them further behind in the league. By mid-February, they sat in eighth, 11 points behind leaders Southampton but having played five games fewer. A draw at Villa was followed by wins against Manchester City and Stoke, keeping Spurs within reach of the summit.

The win over Manchester City provided a moment of history for the club when Ally Dick became the youngest-ever player to start a senior match. Aged just 16 years and 301 days, Dick replaced the injured Galvin.

The young Scot had risen to prominence after he starred in a Scotland Schoolboys match against England in 1980. The game had been televised live and Dick, at his own insistence, still unsigned by any club, had the pick of clubs from either side of the border. Spurs won the race to sign him and he mostly played in the youth team and reserves that season. In an interview with *superhotspur.com*, Dick recalled learning through his landlady and the back page of the local newspaper that he was likely to be involved in the game.

Results in February set the agenda for what lay ahead. Spurs had nine games scheduled in March alone, with the potential for additional cup replays. The fixtures included the League Cup Final against Liverpool, the FA Cup tie with Chelsea and the two-legged European Cup Winners' Cup quarter-final against Eintracht Frankfurt.

The West German cup winners visited White Hart Lane on 3 March. Miller scored his first of the season and Hazard added a second, providing a two-goal cushion and, crucially, Eintracht left without claiming a valuable away goal. It was now five successive home games in all competitions without conceding at White Hart Lane.

The trip across London to Chelsea was fraught with danger, not least for the supporters. Hooliganism was spreading and clashes inside and outside grounds often resembled battle scenes. If you could avoid the fighting, the vile discrimination based on ethnicity, race, gender and sexuality was turning many away from football.

Darryl Telles, then aged 18, is well placed to discuss the environment in and around football stadiums at the time. A Spurs fan of Goan heritage, he was also gay:

> I had lots of Jewish friends and this was only 35 years after the Second World War, so many of them had heard first-

hand the horrific stories from their parents or grandparents about the Holocaust. I was incredibly proud that so many Spurs fans engaged in the Anti-Nazi League. As a person of colour, going to watch games at White Hart Lane was definitely easier than other stadiums. Chris Hughton wrote a column in the local paper about anti-racism and that really resonated with me. Spurs felt like the anti-discrimination club and I never felt threatened because of my race. Homophobia was a different story, though. This was before I went to university and I wasn't outwardly gay at this point but the terraces were a deeply unpleasant place to be.

Stamford Bridge was considered to be one of the most violent away grounds to travel to, a situation not helped by some Chelsea supporters' association with the National Front and overtly racist undertones.

Naturally, Chelsea, as a club, wanted to distance themselves from this element of their fanbase and, following some ugly incidents at away games, felt compelled to discourage any further trouble.

The front page of the matchday programme, usually reserved for an action image, was replaced by a plain black front with white printed writing stating:

IF YOU ARE HERE, MASQUERADING AS A FOOTBALL SUPPORTER BUT YOUR SOLE PURPOSE IS TO CAUSE TROUBLE THEN YOU ARE NOT WELCOME. YOUR BEHAVIOUR AS WITNESSED IN THE PAST, WILL NO LONGER BE TOLERATED. NOT ONLY WILL WE ENSURE THAT YOU ARE EJECTED FROM THE GROUND AND BANNED FOR LIFE FROM STAMFORD BRIDGE, BUT ALSO CHELSEA FOOTBALL CLUB WILL NOT HESITATE TO BRING A PRIVATE PROSECUTION AND CIVIL CLAIM FOR DAMAGES AGAINST YOU.

Chelsea had stunned Liverpool in the fifth round and now hoped to upset Spurs – a team their fans always considered to be their biggest rivals, which only fuelled the flames higher. Ever since the draw had been made, even the most mild-mannered of Chelsea fans had been savouring the opportunity to get one over on Spurs.

Around 15,000 Spurs fans made the journey across London but it was the team that suffered more disruption. The team coach got caught up in heavy traffic through west London and only arrived at Stamford Bridge at 2.45pm. Having already incurred a fine for submitting a late team sheet, Spurs then discovered that the referee wasn't happy with the team playing in navy shorts, as Chelsea were playing in royal blue. Having not brought white shorts, they were forced to play in Chelsea's white away shorts.

Spurs were somewhat flustered and Chelsea got on the front foot, with a vociferous home crowd willing them on. It took until the 43rd minute for the home side to score – the first goal Spurs had conceded in a cup game all season. Stamford Bridge was febrile.

Despite going a goal down at half-time, the players were confident they would turn around the deficit. After all, they were used to overcoming adversity in big cup games. In the second half, they produced one of the best performances of the era – fluent on the ball, with Hoddle and Hazard majestic in midfield. Hoddle had a hand in all three goals. His free kick was spilled by Chelsea's goalkeeper and Archibald slid in the equaliser. Then came the goal that defined the beauty of Spurs.

Hughton galloped forwards from the halfway line and passed the ball into Archibald, who flicked the ball up into the path of Hazard, 25 yards from goal. As was so often the case, the playing surface was imperfect but Hazard overcame that by volleying square to Hoddle, who cushioned the ball perfectly into his forward stride and struck it with the outside of his right foot from a slight angle. Hoddle cut across the ball perfectly, providing sufficient bend with the outside of his boot to set the ball wide of the stretch of the Chelsea goalkeeper but with enough bend to bring it back inside the post. BBC commentator John Motson described it as 'an educated move that says so much about Spurs'.

Within eight minutes, Spurs had a cushion. This time, Hoddle teed up Hazard to guide an arrow-like shot into the bottom corner from 20 yards. Chelsea did pull a goal back but Spurs held on to claim victory and progress to another semi-final.

Once Spurs had won at Brighton in midweek, all attention turned to the following weekend's Milk Cup Final against Liverpool. Hoddle was given a rare night off against Brighton to nurse a minor back injury and was replaced by Roberts but Spurs still won 3-1 with goals from Ardiles, Archibald and Crooks.

Keith Burkinshaw's selection dilemma for the final centred on whether to stick with Paul Price over Graham Roberts in central defence. Price had partnered Miller for 11 of the previous 12 games, including the last five. Much to the disappointment of Roberts, who expected to be picked, Burkinshaw went for the same XI who had beaten both Chelsea and Eintracht Frankfurt in March. Roberts was not even named as the substitute – the place going to Villa, who had returned from injury.

Falco could also consider himself unfortunate not to be involved – he'd scored 11 goals by this point – but the Archibald-Crooks partnership had played the last five games.

Wembley was becoming a second home to Spurs – this was now the fourth visit in ten months – but Liverpool were also more than familiar with the Twin Towers. They'd won the European Cup there in 1978, were the League Cup holders, having played West Ham at Wembley the previous season (though they required a replay win at Villa Park) and had featured in five Charity Shields since 1974.

Liverpool had shown fallibility recently; they went into the final having lost to Brighton the week before and their FA Cup campaign had ended at Chelsea – where Spurs had, of course, just won. Spurs had won just one of their last seven games against Liverpool since returning to Division One but went into the game with great confidence on the back of a 16-game unbeaten streak.

As early as the third minute, Spurs took the lead when Archibald capitalised on a rare moment of uncertainty in the Liverpool defence and poked the ball past Bruce Grobbelaar. The chorus of 'Spurs are on their way to Wembley' was audible around the ground.

Liverpool were capable of the ugly and Graeme Souness was incredibly fortunate to avoid punishment for a horrendous challenge on Tony Galvin. It left Galvin writhing in pain on the ground with a huge gash down his shin, yet not even a free kick was awarded. The winger limped back into the game and adrenaline carried him through.

It was a high-quality game between two excellent teams. Archibald had a chance to score a second but saw his effort scrambled off the line by Souness and Spurs paid the price with three minutes to play. When a Galvin cross was cleared by Alan Hansen, Liverpool broke the length of the pitch to equalise through Ronnie Whelan.

Extra time proved a step too far for a Spurs side running on fumes. In the minutes between the end of full time and the start of extra time, the Spurs team were sat on the turf, physically recovering, while Liverpool remained standing for their team talk. Whelan, again, and Ian Rush scored to inflict Spurs' first-ever Wembley defeat.

For Steve Perryman, it was a case of what might have been:

Looking back, we won two FA Cups but both had required replays and, with all due respect to both Manchester City and QPR, they weren't on the same level as Liverpool. I wouldn't say that losing that game had an adverse effect on us as such but, mentally, I do believe that had we held on to beat the great Liverpool team, it might just have given us that extra confidence and belief in the future.

David Harris, like many Spurs fans of the era, was a regular visitor to Wembley and has his own take on why Spurs lost:

I loved Graham Roberts. I'd actually been at the game at Anfield in 1980 when he made his debut, so have always had an affinity with him. It was a mistake to leave him out in this final. For this game, I was sat very close to where the Liverpool fans were standing. When Whelan equalised so late, I felt a sense of resignation. I remember the newspaper the following day included a really insightful photograph just before extra time where our players were sat on the floor recovering but Liverpool's were all made to stand up.

It was a tough one to take but there was little time to dwell on defeat, as Spurs had to travel to Frankfurt for their European quarter-final second leg. Burkinshaw made just one change – replacing Crooks with Falco – and a tired-looking Spurs team fell 2-0 behind, wiping out the first leg advantage, inside just 15 minutes.

It took courage and determination to stem the momentum of the West German team and, with 13 minutes remaining and the prospect of extra time looming, Hughton found the energy to drive up the left touchline to find Villa, who laid the ball square for Hoddle to guide a left-footed shot into the corner. The away goal provided comfort and saw Spurs through.

The focus for the rest of March reverted back to the league. Spurs played four times in ten days – winning just once, against Southampton at White Hart Lane when Graham Roberts, playing in midfield, scored a hat-trick. Draws against Birmingham and Arsenal sandwiched a defeat to West Brom, leaving Spurs seventh, seven points behind Southampton but still with five games in hand.

Global politics would then have a bearing on the remainder of Spurs' season. On 2 April, Argentinian forces invaded the Falkland Islands, a largely unknown British territory in the South Atlantic. While the invasion dominated the news in both the UK and Argentina, most of the Spurs team were far more concerned with preparations for their FA Cup semi-final the following day as they retired for the evening at their hotel close to Birmingham. However, Steve Perryman was kept awake by animated conversations emanating from the room shared by Ardiles and Villa as the pair took calls from their respective families back in Argentina.

The semi-final was due to be Ardiles's final Spurs appearance of the season. Keith Burkinshaw had agreed to a request from his national team manager, César Luis Menotti, to release Ardiles a month early to prepare for the summer's World Cup tournament. Villa, though, hadn't been selected.

As a nation woke to the developing news, it was clear that neither Argentine was going to be well received by sections of the nation's football community. Ricky Villa didn't play at Villa Park but Ardiles did and was booed by Leicester fans throughout the game. In contrast, the travelling Spurs fans got right behind both men in an act of genuine solidarity.

Spurs always looked the superior side but it took until the second half to make the breakthrough. Hoddle worked a corner to Ardiles just inside the penalty area and he had time to turn and fire the ball across the six-yard box, where Crooks guided the ball in.

Leicester had hoped to wear out Spurs after their recent exertions but, despite a very heavy pitch, Spurs' midfield was able to take control and Galvin enjoyed space out wide on the left. It was the winger's cross that was inexplicably and comically placed into his own goal by defender Ian Wilson with a finish that any of Spurs' great players would have been proud of!

This semi-final victory felt far more routine than the emotional rollercoaster 12 months earlier against Wolves but the outcome was the same – Spurs were going to Wembley for the FA Cup Final!

At a team party that night, Ardiles told his team-mates that he wouldn't be back before the final and warned them that there would be stories in the tabloids about him. He wasn't wrong. *The Sun* ran a nonsense story shortly afterwards stating that he had said he was 'going to kill the English'.

In the other semi-final, QPR surprisingly edged past West Brom to set up another all-London FA Cup Final; it was the fourth in 15 years, Spurs having played Chelsea in the first in

1967. Now, there were suits to be ordered and cup final records to be produced – Chas & Dave had naturally been commissioned to write a new one – but, unlike the previous year, thoughts of Wembley had to be put into the background.

FC Barcelona didn't quite have the same air of grandeur as they would develop in the 20th century but were still a revered and mystical opponent as they travelled to north London on 7 April. Neither Falco nor Archibald were available, so Burkinshaw picked Roberts in midfield and brought Villa back in.

Such was the excitement about the occasion that, ahead of the game, some Spurs fans and their Barcelona counterparts exchanged scarves in the Park Lane. Hostilities on the pitch soon ended that sense of comradeship.

Anyone who attended the game was shocked by the Catalan club's gameplan to kick anything in white and no protection was offered to Spurs by the match officials. Spurs eventually sank to their opponents' level and the game descended into farce – even Hoddle kicked out. By half-time, those red and blue scarves that had been accepted by Spurs fans in the Park Lane were being set on fire.

In the rare moments of actual football, Spurs had the better of the game and played with a technical superiority that seemed to aggravate the Catalan side. Against the run of play, Ray Clemence made a rare howler when, midway into the second half, he let a speculative shot from range slip through his hands to give Barcelona an undeserved lead. Roberts, never one to back away from a physical battle, did score an equaliser shortly before the end but the damage was done.

One newspaper led with the back page headline: ANIMALS! THE BUTCHERS OF BARCELONA SHAKE BATTLING SPURS

Back-to-back league wins at Easter gave faint hope that Spurs could still win the title. The second of those came at Highbury, with goals by Hazard and Crooks (2), but, ominously, Liverpool were now top, having won six successive league games. Spurs did have three games in hand but still had 12 league matches to play in little over a month. The first of those proved decisive. Against Sunderland, one place off the bottom of the league, Spurs led 2-0 and looked comfortable, only to concede twice in the final 15 minutes.

Steffan Chirazi had been at both games:

We were in the middle of a schedule pressure cooker. Managing minutes was not a luxury and players were giving their all, despite not being 100 per cent.

Tony Galvin suffered an awful foul at the boot of Graeme Souness back in March during the Milk Cup Final, a particularly egregious foul I personally believe resulted in him never quite being the same player again. Yet, we went to Arsenal that Easter Monday knowing a win would keep us on course for the title. The match went as well as you could imagine; a 3-1 win, some wonderful football, the superlative Garth Crooks grabbing a brace and the chronically underrated Mickey Hazard getting the other. Indeed, I left the Clock End bouncing and ready for what would surely be a trouncing of Sunderland 48 hours later at The Lane.

It seemed an accurate feeling on that Wednesday night after 45 minutes. Two-nil up and cruising, it felt our goal difference would get some serious second-half weight. But somewhere in the second half, it felt like we lost focus; albeit hindsight now suggests that it was physical and mental fatigue. I believe Galvin tripped Stan Cummins somewhat unnecessarily to concede a penalty with under 15 minutes left and then I just remember the palpable surge of nerves through The Shelf. We gave up the equaliser some five minutes or so later and, as I left The Lane at the final whistle, I suddenly felt that not only were our title hopes done, I feared we might not finish with any reward for our brilliant football.

The sheer physical absurdity of playing 18 games in 51 days, with one substitute per game and a small squad, was too much – as well as an extra level of brute physicality we were consistently on the receiving end of. This was not just in the league but in Europe, too, where Barcelona's visit for the Cup Winners' Cup semi-final first leg saw them forever etched in my memory as the filthiest side I have ever seen visit N17 (a whole other story).

Looking back, it was wholly inevitable that a Sunderland would happen … but try telling that to this 15-year-old at the time!

A 2-0 defeat at Old Trafford three days later seemed to end the title bid once and for all. Spurs were sixth but 14 points behind Liverpool, who kept winning.

Further fixture congestion was alleviated when Barcelona narrowly beat Spurs 1-0 at the Nou Camp. There were disagreements within the changing room as to whether Spurs should fight fire with fire and adopt an equally physical approach but, ahead of the game, the referee came in to address the team and advised them that any repeat of the first game could result in an abandonment and both teams being disqualified from the competition.

Spurs elected to play football and created the better chances in the first half but when the Dane, Allan Simonsen, put the home side ahead just after the restart, it proved to be a hurdle too far for a tired Spurs team. The European adventure had ended but much had been gained and lessons learned that would be of great use within the next two years, as Tony Parks, on the bench for both games, recalls:

I've never seen a team adopt such a rough approach – it was way beyond what you expected on a football pitch. They knew we were a better football team than them, so decided they'd just try and kick us off the park. If anything, it was even worse in the away game. Before the game, the referee came into us and told us that if WE retaliated, there was a chance UEFA would kick us out the competition! We felt really hard done by and there was a strong sense that UEFA had it in for all English clubs. However, we learnt a lot from all our European experiences in this season, especially now we'd had to deal with being literally kicked out of the competition by Barcelona! It was little things like coping with the travel and the recovery afterwards. We were building something and used the experience with Barcelona to make us stronger and more determined the following season.

Domestically, the pressure of the title race had seemingly subsided and this provided an opportunity to rotate players, giving the likes of Garry Brooke and Gary O'Reilly appearances, as well as debuts for Tony Parks and midfielder Ian Crook.

The title was mathematically lost after a defeat at West Ham on 10 May – the second in a run of three games played within five days. Spurs lost their remaining two matches but ended the season in fourth position – enough to secure a place in the UEFA Cup the following season should they fail to win the FA Cup and return to the Cup Winners' Cup.

For the second year in a row, a Spurs squad appeared on *Top of the Pops* to perform their cup final song. 'Tottenham, Tottenham', written by Chas & Dave, was inspired by Chubby Checker's 'Lets Twist Again' – specifically the line about 'doing it like we did last year'. The song peaked at No.19.

With the Falklands War ongoing, Ricky Villa made the sad but understandable decision not to play. Villa felt that the prospect of appearing in the showpiece final – a culturally significant event that involved the royal family – was insensitive.

The only change from the semi-final line-up was Miller replacing Ardiles. This meant that Roberts played in midfield. Hazard started alongside him, having enjoyed an excellent season with ten goals, four of which had come in cup games. Tony Galvin had missed the last seven league games but was passed fit while Steve Perryman, having appeared in all 64 first-team games that season, required a painkilling injection in his thigh to be able to lead out the team again at Wembley. Perryman had been named as the Football Writers' Association player of the season.

Spurs were up against Queens Park Rangers, who were playing in their first FA Cup Final. The Division Two side were managed by the ex-Spurs midfielder Terry Venables, who was making a name for himself as a tactically astute coach and a charismatic and ambitious manager who also had become a club director.

Venables's involvement was one of several intriguing narratives that are common in showpiece games. Venables had played for QPR in the 70s and was signed by former Spurs double-winning striker Les Allen. Allen's eldest son, Clive, was a talented youth footballer but had been overlooked by Spurs, eventually being picked up by QPR. He enjoyed a breakout season in 1979/80, scoring 30 times, which led to him becoming the first £1m teenager when he was signed by Arsenal in the summer of 1980. In one of the decade's most bizarre transfer stories, Allen was an Arsenal player for 63 days, only appearing in pre-season games before he was sold to Crystal Palace in order for Kenny Sansom to move the other way.

At that point, Crystal Palace were managed by Venables but within six months he had moved on to QPR, where he promptly signed Allen, reuniting them in west London for the start of the 1981/82 season and completing the ultimate transfer merry-go-round.

Drawn as the 'away team', Spurs had to play in their change strip of all yellow; the first time they not worn their traditional white for a cup final.

The final few weeks of the season had been a slog for Spurs and Venables knew that the best way to cause an upset was to neutralise Hoddle. What followed was a largely uneventful 90 minutes in which neither team scored. Lawrie McMenemy, a pundit for BBC's *Match of the Day*, described the game as 'boring'. That said, QPR goalkeeper Peter Hucker was named man of the match, which indicates that Spurs created the better chances, the best falling to Archibald, who saw his shot tipped wide.

The game went into extra time. Hoddle had been Spurs' standout player and eventually broke the deadlock in the second half. Having been man-marked throughout the game, Hoddle won a tackle in midfield against his marker, Gary Waddock, although it looked like a foul. The ball broke for Roberts and he carried it forwards before laying it back to Hoddle, who set himself and, from 20 yards, guided a shot into the bottom corner. It took a slight deflection off Tony Currie but was undoubtedly Hoddle's goal.

Spurs looked to be able to play out the remaining 11 minutes but, after substitute Brooke gave the ball away, Price was forced to hack the ball clear into touch. QPR were strong from set pieces and Stainrod's long throw was flicked on by Hazell and Terry Fenwick became the first full-back to score an FA Cup Final goal from open play, forcing an unlikely draw and a replay.

For the replay, Burkinshaw named an unchanged team. The previous season, the retention of Ricky Villa had been the main talking point and this year Villa also made the headlines. He was part of the non-playing group resplendent in club suits and ties (the tie was produced by Paul Miller's design company) and made his way out to huge applause from the Spurs fans at the tunnel end.

The replay began in much the same pattern as the first game. Spurs had plenty of the ball but the decisive moment of the final came as early as the sixth minute. Roberts took possession on the halfway line and channelled his inner-Ricky Villa, slaloming between QPR defenders. Stand-in QPR captain Currie made a rash decision to try and tackle Roberts and proceeded to bring him down, giving the referee an easy decision to point to the spot.

Hoddle sent Hucker the wrong way to provide a lead that Spurs managed to hold on to for the remaining 84 minutes. It wasn't a classic and neither game against QPR will live long in the memory. Nor does it produce the same emotional memories of 1981 but, nevertheless, Spurs had won their second major trophy in two seasons. They had now won the FA Cup on seven occasions, level with Aston Villa, and had won it as many times as anyone in the competition's 101-year history.

Perryman, having played all 66 games in a gruelling season, just about found the energy to climb the familiar 39 steps to lift the cup aloft and close an incredible season that had, at some points, promised to return more than just one trophy. Bill Nicholson had famously stated back in the 1960s that 'we set our sights very high, so high that even failure will have in it an echo of glory'.

It was a sign of the feeling within the club that 'only' winning the FA Cup was something of a disappointment. Five years previously, the club had been relegated to Division Two!

League position	Fourth
Average home league attendance	35,105
Most appearances	Perryman (66)
Top goalscorer	Crooks (18)
League winners	Liverpool
FA Cup winners	Spurs
League Cup winners	Liverpool

82/83 – BATTLE WEARY

CLEMENCE
O'REILLY PERRYMAN LACY HUGHTON
MABBUTT BROOKE VILLA GALVIN
ARCHIBALD CROOKS

AS IF the back-to-back FA Cup successes weren't reason enough for celebration, the 1982/83 season marked the club's 100th year in existence. A new home shirt was designed by Le Coq Sportif, with the centenary recognised on the club crest.

In a century, the custodianship of the club had changed on several occasions but now, unbeknown to all bar a few, the ownership was about to change hands. Irving Scholar had continued to purchase shares in the company and, during the summer of 1982, made a significant breakthrough when Sidney Wale agreed to sell him his 700 shares. Wale still carried the scars from the coup led by Geoffrey Richardson that saw him ousted as chairman in 1980.

As the World Cup played out in Spain, there was no sniff of a Spurs takeover and Scholar remained an unknown. That summer's competition became one of the most iconic World Cup tournaments of all time. Italy beat West Germany in the final, although it was once again the Brazilians, resplendent in their traditional yellow shirts, who, with the aid of colour television, captured the public imagination. Like Spurs on the domestic scene, Brazil were unable to win the ultimate prize that their style and flamboyancy deserved. England, playing in the World Cup for the first time since 1970, didn't lose a game but were knocked out after the second group stage. Hoddle was, once again, criminally underused.

Meanwhile, Ossie Ardiles represented Argentina as the Falklands War came to an end some 5,000 miles away in the South Atlantic. Ardiles's cousin had been killed, one of just over 900 soldiers who lost their lives from both sides. The ceasefire was declared the day after Argentina had lost their opening game against Belgium and, although they bounced back, with Ardiles among the scorers in the next match against Hungary, the holders could only finish second in their group, which presented them with the unenviable task of taking on Brazil and Italy in the second group stage, where they were eliminated.

Writing in his autobiography, *Ossie's Dream*, Ardiles describes the period after the World Cup as 'a black part of his life'. Though he doesn't feel the war had any impact on his or his team-mates' performance, he realised that he was in a 'lose-lose situation' ahead of the domestic season and would be lambasted by both the English and Argentine media if he returned to ply his trade in London.

Keith Burkinshaw and the club remained steadfast in their support for Ardiles and were loath to sanction a transfer but Ardiles was adamant that he needed to move abroad, despite the fact that his compatriot, Villa, was committed to remaining a Spurs player. In the end, a compromise was made when Paris Saint-Germain offered to take Ardiles on loan for the season.

Ardiles's absence towards the end of the previous season had undoubtedly affected Spurs, so the question of how they would cope without for him for a whole season, if not forever, loomed over the club as pre-season began in July.

Spurs fan Tim Vickery is well-known now as a South American football journalist. However, he was still living in London during the 1980s and is well placed to assess the impact of Ardiles' departure:

> Those of us who watched Ossie play every week realised that he was so vital and would be a huge loss. Hoddle and Villa often took the headlines and were capable of the spectacular but it was Ossie who kept everything ticking over in midfield. The dual identity of him and Spurs was

total; stylistically he was the perfect fit. The political situation was clearly a very difficult time for him personally – Ossie really embraced life in England. He moved away to Paris but his heart was always back in England.

The only new player arriving at White Hart Lane was the versatile England Under-21 star Gary Mabbutt, who joined from Bristol Rovers for a fee of £105,000. Mabbutt was best known within football for being a diagnosed type-1 diabetic, a condition that would normally have curtailed a professional sports career.

Speaking to the *Off The Shelf* podcast, Mabbutt explained how, after a series of poor performances around Christmas 1980, he had been referred to the Bristol Rovers club doctor. Tests revealed that he had type-1 diabetes – a condition about which there was relatively little known and, so, it was assumed that his career was over. After seeking guidance from several specialists – of which there were still very few – he was encouraged to trial a course of medication that would involve round-the-clock insulin injections.

Undeterred by the potentially fatal consequences, Mabbutt returned to first-team action at Bristol Rovers, impressing sufficiently in a struggling side in the second and then third tier of English football to earn a call-up to the England Under-21 squad.

When his contract expired at his hometown club at the end of the 1981/82 season, Mabbutt wrote to all Division One and Two clubs seeking a trial. He received just one positive response from Birmingham City, who offered him a contract.

Agreeable to the offer from Birmingham, Mabbutt was close to signing – until he received a phone call that changed his life. The call came from Bill Nicholson, who had read with interest the letter that Mabbutt had written some weeks earlier. In his capacity as chief scout, Nicholson was aware of Mabbutt and had seen him play for both his club and England Under-21s.

Nicholson asked Mabbutt to put the Birmingham offer on hold and visit him at White Hart Lane the following morning.

Mabbutt discussed on *Off The Shelf* the feeling of destiny as he drove through the famous wrought-iron gates at White Hart Lane. He and Nicholson then travelled to the training ground in Cheshunt, where he was introduced to Burkinshaw and several senior players. He was offered a three-year contract on the promise that they would endeavour to make him 'a Tottenham Hotspur player' within two years if he was prepared to work hard and be patient. That was good enough for Mabbutt, who agreed to join Spurs and embark on what would be a 16-year playing career with the club.

Joining his team-mates on a pre-season tour to Norway, Mabbutt was stunned just how quickly he was incorporated into the first team, initially through necessity. With Ardiles now out on loan, Spurs' midfield was decimated; Villa and Hazard missed the whole of the pre-season schedule through injury, as did Steve Perryman, who had played in each of the 66 first-team fixtures the previous season.

As FA Cup holders, Spurs once again appeared in the Charity Shield to open the domestic season, meeting Liverpool in a repeat of the Milk Cup Final five months earlier. By the time the game came around, both Roberts and Price had also picked up injuries that required minor surgery. Perryman's absence, the first time in 140 first-team games, meant Hoddle led the team.

Spurs' starting XI included Mabbutt on the right side of midfield and there were rare appearances for Gary O'Reilly and John Lacy in defence.

The new season saw several law changes that were discussed among the TV pundits for ITV's highlights show. Most notably, goalkeepers were now restricted to taking just four steps when holding the ball in their hands – a rule change aimed at reducing timewasting. In reality, the rule achieved little and it was a further ten years until the backpass rule made a significant impact.

Additionally, referees were being asked to clamp down on cynical challenges or tackles that deliberately aimed to deny an attacker a goalscoring opportunity. Such challenges were known as 'professional fouls' and the ruling was a delayed reaction to the infamous incident in the 1980 FA Cup Final when former Spurs defender Willie Young, playing for Arsenal, scythed down a future Spurs player, Paul Allen of West Ham, when he was through on goal.

Perhaps the lawmakers should have been more concerned with the sort of challenge that Graeme Souness had made on Tony Galvin in the Milk Cup Final. There may have been mutual respect between the two teams but there was no love lost, as evidenced when Hoddle clattered into the back of Souness early in the first half. Souness responded with a stamp that caught Hoddle just below the hip. First on to the scene was Crooks, who appeared to butt Souness and throw punches at both him and Dalglish. It was a moment of madness.

Incredibly, the referee kept his cards in his pocket, merely speaking to the three players. Finally, a football match broke out and it was Liverpool who scored the only goal. Speaking after the game, Burkinshaw condemned Crooks's actions, though was pleased with his team's performance, citing the four good saves that Grobbelaar had been forced into.

The Spurs manager also emphasised his admiration for the way that Brazil had played in the World Cup, saying it inspired him to continue to want his Spurs team to go out to entertain. Having won back-to-back FA Cups, the natural progression for this team was either to win a European trophy or to finally win the league championship that had eluded the club since 1961. Steve Perryman spoke regularly with Keith Burkinshaw and recalls a conversation they had around this time about what they'd need to do to become title challengers:

I remember speaking with Keith after one of those cup victories and I said that if we wanted to win the league we needed to be, dare I say it, more like Arsenal. Keith told me that you couldn't say that if you sat on his side of the table! When they played badly, they could still earn a draw but when we played badly, we were liable to get beaten, sometimes heavily. You can't win a league championship with that mentality.

Spurs' opening league game saw newly promoted Luton Town visit White Hart Lane. The Bedfordshire club had enjoyed the briefest of forays in the top flight in the mid-70s but had rebuilt an exciting team in Division Two under their erudite young manager David Pleat.

The fit-again Perryman returned to the team at the expense of O'Reilly. Mabbutt started in midfield and marked his White Hart Lane debut with a goal. Hoddle's floated free kick was met by the head of Mabbutt, who told *Off The Shelf* that this was the beginning of a wonderful relationship between him and the fans that has lasted for more than 40 years. Hazard added a second before the 20th minute but Luton fought back to draw 2-2.

The inconsistencies evidenced during that match were mirrored by a mixed bag of results throughout the autumn. Big wins over Southampton and Nottingham Forest at White Hart Lane were negated by disappointing defeats at home to Manchester City and away at Swansea. Injuries continued to have an impact, with Burkinshaw unable to name an unchanged starting XI until April. It was not just the scale of the injuries, either. With Ardiles in exile, Hoddle developed issues with both his Achilles tendons and missed 13 games from September through until November.

Roberts wasn't able to start a game until December and Price and Miller were both in and out. Even Perryman was forced to sit out the whole of October. It appeared that the battle scars collected through the gruelling previous season were taking their toll.

Injuries did, however, present the opportunity for Mabbutt to establish himself as a genuine first-team player. Constantly rotating between positions, he not only demonstrated versatility but also an ability to score goals from all positions. He scored in each of his first three home league games.

Mabbutt's club form soon earned him a call-up to the senior England team and he made his full debut in a home friendly against West Germany in October, filling in at right-back.

Also enjoying a fine run of form was Garry Brooke. The midfielder, now 21, had been unfortunate to have to compete for a place in midfield with the likes of Hoddle, Villa, Ardiles and Hazard but had been the substitute for the 1981 and 1982 FA Cup Finals, coming on in both. Brooke had suffered a knee injury in September 1981 that kept him out for four months.

Throughout the back end of the 1981/82 season, Brooke had proved a more than capable stand-in for Hoddle and Ardiles and his confidence was evident, having taken responsibility to take, and score, penalties. Back in the team due to injuries, he started 19 successive games between August and November and chipped in with eight goals, which included a hat-trick against Coventry at White Hart Lane.

Having qualified again for the European Cup Winners' Cup, Spurs hoped to go beyond the semi-final stage, where they had been kicked out by Barcelona the previous season. The first round presented another trip to the Emerald Isle – this time north of the border, where Spurs met Coleraine. This time, there were no unnerving Bovril announcements and Spurs progressed comfortably, winning 7-0 on aggregate.

The draw for the second round was not so kind. Still smarting from their shock defeat in the 1982 European Cup Final at the hands of Aston Villa, Bayern Munich were desperate to overcome English opposition. The first leg at White Hart Lane saw an evenly contested match end in a 1-1 draw.

Archibald gave Spurs an early lead but Bayern, boasting a star-studded line-up headlined by Karl-Heinz Rummenigge, equalised after the interval to claim a crucial away goal.

Before the return leg in Bavaria, Spurs travelled to Villa Park for a league match on 30 October. With the club still reeling from injuries, Hughton at least returned to the starting XI and Spurs had the opportunity to go top.

However, they found another goalkeeper in inspired form, with Jimmy Rimmer making several top-class saves before Mabbutt was adjudged to have fouled Villa striker Peter Withe in the area. Gordon Cowans converted the penalty. Spurs continued to create chance after chance, only for Rimmer to repel them. Villa scored a further three goals without reply but the 4-0 scoreline did not reflect the balance of the game. Both

Manchester United and second-placed West Brom were also beaten, meaning Spurs had missed the opportunity to claim top spot. It would be the closest they'd get to the summit for two years.

Ahead of the trip to Germany, Spurs were boosted by the news that both Hoddle and Perryman were available, albeit only to take their place on the bench. Spurs fans and the team enjoyed gorgeous sunshine in Bavaria through the afternoon but as the evening arrived, so did a fatal bout of freezing fog. By kick-off, visibility was so bad you couldn't see from one goal to the other, let alone see the pitch from the upper tiers of the Olympic Stadium. UEFA had a clear directive for referees, which stated that the game must go ahead if both goals could be seen from the halfway line. The official decided he could see both and the game went ahead.

Spurs were well beaten, going down 4-1, but even Keith Burkinshaw could find no reason to protest to UEFA and request a rematch. Chris Hughton scored Spurs' consolation goal, though the German TV director and commentator thought it was John Lacy! Either they hadn't done sufficient research on the Spurs players or the fog really was that bad.

Defeat in Europe stung but hopes of going all the way in the Milk Cup were raised, having progressed to the fourth round after wins over Brighton and Gillingham.

The top of the league had been tantalisingly close but back-to-back defeats at home to newly promoted Watford, the first time the clubs had ever met in a league match, and away at Old Trafford dropped Spurs down to tenth.

The home game against Watford saw a very clear clash of styles. Watford, under the ownership of Elton John and management of Graham Taylor, had miraculously risen all the way through the Football League from the fourth tier to the first within five years. In September, they had even briefly topped the table. Watford's success had been largely down to a unique playing style that involved very physical and direct football. It was the polar opposite to Spurs but proved effective. Taylor's team won 1-0.

After the game, Burkinshaw commented that he would never resort to Taylor's direct tactics. It has been reported that Burkinshaw would scream 'Watford' during training sessions if he felt his defenders were simply kicking the ball long from the back!

* * *

With the club's AGM due to take place in December, Irving Scholar was busy executing the final stages of his plan to take over the club.

With attention drawn towards Spurs' upcoming home match with West Ham, the *Daily Express* ran an exclusive article on 19 November under the headline 'Spurs in Takeover Shock'. The article didn't mention Scholar by name but revealed that Spurs' finances were in a perilous state and that the estimated costs of the West Stand had been grossly miscalculated, meaning a takeover attempt seemed certain.

Scholar was alerted to the story while on holiday in Las Vegas and hastily arranged to return to the UK. The following morning, the day of the West Ham game, other media outlets were running with the story about a mystery investor who may be about to take over the club.

Scholar was able to arrange a meeting with the current board to take place immediately after the match, which Spurs won 2-1, with both goals from Archibald.

Initially, Scholar proposed that the club issue the remaining 3,108 shares that remained from the original company inception in 1908. Scholar would purchase these at £200 each, injecting around £600,000 into the club.

After further dialogue over the coming days, by which time Scholar's name had been leaked to the press for the first time, the proposal was rejected by the board, who were still adamant that there were no financial concerns. They would, however, welcome an investment, which Scholar offered in the form of a £700,000 interest-free loan, repayable by July 1985, in addition to the original share issue.

With his name and intentions now out in the open, Scholar was approached by a fellow West Stand box holder, Paul Bobroff.

Scholar and Bobroff had briefly spoken beforehand, though Scholar doubted that Bobroff was as fanatical a supporter as he was. Cutting straight to the point, Bobroff revealed that he was in a position to purchase 13 per cent of the company shares from the Bearman Estate – the third-largest shareholders – and enquired whether, if he was to do so, he and Scholar would be able to join forces. This was a proposal that Scholar toyed with – he was not living in England and could see that Bobroff's knowledge and contacts in the City may be beneficial. Crucially, by combining forces, the pair would own more than 50 per cent of the company shares.

In a bizarre twist, Bobroff then offered to sell his new shares to Scholar. His decision not to purchase them was one he came to regret.

On 1 December, the same day that Spurs played Luton in the Milk Cup, a notice was formally served on the present board of directors that an EGM was being called by a number of shareholders to remove Arthur and Geoffrey Richardson and their ally, Ken Kennard. Knowing that their game was now up, all three resigned the following morning. In a conciliatory gesture, both Richardsons were made life vice-presidents of the club.

Irving Scholar was now legally the majority shareholder of Tottenham Hotspur – perhaps every supporter's dream – and had keys to the office, though he elected not to sit on the newly constituted board. Instead, current director, Douglas Alexiou, the son-in-law of Sidney Wale, became chairman and Frank Sinclair, who, like Alexiou, had previously been on the board, was elected as vice-chairman. Paul Bobroff and Peter Leaver, an associate of Scholar, were appointed directors.

Scholar wrote in *Behind Closed Doors* about the moment he realised what he'd just done:

> Everything had happened so quickly that I found it difficult to take it all in. Tottenham had always been my greatest passion: from the days of standing on the terraces as a young boy, to the time I got my first season ticket in the East

Stand ... It was a situation I could barely have imagined when my Uncle Gerry took me to see Tottenham on 6 September 1952.

Alan Fisher describes the state of the club and the challenges that the new owner faced:

> Irving Scholar inherited a settled, experienced team doing well in cup competitions without making a serious title challenge. Off the field, money was tight, as the club were burdened by the spiralling cost of building the new West Stand, opened in February 1982, and restricted transfer funds stifled the necessary team rebuilding in the mid-80s.

The first win under the new ownership came in mid-December when Spurs beat Birmingham 2-1 at White Hart Lane. Roberts and Galvin returned from injury, though Miller was now unavailable. Mabbutt started as a striker and scored both goals but the day was more significant for the news that Ossie Ardiles would be returning to London in the New Year.

On Boxing Day, Spurs lost 2-0 at Arsenal, meaning they'd now gone eight away league games without a goal. The Gunners were languishing just above the relegation zone going into the game, with Terry Neill under real pressure. This victory over his former assistant, Burkinshaw, provided much-needed respite.

As was often the case at the time, there was a full fixture list scheduled for the following day, with Spurs at home to Brighton. It was the first occasion that Scholar, living in Monaco, attended a home game as the club's owner. As he arrived at the West Stand just after midday (ahead of an evening kick-off), he was bemused to see fans queueing outside an unattended and locked-up ticket office.

Scholar himself opened up and, with a couple of senior colleagues, served supporters, issuing match tickets that were produced and printed by an external agency. He was made aware of the general chaos surrounding club operations and that it was common to find wads of old tickets and cash strewn across the floor. This seemed indicative of the way the club operated on many levels and his early impressions were of a club that 'gave the appearance of being a run-down family business still imprisoned in its Victorian surroundings and shaped by Victorian attitudes'.

Only 23,994 attended the Brighton match but those who did persevere were at least rewarded with a 2-0 win.

Nineteen-eighty-three got off to a terrible start, with a 3-0 defeat at West Ham on New Year's Day in which Georgio Mazzon was given his first start of the season following an injury to Roberts. Two days later, Spurs beat Everton 2-1, with both goals scored by Terry Gibson, who was making just his second league start in three years since his debut. He would go on to play the next 18 games. The win over Everton also provided a debut for another youth team graduate, Simon Webster.

As the FA Cup came back around, Spurs were looking to win the famous competition for the third successive year – a feat not achieved since Blackburn Rovers did it in the 1880s. The draw gave Spurs a home tie against Southampton.

Hazard scored the only goal of the game – a sweetly struck shot from range – despite being momentarily knocked unconscious in the first half. He had temporarily lost full vision and played in a blur until after half-time. It seemed perfectly in keeping with Spurs' injury misfortunes that Hazard would miss the next six weeks, just as Ardiles returned.

The Argentine did finally reappear in a league game at Luton in which Spurs finally scored away from home in the league. Hoddle's second-half equaliser was the first away goal since mid-September.

The remainder of January produced mixed fortunes. An underwhelming draw at home to Sunderland followed a bizarre exit in the League Cup when Second Division Burnley, who had just sacked their manager and sat second from bottom, won 4-1 at White Hart Lane, with Roberts scoring two own goals. It left the FA Cup as Spurs' only route to silverware.

West Brom were the fourth-round opponents at White Hart Lane and they scored the opening goal of the game to jeopardise Spurs' run of 18 successive FA Cup games without defeat. However, a goal from Crooks, who returned from injury, and a fine solo effort by Gibson saw Spurs into the fifth round, where they were given a tricky away tie at Everton, scheduled for mid-February.

Gibson made it four goals in four games by scoring in a 2-2 draw at Manchester City but the game was marred by a serious injury to Ardiles who, it transpired, had broken a bone in his leg, ruling him out for the rest of the season.

However, Ardiles' injury wasn't the most significant suffered by a Spurs player that month.

Brooke had continued his excellent form, enjoying an extended run in the first team. The following weekend, with temperatures in London plummeting, Brooke attended a wedding reception following the home game against Swansea. He was being driven home through Enfield when the car skidded on black ice, hit a lamppost and crashed in a ditch. Interviewed in *The Boys from White Hart Lane*, Brooke revealed that he was in agony but didn't realise how much danger he was in. He was rushed to hospital and his parents were told that his chances of survival were slim.

Miraculously, Brooke pulled through but spent eight days in intensive care, having broken nine ribs and punctured a lung. He spent the next two months recovering at home. Incredibly, he was able to play again.

Brooke headlined Spurs' midfield injuries as they travelled to Goodison Park. Everton were starting to build a formidable team hell-bent on challenging city rivals Liverpool. They saw the game with Spurs as an opportunity to build momentum and on the day, with home advantage, were too strong. Two second-half goals sealed Spurs' fate and they suffered their first FA Cup defeat since 1980.

It was a huge disappointment to fans like David Harris, who had enjoyed the two previous FA Cup successes:

> I was still only ten and, after the last two years, expected
> we'd win it every year. As the season progressed, we'd just
> lost too many players – Hoddle to injury, Ardiles initially

was in Paris and then got injured. There were lots of others, too, and the squad hadn't been added to, beyond Mabbutt. I think they suffered a psychological blow when they were knocked out of the Cup Winners' Cup, too, so when it came round to Everton – who were a really good side on the rise – I had a bad feeling. I didn't go to the game, as I was at a bar mitzvah, and had to rely on radio updates. If we'd won the cup again for a third season in a row, we'd have got to keep the trophy!

Twelve months earlier, Spurs still had ambitions to win four trophies but now, in February 1983, had only their remaining 15 league games to look ahead to. Spurs sat in eighth, knowing that fifth place would guarantee a spot in the 1983/84 UEFA Cup competition. This incentive provided the motivation for a strong end to what had been an inconsistent season not helped by so many injuries.

With injuries still riddling the squad, Spurs failed to win any of their next three games, with a 3-0 defeat at newly promoted Notts County the nadir of the season.

In the boardroom, Irving Scholar had now had a chance to assess the true state of the club's finances. He states that he had inherited the biggest debt in football, with the club £5.5m in the red. Internally, the new board discussed plans to change the way the club, as a company, were listed. At this point, no English football club were owned publicly but the UK economy had seen rapid changes, with several previously state-owned institutions floating on the London Stock Exchange. It meant that any member of the public could buy shares, thus becoming 'part owners' and earning dividends based on profit.

These ideas were not discussed outside of the boardroom but Scholar had already proved to be a very different character to his predecessors and, as club captain, Steve Perryman already had his concerns:

I remember when I first broke into the team and, after six months or so, questioned who were the older gentlemen who sat alone at the front of the train or bus. It was explained to me that they were the directors and that illustrated what a passive role they had with us as players. As far as we were concerned, we played for the manager, initially, for me, Bill Nicholson. It was the manager who controlled your career and you didn't even consider anyone else at the club.

As I became a more senior member of the team, the directors took more interest in me personally and would exchange pleasantries and there was some care but it never went beyond surface level.

On first impressions, Scholar was ultra-smooth. He was significantly younger than the previous board members, better dressed, but that made me wary of him. He was too smooth for his own good. Bobroff was less personable and out of choice, you'd always speak to Scholar but this was clearly a new era, with a new glossy image and they seemed determined to take us in a new direction.

Bobroff was put in charge of exploring the public listing but, in the short term, the team needed new blood. Despite all the injuries, Spurs had not signed a player since Mabbutt joined the previous summer but, keen for reinforcements, a deal was reached with Ipswich for their striker, Alan Brazil. The transfer fee of £425,000 had to be personally underwritten by Scholar and Bobroff, pledging repayment once the following season's season ticket income was received.

Although still only 23, Brazil had great pedigree, having been part of a highly successful Ipswich team that had won the UEFA Cup in 1981 and had come close to winning the league title. The Suffolk outfit and Brazil had regularly been a thorn in Spurs' side. The signing of Brazil provided another striking option for Burkinshaw, as Crooks and Archibald had now picked up injuries – the former would miss the rest of the season.

Brazil went straight into the starting XI for the trip to Watford on 19 March. The game became something of a grudge match – not only were Spurs Watford's nearest geographic rivals (their traditional rivals were Luton) but the war of words between Burkinshaw and Taylor following the match earlier in the season added spice.

Watford hadn't lost at home since December and Spurs were seeking a first away win since September, so form suggested a home win. However, it was debutant Brazil's strike partner, the all-too-often overlooked Mark Falco, who scored the only goal of the game after Brazil's header had been cleared off the line.

It was a feisty affair that saw several bookings and Steve Perryman sent off for the first time in his Spurs career, somewhat harshly for a challenge ten minutes from the end. The *Watford Observer's* match report was scathing about Spurs' physical approach to the game and accused Burkinshaw of hypocrisy, having stated earlier in the season that he would never play like Watford. The article singled out Mabbutt being tasked with man-marking his opposite number and referred to a number of poor refereeing decisions that went against the home team.

Spurs made it back-to-back league wins for the first time since September with a 2-0 win over Aston Villa – with Falco scoring twice – but then lost against relegation-haunted Brighton on the South Coast on Easter Saturday. Spurs led 1-0 through Roberts's first goal in more than a year and looked set for a third successive win when Brighton were reduced to ten men. However, a needless red card for Tony Galvin led to a ridiculous four-minute spell in which the home team scored twice to win 2-1.

Spurs were down to tenth going into the final nine games of the season and only one point ahead of Arsenal as the two teams met at White Hart Lane on Easter Monday.

Sadly, the north London derby hadn't been selected by BBC or ITV as their feature game, so the only footage that exists is from Spurs' own TV cameras in the West Stand and there is no commentary. The grainy images, filmed on a bright sunny afternoon in front of a raucous home crowd, record one of the most remarkable performances and results of the decade, with Spurs tearing into Arsenal and recording an emphatic 5-0 victory.

The second goal, scored by Falco, must be one of the greatest goals scored at White Hart Lane to have been seen, in its full glory, by so few people.

Gibson recalls his role in that goal and the win:

When Alan Brazil joined, I started playing on the wing. It wasn't really my position but I was happy to play there if it kept me in the team. This was my first game against Arsenal. I'm not a hateful person but I hate Arsenal and I'd been distraught on the terraces in 78 when they'd beaten us 5-0. I was personally out for revenge but what I most relished was the chance to play against Kenny Sansom, who was the England left-back.

We must have had a lot of injuries going into that game. Archibald played centre midfield and I was on the wing. There was no Hod, Hazard, Ossie or Ricky.

I remember the Falco goal. Clem passed short from the goal kick. It was something we were encouraged to do, unlike nearly every other team in the division. The ball went to O'Reilly, who looked up and played it to me on the touchline. I could feel Sansom charging into me, so, instinctively, I flicked the ball around him. I could feel the roar of The Shelf as I did it and I was now facing forwards. I was quick, so made up a lot of ground. Out the corner of my eye, I could see 'Bilko' [Falco], so crossed towards him. I assumed he'd bring it down on his chest but, instead, he just stepped on to it and hit the sweetest volley you'll ever see with his weaker foot. The finish was outstanding but, on a personal level, beating Sansom like that was the biggest thrill!

Hughton added his second – and Spurs' third – before half-time and after the break, Spurs continued with their relentless attacks. Falco scored his second and Brazil rounded off the scoring with his first for the club. On another day, he could have had a hat-trick. It was Spurs' biggest win in the *north* London derby – they had beaten *Woolwich* Arsenal by the same score on

Christmas Day 1911 – and it was payback for the 5-0 reversal in December 1978, as Mike Leigh recalls:

> I was 11 in 1978 and that defeat to them remains one of the worst days of my life. I grew up in a big Spurs and Arsenal area, so it was a constant source of embarrassment. I remember that, going into the game in 83, we had several players out injured and we hadn't been playing that well beforehand, so there was no sense of what was coming. Falco's goal was incredible but to win 5-0 felt like retribution – it was finally closure for what had happened five years earlier. I bought the full match on VHS and my friend and I watched it back on a very regular basis, even recording our own commentary over the top of it!

The win set up Spurs nicely for the end of season run-in, which saw a draw and four successive victories in the next five games – the last of which, on 30 April, denied Liverpool, momentarily, from clinching the league title that they had all but sewn up in early spring. After his goal against Arsenal, Alan Brazil found goalscoring form, with four further goals in six games in which he and fellow Scot Archibald formed a promising partnership.

Despite a defeat at Birmingham, Spurs secured the points to guarantee UEFA Cup football for the following season. Wins over Manchester United and Stoke meant Spurs finished the season in fourth place, repeating the previous campaign's position. David Harris recognises the impact Alan Brazil made:

> Brazil's goals made a really big difference. He scored six times and most of them were vital ones to secure points. Before the Stoke game, Keith Burkinshaw spoke to the crowd on the microphone to tell us how important the game was for us to qualify for Europe. Nobody knew at the time just how important that late run of results was going to prove.

The early cup exits had been a disappointment, especially when Spurs had such high expectations, but perhaps having a clear run of league fixtures at the end of the season contributed to the fine run of form. It was an understated success, considering the impact of the wretched run of injuries – no doubt a hangover from the gruelling 1981/82 season. The mainstays of that season played too few games – Hoddle (24 league appearances), Crooks (26), Galvin (26), Miller (23) and Roberts (24) all missed large spells of the season. Even Perryman was unavailable for 11 games. Additionally, the aftermath of the Falklands War denied Spurs the services of Ardiles for the first half of the season and then injury ruled him out from February.

Ardiles was recovering from his broken leg but would return the following season, unlike compatriot Villa, who, following the end of his contract, decided he wanted to fulfil a lifetime ambition of living in Miami, where he would play in the North American Soccer League for Fort Lauderdale. Villa is, of course, best remembered for the 1981 FA Cup Final replay but his five years in north London make him a club legend who is still fondly remembered some 40 years on.

On an individual level, the highlight of the season was the form of Gary Mabbutt, who ended the season with ten goals, despite being played in a variety of different positions. He had made a seamless transition from the third tier to the top flight.

Graham Roberts earned a senior England debut, starting the Home International games against Northern Ireland and Scotland. It meant he had gone from non-league to playing for his country in just over three years. His next 12 months wouldn't be too bad either!

League position	Fourth
Average home league attendance	30,692
Most appearances	Hughton & Mabbutt (46)
Top goalscorer	Archibald & Crooks (15)
League winners	Liverpool
FA Cup winners	Manchester United
League Cup winners	Liverpool

83/84 – THERE USED TO BE A FOOTBALL CLUB OVER THERE

CLEMENCE
D. THOMAS   PERRYMAN   MILLER   HUGHTON
STEVENS   ROBERTS   HODDLE   GALVIN
ARCHIBALD   FALCO

SPURS MOVED swiftly to bring two new players to the club. Danny Thomas, selected in the previous season's PFA Division One team of the year, joined from Coventry and Gary Stevens, who had starred in Brighton's unexpected FA Cup Final appearance, was also signed. Both could cover multiple positions.

Leaving White Hart Lane were John Lacy (Crystal Palace), Pat Corbett (Orient), Georgio Mazzon (Aldershot) and Terry Gibson (Coventry). As a boyhood Spurs fan, Gibson was gutted to leave:

> I really wanted to stay. I'd had a good run of goals at the start of the year and Peter Shreeve suggested that a new contract wouldn't be a problem. Eventually, I was offered a one-year deal and a rise of £50 per week. The money wasn't important but I thought I deserved a longer deal. Two years would have been enough but they wouldn't budge.
>
> During pre-season, I played for the reserves at Lewes and scored five in a 6-4 win. Lewes were managed by the brother of Bobby Gould – then manager of Coventry. The next morning, Keith called me aside but, instead of telling me that they'd offer me the two-year deal, he told me that

the club had accepted bids of £70,000 from Coventry and a Belgian side.

I'll never understand why, in 1980 as a 17-year-old with three appearances, I was given a four-year deal but now, three years later, having played well and scored goals, I was only offered one year. They were dragging their heels with a new deal for Steve [Perryman] at the time, so what chance did I have?

A year later, just after Peter had become manager, I bumped into him at Ian Crook's wedding. He told me that he wanted to bring me back. I think they offered Coventry £200,000 but I'd scored 19 goals that season, so it was well below what they'd have taken.

Spurs were still my team but I carried a grudge when I played against them for the rest of my career. I scored a few times, too, for Coventry and Wimbledon but, to be fair, I also scored a few against Arsenal and that was always extra special. Since retiring, I've come full circle and am a passionate fan again. It's a weird journey supporting a team and being a professional footballer!

Steve Perryman eventually signed a new three-year contract but it was a long, drawn-out affair. The captain had hoped to sign a three-year extension that he felt had been agreed earlier in the year but was only offered one further year. Bill Nicholson became involved in the mediation and a deal to run through to 1986 was agreed.

A similar stand-off had occurred in 1981 between Burkinshaw and Steve Archibald, with the forward believing it was stipulated in his contract that he would receive salary increases based on the number of goals he scored. Having passed the required goals threshold in his first season, he was irked when Burkinshaw seemed to deny any knowledge of the agreement. The striker and manager had a strained relationship from that point onwards … and it was about to get worse.

Scholar, who had also mediated the row between captain and manager, was undoubtedly beginning to question whether

Burkinshaw should be the sole arbiter of player contract negotiations.

The week before the season started, Bill Nicholson was rewarded for his service to the club with a testimonial at White Hart Lane. The afternoon included a double header, with a 60s Spurs team taking on their 70s counterparts. Jimmy Greaves, still the club's record goalscorer and now a well-known TV personality, was the star attraction and, inevitably, scored. This game was followed by the first team drawing 1-1 with West Ham.

Scholar could take some credit for the belated testimonial for Nicholson. It was evidence of Scholar the Spurs fan recognising Nicholson's role and legacy. Another side to Scholar which was apparent in the summer of 1983 was that of a progressive and innovative club owner. Scholar commissioned the London-based PR firm Saatchi and Saatchi (who had recently contributed to the Conservative Party's landslide election victory) to help attract supporters to games and also woo potential investors ahead of the Stock Exchange flotation scheduled for October.

Throughout August, a TV and radio advertising campaign featured well-known comedian Peter Cook and the fictitious Mrs Ridlington, a grey-haired granny, adorned in a navy and white scarf, attending White Hart Lane with her family. The clear message to supporters was that they should attend games to 'really be a part of the team'.

Since Scholar's initial experience in the ticket office shortly after taking over, he had taken his ticket office and commercial manager to the USA to explore digital ticketing systems. His vision was to change the feel of a home matchday experience as he attempted to marginalise the hooligans and entice a new breed of fans – including families – to White Hart Lane.

Additionally, the merchandise range was increased and the club shop operations were improved. Many aspects of American sport intrigued Scholar, who was keen to embrace the angle of a 'family day out'. He also became aware of the concept of 'dynamic pricing' – a system that saw ticket prices vary depending on the opposition. Spurs became one of the first clubs to introduce different pricing categories for home games.

Sales of executive boxes, albeit initiated before Scholar arrived, continued to go well, with all bar one of the 72 taken for the upcoming season (the remaining one was deliberately kept back by the club). The release of those remaining shares purchased by Scholar and Bobroff had generated more than £1.3m in revenue, which helped to manage the club's debts.

However, while the club were developing commercially, it was easy to forget that their main business was football and there were already signs of conflicts. Since the old West Stand was knocked down, the players had had to park their cars a few hundred yards up the High Road and walk the remainder of the way. With the new stand and its car park now opened, it was expected that they would now park inside the stadium car park but captain Perryman was summoned to see Scholar, who advised him that the parking bays would be reserved for executive box holders and that the players would have to continue their walk along the High Road. A compromise was reached but it set the tone for problems ahead.

Ultimately, players and supporters all wanted to see Spurs win matches and win trophies, so it was hugely deflating for Mrs Ridlington et al when Spurs were beaten 3-1 at Ipswich on the opening day of the season. Thomas and Stevens both made debuts, starting in defence alongside Roberts and Perryman. Ardiles, Crooks, Hughton, Price and Miller were all unavailable – a hangover from the previous season – while Hazard had to go off injured and would miss the next six months.

Two days later, on Bank Holiday Monday, Coventry were the visitors to White Hart Lane. Young full-back Mark Bowen came into the starting XI for his debut but the away side, featuring Terry Gibson, scored a late equaliser, cancelling out Hoddle's first-half penalty.

Spurs ended the game with ten men. Having replaced Brazil through injury, Steve Archibald picked up a knee injury and knew instantly that he couldn't continue. Post-match, Burkinshaw said that Archibald was 'cheating' the club – a comment that understandably only served to further strain the relationship between the two. The striker was subsequently placed on the transfer list and didn't feature in the next five games.

Spurs' winless start continued with a home defeat to West Ham and a draw at West Brom. Though Spurs beat newly promoted Leicester – before thumping Irish part-timers Drogheda in the first leg of their UEFA Cup first-round tie – a further home league defeat, this time to Everton, marked a very disappointing start to the season.

The Everton defeat left Spurs fifth from bottom in the embryonic league table, leaving rival supporters to jest whether Mrs Ridlington might actually get a game!

Spurs made the short trip to play Watford in a fixture that had attracted attention due to the previous season's war of words between the respective managers. Archibald was named on the bench, with Brazil and Falco in attack. While Archibald watched on awkwardly on the same wooden bench as Burkinshaw, Watford took a first-half lead.

In the second half, Spurs, kicking towards the away end, began to find some fluency. Brazil tested Steve Sherwood with a sharp shot, having performed an exquisite 'Cruyff turn' inside the Watford penalty area to create the space to get his shot away.

At the start of the previous season, Burkinshaw had commented on how he'd been inspired by the Brazilian national team's stylish play at Spain 82. Now, 14 months later in the less illustrious surroundings of south-west Hertfordshire, Hoddle appeared to have been inspired by Brazil … his team-mate, Alan.

Receiving the ball from Brooke just inside the corner of the area, Hoddle performed an equally exquisite 'Cruyff turn' in one fluid motion, taking his marker completely out of the game. Brazil had elected for power, only to see his shot saved, but Hoddle deftly clipped the ball over the goalkeeper and watched as it dipped perfectly to find the far corner. It was voted the BBC goal of the season and remains one of the club's most iconic goals, regularly featuring on official Spurs video montages.

The goal inspired Spurs, who built momentum. With over an hour played, Burkinshaw turned to Archibald, sending him on in place of Brooke. With Falco and Brazil causing problems in the frontline, Archibald played deeper, in midfield. Adorned by several renditions of 'We'll take more care of you' from the away end, the stage was set for Archibald to steal the headlines when he hit a rasping drive from 25 yards into the top corner to give Spurs a late lead.

Hughton then added a third before Watford scored a late consolation from the penalty spot. The win ended the league drought and provided a route back for Archibald – though the relationship with Burkinshaw was terminally damaged.

Drogheda came to White Hart Lane already 6-0 behind after the first leg in Ireland. Spurs' record European victory was a 9-0 win against Icelandic outfit Keflavík in 1971. That record looked like being surpassed when Spurs took a 7-0 lead on the night with half an hour still remaining. Not wanting to go down in infamy, the Irish part-timers dug in, restricting Spurs to just one more goal, resulting in an 8-0 win (14-0 on aggregate).

With spirits lifted, Spurs could look forward to a home league game against Nottingham Forest which was significant for a couple of non-footballing reasons.

Unusually, the game was scheduled for Sunday afternoon instead of the traditional Saturday 3pm slot. This was because the Football League had reached a £5.2m agreement with the two main terrestrial TV broadcasters – BBC and ITV – to screen ten live matches throughout the season.

Clubs had been always been reluctant to allow live TV coverage of games, fearing it would reduce attendances and gate receipts but, finally, a breakthrough was reached at the start of the 1983/84 season. Until then, other than a brief and failed experiment in 1960 for ITV to screen Football League games live, the FA Cup Final was the only domestic club football available to watch live on TV in England. With ITV selecting Spurs v Nottingham Forest as their first live game of the season, there was much interest in the match but also how many supporters would attend … and, in front of a national audience, how they would behave.

The game was scheduled for 2.35pm on Sunday, 2 October – a move that upset Burkinshaw, who felt that regular match-going fans would be put out by the break from the norm of a Saturday 3pm. He claimed: 'I still feel we are penalising our season ticket holders. They bought their seats to watch soccer on a Saturday afternoon, not a Sunday. Sometimes we forget the people who stand by us on all occasions.'

By coincidence, Australian media mogul Rupert Murdoch had recently announced plans to launch satellite television in the UK.

Spurs were keen to capitalise on the attention generated by the TV fixture, principally to ensure that fans turned up at the gates on the day. A marketing budget was set aside to give free transportation to and from the ground from Hertfordshire and other Spurs heartlands in the Home Counties and for the first 1,000 under-16s who arrived at the ground to receive free gifts. The club even arranged for the match ball to be dropped into the ground by a parachutist immediately before kick-off. The parachute gimmick lasted for a few home games but wasn't continued after an incident in which the parachutist holding the match ball landed safely – but on the High Road rather than within the stadium!

To alleviate concerns about potential lost revenue, the Football League created a pot of £300,000 to support home clubs if their gate receipts were significantly lower as a result of live TV coverage. As it transpired, the club's marketing campaign was successful, with a crowd of 30,596 turning up – over 1,000 more than had attended the previous league game against Everton.

TV figures were disappointing, though. An audience of just over 5m tuned in – about half the number that had watched England play Denmark in a European Championship qualifier on BBC the previous month and around the same figure for that evening's *Songs of Praise* on BBC. However, both ITV and the Football League remained stoical, arguing that it was only the first game and still something of an experiment.

Those who did watch, either live or on TV, saw Nottingham Forest take an early lead and Spurs looking lethargic. However, the game turned on its head after the break when Brooke replaced Brazil and Stevens and Archibald scored to give Spurs their first home league win of the season.

Post-match, chairman Douglas Alexiou joined the ITV studio, in one of the West Stand boxes, to say how pleased he was with the afternoon and the way the crowd had reacted.

The game also marked the day before the club were to be officially launched on the Stock Exchange.

There had been several hurdles to overcome since the idea had first been mooted by Scholar – most notably an old Football Association doctrine that stated clubs could not provide owners any sort of dividend which, of course, would be a significant challenge for a publicly listed company. The solution was to create a holding company – Tottenham Hotspur plc – with the football club listed as a subsidiary.

The rights issue prospectus, included within the matchday programme, detailed the club's financial situation and stated how the new West Stand's 72 executive boxes and hospitality facilities were helping to generate additional income, despite a small drop in average attendances and gate receipts.

The section titled *The Future of the Group* provided an insight into the direction that the directors wanted to take the club:

> The Directors intend to ensure that the Club remains one of the leading football clubs in the country. They will seek to increase the Group's income by improving the return from the existing assets and by establishing new sources of revenue in the leisure field … The Directors believe that the listing of the Company's shares on the Stock Exchange is an important and logical step in the development of the Company as a broadly based leisure group and that it will assist the Group in taking advantage of the Spurs name and reputation.

The references to the leisure field and the company being a broadly based leisure group were significant.

The initial launch was a success. Shares were subscribed three and a half times and the share price immediately rose from £1 to £1.08 and, therefore, generated in excess of the £3.3m which had been forecasted, effectively wiping out the club's debts.

Daniel Wynne received 100 shares as a gift and still holds them today:

> I was able to tell friends at school that I 'partly owned' Tottenham Hotspur. It meant that when I picked up a newspaper, I was now not just reading the back pages but would inspect the financial pages and share index, too. It definitely developed my teenage interest in finance and I've worked in the industry since leaving school. It's probably not a coincidence that many peers of my age in the City are Spurs fans!

Keith Burkinshaw was focused solely on football matters through October, with the win over Forest the first of four straight league victories in the month, along with a League Cup success over Lincoln. However, the main on-field talking point of October was the hotly anticipated UEFA Cup second-round tie with Feyenoord.

The fixture came less than ten years after the infamous 1974 final featuring the two clubs, which was marred by crowd disturbances at the second leg in Rotterdam. There was needle off the pitch but the game was billed as Hoddle v Cruyff, who was playing out the end of his career for Feyenoord. The Dutch maestro had enjoyed his peak years during the 70s as part of the all-conquering Ajax team and talisman of the iconic Dutch national team that won so many hearts. Hoddle himself had been inspired by Cruyff during his teenage years.

Cruyff had been dismissive of Hoddle in the build-up to the game, his comments only adding to the anticipation. Feyenoord also included a 21-year-old named Ruud Gullit in their starting XI. Coming just three weeks after Hoddle's incredible goal against Watford – a goal that involved the turn *invented* by Cruyff – the Spurs man gave perhaps his greatest-ever performance in lilywhite. Strangely, Cruyff's role was to man-mark Hoddle – a move that spectacularly backfired.

Though he didn't score, Hoddle had a role in all four goals scored by Spurs before half-time. The second goal, scored by Galvin, will, in particular, live long in the memory for Hoddle's inch-perfect lofted pass from the halfway line.

Steve Perryman wrote in *A Spur Forever*:

> Glenn didn't score but he was unplayable. I always said he was the leader of the orchestra. He led the orchestra that night and we were all in tune. Credit to Cruyff; he admitted that he had been wrong about Glenn afterwards.

By the second half, Cruyff dropped the man-marking plan and the Dutch team played with far more freedom, scoring twice to keep the tie alive heading into the second leg. However, any Feyenoord optimism was short-lived, with Spurs putting in a mature performance to win 2-0 and set up the chance to gain revenge on Bayern Munich in the last 16.

Success in the UEFA Cup became even more important when Spurs were knocked out of the League Cup by Arsenal at White Hart Lane on 9 November. Spurs fell two goals behind before Hoddle pulled one back from the spot, beating Pat Jennings.

Jennings was then the focal point at the final whistle as he became the latest unsuspecting subject of ITV's *This Is Your Life*. He was approached by presenter Eamonn Andrews as he walked off the pitch and presented with the famous red leather-bound book. Steve Perryman had to join Jennings on the Arsenal team coach to whisk him, along with the rest of the Gunners squad, straight to the London studios!

In the league, Spurs drew with Stoke and Liverpool before recording wins against Luton and QPR. Burkinshaw again had to dip into the reserve team, with young winger Richard Cooke scoring on his debut at Luton. Cooke and Ally Dick were both selected for the home win over QPR, a result which pushed

Spurs up into fourth. Liverpool, though, had gone top at the start of November and never looked back as they went on to record a comfortable third league title in a row.

The first leg of the UEFA Cup saw Spurs travel to Munich. Despite going down 1-0, Spurs were encouraged by their performance and had belief that they could overcome the deficit at White Hart Lane on 7 December.

The performance may not have been as swashbuckling as the dazzling first half against Feyenoord but it was another glorious night under the lights at White Hart Lane. Archibald levelled the tie and, with Bayern chasing an away goal, Hoddle was able to find more space to dictate the play. It was his pass that released Falco, who still had a lot to do but found the bottom corner from a tight angle. It proved to be the decisive goal and Spurs could look forward to further European action when the tournament resumed in March.

As was customary for European ties, Spurs played in all white but against Bayern at White Hart Lane, the front of the lilywhite shirt was emblazoned with the name of a sponsor – German beer brewery company Holsten. A Turkish carpet and rug manufacturer 'Sultan Hari' had been the first ever company to sponsor the front of a Spurs shirt but this was just for a two-game tour of Istanbul in the 1981 post-season.

Just ten years earlier, the Spurs board, then led by Sidney Wale, had been reticent to allow pitchside advertising at White Hart Lane, believing that it was crass and incongruous with the values of the club. In this regard, the Richardsons had been more progressive thinkers and, by the end of the 70s, several local and national brands were visible around the perimeter of the pitch. The Milk Marketing Board's sponsorship of the League Cup in 1981 set the tone for what was to follow. At the start of the 1983/84 season, Canon agreed a £3.3m deal to sponsor the Football League.

Once the Football League gave the go-ahead for shirt sponsorship, Coventry had been the first Division One club to secure a deal and, by the 1982/83 season, the biggest clubs had followed suit; Liverpool, Arsenal, Manchester United and

Everton had all agreed deals that saw sponsor's names on the front of their shirts.

Holsten was one of the new West Stand hospitality members and was approached to provide sponsorship for the return game with Bayern. The company accepted and subsequently agreed to maintain the arrangement throughout the rest of the season. The brand became synonymous with Spurs and remained the main shirt sponsor until 1995.

December was a hugely disappointing month. Spurs failed to win any of their five league games, which included another home defeat to Arsenal on Boxing Day. Ardiles returned to the team for a fixture televised live by the BBC at Manchester United but, despite assisting a Falco equaliser, he was on the losing side.

By the time of the game at Old Trafford, Garth Crooks was a Manchester United player, albeit temporarily, after agreeing a short-term loan deal. Crooks had suffered a further injury at the start of the season and the form of Archibald (still transfer listed), Falco and Brazil severely limited Crooks's game time. He agreed to join Ron Atkinson's team, who were chasing Liverpool at the top of the table.

The calendar year ended abysmally, with a 4-1 defeat at West Ham. Spurs were without Roberts, Miller, Hughton, Mabbutt and Hoddle, meaning that Bowen, O'Reilly and Webster all started.

However, the result seemed trivial after the death of Peter Southey had been announced following his brave battle with leukaemia. On the insistence of the players, a picture of Southey was placed in the players' lounge next to the changing room. A minute's silence was observed ahead of the next home game against Watford, the opening game of 1984.

Spurs trailed 2-0 within 20 minutes, with Ray Clemence unusually error-prone. Hoddle appeared to have inspired a second-half comeback but Watford won through a disputed penalty 13 minutes from the end.

The following day's *Daily Mirror* led with the headline 'Calamity Lane', its report stating that Spurs had replaced

Arsenal as the calamity club of north London – a reference to the fact that Arsenal had recently sacked Terry Neill and sat in the lower half of the league table.

Post-match, Burkinshaw admitted: 'We look a million miles away from a championship side now ... we were looking to get 12 points over the holiday period and we finished up with one ... it's difficult to say what would be my best back four. Whoever comes in seems to make mistakes.'

Even the FA Cup couldn't provide respite. Spurs were fortunate to escape at Fulham with a 0-0 draw. Clemence, retained in the starting XI, was forced to leave the field with a recurrence of a shoulder injury. On this occasion, it was Roberts, not Hoddle, who took the gloves and he was able to keep Fulham at bay.

Spurs won the replay back at White Hart Lane, with Tony Parks making just his fifth appearance for the senior team. Still just 20, Parks had a reasonably quiet evening, with Roberts and Miller back in the team alongside Perryman in defence, as Spurs won 2-0. However, Spurs' FA Cup campaign lasted just one more round, Norwich beating them 2-1 in a replay at Carrow Road.

By that time, Spurs had, at least, ended their run without a league win, having beaten Ipswich 2-0 at White Hart Lane. Crooks had returned from his loan spell, coming on as sub.

The defensive selection and form issues Burkinshaw had lamented had at least calmed down. By February, the back four of Perryman, Roberts, Miller and Hughton – the foundation of the successful 81 and 82 teams – were reunited.

Hoddle's troublesome ankle injury finally took its toll. After Spurs lost to Birmingham at the end of February, he and the club decided it was time to have an operation that would likely keep him out for the remainder of the season.

Spurs continued to go through the motions in the league in spring, which was reflected in the attendances at White Hart Lane. Only 18,271 turned up for the home win against Stoke but that number almost doubled for the first leg of the UEFA Cup quarter-final against Austria Vienna three days later.

The matchday programme included a table compiled by *World Soccer* magazine that emphasised Spurs' pedigree in European football. Calculating the combined percentage of European games won since continental competition began in 1955, Spurs proudly sat top, averaging 1.428 points per game (based on two points per game) above Borussia Mönchengladbach and Liverpool.

Feyenoord and Bayern Munich may have been bigger names than Austria Vienna but the Austrian outfit proved a far tougher test in the first half, proving to be resolute. Spurs remained patient, with Ardiles and Hazard dictating the tempo in midfield. It was Hazard's sharp footwork that created the first goal for Archibald, who prodded home from close range on the hour. Brazil added a second and, having avoided conceding an away goal, Spurs were in pole position to qualify for the semi-finals.

Two weeks later in Vienna, Brazil calmed any nerves by putting Spurs ahead inside 15 minutes. The home side equalised on the night, only for Ardiles to put Spurs back ahead. The game ended 2-2 – 4-2 on aggregate – and the Yugoslav outfit Hajduk Spilt awaited in the semi-final.

However, a seismic conversation that took place in the team hotel ahead of the game in Austria would alter the future of the club. Keith Burkinshaw was sat in his hotel room in the early afternoon ahead of the game when Irving Scholar and Paul Bobroff knocked on his door and asked to come in. Burkinshaw was told in no uncertain terms that the way the club was to be managed was to change and that he, as manager, should expect to have no further role in transfers or contract negotiations.

A proud and outspoken Yorkshireman, Burkinshaw felt that his position was untenable. Unbeknown to anyone at this point, Spurs' most successful manager since Bill Nicholson would be leaving the club at the end of the season.

Scholar was a Europhile and had seen how continental clubs operated and felt that Spurs needed to be pioneers and act progressively. In *Behind Closed Doors*, Scholar provides a different take on the situation, suggesting that Burkinshaw was on the brink of a breakdown, citing the pressures of management and the episode with Archibald, which had really taken its toll. Scholar also referenced a lack of trust between Bobroff and Burkinshaw that had developed over a 15-month period (Scholar, of course, was not actually on the board, so didn't sit in on board meetings).

Scholar suggests that Burkinshaw was relieved to be standing down, though it was agreed that the news wouldn't be made public until the end of the season.

Continued participation in the UEFA Cup ensured the club remained profitable. In the share issue prospectus, it was anticipated that the club would compete in at least eight cup matches and qualification for the semi-finals guaranteed at least two more, in addition to the nine (four UEFA Cup, four FA Cup – including replays – and League Cup) already played. The prospectus had also promised investors that a profit of at least £900,000 would be recorded in the year.

In the three weeks between their quarter-final and semi-final, Spurs won two and drew one of their three league games. They remained outside the UEFA Cup qualification spots and, with a number of tough league games still to come, knew that winning the competition was the only way to guarantee participation the following season.

Hajduk Split had history as a European club; they had actually met Spurs in the 1967/68 European Cup Winners' Cup, with Spurs winning that tie 6-3 on aggregate.

Clemence had briefly returned to the first team in March but broke a finger while facing shots in a training session, leaving Parks as the No.1 for the semi-final tie.

It was a wet night on the Adriatic coast, with both goalmouths saturated, but the sense of occasion was clear when a member of the Split 'ultras' sacrificed a chicken (a reference to the cockerel on the Spurs badge) on the pitch ahead of kick-off!

The Spurs team were either unaware or unfazed by this and started the game better, taking the lead and, in doing so, scoring what would prove to be a vital away goal. Falco's penalty was initially saved, as was his first follow-up, but the home side failed to clear the ball and the striker's blushes were spared when he swept home from close range.

With a raucous crowd behind them, the home side rallied after the break and scored twice. Both teams had chances to add to the scoring but the game ended 2-1 to Split. However, this was a Spurs team with experience of overturning first-leg deficits and weren't fazed by the task awaiting them back at White Hart Lane.

Burkinshaw named the same XI for the Division One win against Luton three days later but, by this point, speculation had begun to grow about his future. An exclusive in the *London Evening Standard* appeared to reveal the finer detail of Burkinshaw's meeting with Scholar and Bobroff in Vienna and, by the time of the Luton game, the club felt compelled to confirm within the matchday programme that, indeed, Burkinshaw's resignation had been 'reluctantly accepted' and that he would leave the club at the end of the season.

Tony Parks was bitterly disappointed with the decision that had gradually become known to the squad ahead of the public announcement:

> I'm sure the senior players knew much earlier than the rest of us and that's where they – and Steve [Perryman], in particular – were so fantastic, because they shielded us from what could have been a really unsettling situation. I didn't have much to do with Scholar but it was clear he was a new breed of football chairman who was very happy to be a face and wanted to be in front of the camera. The previous regime was the complete opposite but he wanted to sit on the team coach and get involved in the football decisions. I think Scholar thought he could do a better job than Keith of raising the profile of the team. He had a completely different philosophy to Keith, who was incredibly principled, so there was always going to be a clash.

The majority of the players were stunned at the news. Hoddle wrote in *Playmaker* that he was shocked and that 'Keith deserved better'. Paul Miller stated in *The Boys from White Hart Lane* that the players knew that he had differences with Scholar.

Jill Lewis was shocked and very disappointed to learn of Burkinshaw's departure:

> There had been a sense that all wasn't right with Burkinshaw once Scholar took over. We really didn't want him to go. It felt like the end of an era – the 'Argentina glory years' were coming to an end and Burkinshaw was fundamental to that wonderful period for the club. It caused some resentment towards Scholar, as it felt like football wasn't the sole focus anymore.

Prior to the UEFA Cup second leg, Spurs beat Aston Villa but lost 3-2 at Highbury – the third defeat of the season in a north London derby. Arsenal led 1-0 with just 12 minutes remaining and looked to have scored the decisive second goal until Archibald fired Spurs straight back into it. Within two minutes, Arsenal scored their third, only for Archibald to again reply instantly. With Falco suspended, Crooks partnered Archibald for what turned out to be the final occasion the pair started a game together in lilywhite.

Julie Welch dedicated a chapter to the pair in her 2024 football shorts book *Double Acts*:

> At this point in 1984, we didn't know that they'd never start a game again but you could tell that both had their days numbered. Crooks had suffered a number of injuries that slowed him down and Archibald had that fatal falling out with Burkinshaw.
>
> As a result, they never really hit the incredible heights of that first season together in 80/81, when they scored 46 goals between them. When writing *Double Acts*, I studied the dynamic of some of the club's greatest-ever partnerships – like Greaves and Gilzean, Gascoigne and Lineker and Kane and Son – but none are quite like Crooks and Archibald. Both had their own unique qualities and moments but

they're invariably remembered as a partnership. You can't say one without the other.

True enough, Falco replaced Crooks in the starting XI for the return leg against Split on 25 April and Roberts and Hazard passed late fitness tests. Mabbutt, who was struggling with a groin injury, was named as a sub, with Stevens starting in midfield. Parks kept his place in goal, despite Clemence being available.

Stevens had the first chance of the game, failing to convert a header from a left-wing cross, but it was Micky Hazard who scored Spurs' goal in the seventh minute.

Spurs were awarded a free kick 25 yards out from a central position. With Hoddle not playing, Hazard called rank and lined up a shot that went low around the wall, surprising the keeper and bouncing into the bottom corner. In the melee that ensued, Hazard lost a contact lens, which he miraculously managed to spot in the glare of the floodlights. He ran straight down the tunnel to the changing room to try and replace it and required the help of Peter Shreeve, who'd come running down from his seat in the directors' box, to put it back in.

Spurs held their nerve. Archibald saw a well-hit shot saved and then, at the other end, Parks was relieved when he juggled a long-range free kick on to the bar and just about managed to gather the ball before an on-rushing Split player could equalise. It proved to be the final moment of significance before the referee blew the final whistle, which sparked euphoric scenes. Spurs had reached a fourth major European final.

It should have been an all-English final but, just as Spurs had suffered in 1962, Nottingham Forest were cheated in their semi-final against Anderlecht. In 1997, it was revealed by UEFA that the referee had been bribed by an Anderlecht director ahead of the game.

As had been the case when Spurs won the inaugural UEFA Cup in 1972, the final of the competition was played over two legs. The first game was due to be played in Brussels on 9 May, with the return leg at White Hart Lane two weeks later.

Before the first leg, Spurs had three league games to negotiate and the priority was very clearly to nurse players who were carrying injuries and to get those already out back to full fitness. Hoddle appeared to be fighting a losing battle but there was hope that Ardiles and Roberts might be okay. Neither played in Spurs' 2-1 defeat at QPR or the 2-0 win over Norwich.

The Norwich game was just four days ahead of the first leg in Brussels but a full Division One fixture list was scheduled for the Bank Holiday Monday, with Spurs travelling to Southampton. Spurs were now five points behind fifth-placed Nottingham Forest with just two games to play, so Burkinshaw made the pragmatic decision to make wholesale changes. Even Tony Parks, who was by now the preferred choice in goal, was given the afternoon off:

> I'll always be so grateful for the faith that Keith put in me. I think because he had started coaching the reserves and had Peter alongside him meant that he really trusted all of us that had come through the youth team. If you came in and impressed, he kept faith with you. He was prepared to make big calls like that, especially with the young lads. I believe the board were encouraging him to put Clem back in for the final but he stuck to his guns. That gave me so much confidence.

Clemence came back at Southampton in a team that included Ian Culverhouse, Mark Bowen, Gary O'Reilly, Ian Crook, Richard Cooke, Robbie Brace and Allan Cockram. Spurs were beaten 5-0 and were subsequently fined by the FA for fielding an under-strength team.

Whenever an English club – or, more particularly, their fans – travelled to the continent, tensions were heightened. Spurs had been fined £7,500 by UEFA for their fans' behaviour in Feyenoord earlier in the season. The Belgian authorities, who had hosted Nottingham Forest fans just weeks earlier, arranged for decrepit old wartime railway stock to transport fans from Ostend to Brussels and, as a precautionary measure, freed up horse stables near the stadium as a temporary prison. Regrettably, there were incidents in the town centre and, tragically, an 18-year-old Spurs fan was shot dead by a barman. The players, some of whom knew the fan in question, learned about the catastrophe on the morning of the match.

Hoddle had already been ruled out of both legs of the final and Ardiles was also not risked in Brussels, though it was hoped he might return for the second leg.

The starting XI was Parks, Thomas, Perryman, Miller, Hughton, Stevens, Roberts, Hazard, Galvin, Falco, Archibald. Mabbutt was declared fit enough to take his place on the bench alongside Clemence, Culverhouse, Cooke and Crooks. That Cooke (11 appearances) and Culverhouse (three) were selected in the 16 for a final highlights just how depleted Spurs were.

Anderlecht were narrow favourites to win the final and retain the trophy they had won in 1983. By the early 80s, the UEFA Cup was considered by some to be the toughest of the three competitions to win. The European Cup contained just the previous season's champions, whereas the UEFA Cup included multiple teams from the strongest leagues.

Belgian football was also enjoying a resurgence; like England, they had qualified for the 1982 World Cup after a 12-year hiatus, and had stunned Ossie Ardiles's Argentina in the opening game. They had qualified for the finals of Euro 84 (England hadn't) and had the nucleus of a young, talented squad that would go on to reach the semi-finals of the 1986 World Cup.

As was the case in most countries across Europe, Belgian club football was largely insular, with most teams made up of homegrown players. Eight of the 20 members of the Belgian Euro 84 squad were from Anderlecht, including prolific striker Erwin Vandenbergh and prodigious midfield talent Enzo Scifo. Additionally, three members of the Danish squad also played their club football for Anderlecht. As a result, Anderlecht supplied more players at the Euro 84 finals that summer than any other club side in Europe.

Glenn Hoddle established himself as a world-class talent with 22 goals in 1979/80

Crooks and Archibald hit it off immediately. Villa and Hoddle join in the celebration after Crooks' debut goal in August 1980

Ricky Villa reels away having scored the iconic winner in the 1981 FA Cup Final

The team celebrate after the 1981 FA Cup Final replay success.

Ray Clemence provided quality and experience after joining from Liverpool in 1981

Captain Fantastic Steve Perryman played in every one of the 66 first team games in 81/82 including all three Wembley cup finals.

Micky Hazard in action for Spurs in the 1982 Milk Cup Final.

Another cup final and another cup final song! Chas and Dave wrote 'Tottenham, Tottenham' for the 1982 FA Cup Final.

'The Animals of Barcelona' – Tony Galvin looks to evade the challenge of two Barcelona players in the Cup Winners' Cup home leg tie April 82.

It took a couple of months for Gary Mabbutt to earn a full England cap having joined Spurs from Bristol Rovers in 1982. He was Spurs' star performer in 82/83

TV cameras in position for Spurs v Nottingham Forest in October 1983.

Graham Roberts slots in Spurs' equaliser with the Shelf looking on v Anderlecht

Playing in their all sky blue away kit, Spurs kicked off in what proved to be a first half of few clearcut chances. Falco came closest to putting Spurs ahead when he met Galvin's cross but couldn't direct it goalwards. It became a tense affair, both on and off the pitch. Strong words were exchanged between the sets of players on several occasions and a crowd disturbance resulted in at least one fan being taken out of the ground on a stretcher. More would follow in the second half.

After the interval, the game opened up. Alexandre Czerniatynski slipped a shot inches past the post while Anderlecht nearly presented Spurs with a goal, only escaping when Falco's shot was cleared off the line. Not helped by the wet surface, tackles came thick and fast – Stevens, Galvin and Thomas all on the receiving end of fouls that were lucky to escape further action.

Following a flurry of corners, Miller rose above his marker to head powerfully into the net in front of the travelling fans to give Spurs a 53rd-minute lead. It was the defender's first goal in more than a year.

Miller's central defensive partner, Perryman, was involved in the next notable action. Having seen the Swiss referee take a very lenient approach to some of the Anderlecht challenges, he was horrified to see a yellow card brandished following his foul on Morten Olsen. This was the second caution he had received in the competition and meant that Spurs' skipper would be suspended for the second leg.

Four minutes later, Galvin followed Perryman into the book. The Spurs winger committed the initial foul but he was then kicked whilst getting to his feet. Disciplinary action was only taken against Galvin. It may have been nothing compared to the disgraceful officiating in Anderlecht's semi-final but Spurs had reason to feel aggrieved.

The away team looked comfortable but were forced into a change when Stevens, who didn't appear to have recovered from a heavy challenge earlier in the half, was replaced by Mabbutt, who himself was nursing an injury. Then, with just four minutes remaining, the first real shot in anger from the Belgians was spilled by Parks and Olsen was on hand to fire in an equaliser from close range.

The game ended in a draw that, on the face of it, was a decent result for Spurs, especially having scored an away goal, but there was a feeling of disappointment over the late concession of a goal after Anderlecht had offered little threat. The 7,000 or so Spurs fans in the stadium celebrated the result, singing Keith Burkinshaw's name, but were unaware that UEFA had opened an investigation into the troubles that had occurred both in the stadium and in central Brussels, where several outbreaks of violence had occurred, with two police officers attacked and 40 Spurs fans arrested. The morning newspapers speculated that UEFA might yet disqualify Spurs from the competition.

Talking about the performance of his team, Burkinshaw was pleased. 'The thing that really pleased me tonight was that Brian Clough had told me what a fantastic side Anderlecht are. Tonight, we matched them and possibly even bettered them … if we had got a second, I don't think Anderlecht would have come back.'

Perryman, when asked about his yellow card, was typically phlegmatic, admitting that he might have seen red in the incident for which he had been booked earlier in the tournament. He was, though, clearly disappointed. 'It's as though I've been sent off at half-time … I haven't got too many finals left.'

Upon returning to England, Burkinshaw then had to prepare his team for their final league game of the season – a home match against Manchester United, who had the slimmest of chances of overhauling Liverpool to win the championship. Mabbutt replaced Stevens in an otherwise unchanged XI.

While the home crowd continued to show their solidarity with Burkinshaw in what was his penultimate game in charge, it was Steve Archibald, whose soured relationship with his manager remained, who scored in a 1-1 draw.

In the ten days ahead of the second leg, the media were compelled by the narrative of Burkinshaw's final game as Spurs manager. There was still incredulity at the club's decision to allow Burkinshaw to leave. Writing in *The People*, reporter Brian

Madley – a friend of Burkinshaw's – commented on how relaxed the manager now appeared. He wrote of Scholar: 'He looked like a man whose divorce celebrations had been cut short by the news that his wife had won the pools.' Madley posited; 'How can they find a manager better than Burkinshaw who is prepared to accept the restrictions he wouldn't?'

Burkinshaw's wasn't the only contract due to expire. Graham Roberts put pen to paper on a new five-year deal but Paul Miller and the club had reached stalemate in a quest to extend the defender's stay at White Hart Lane. Miller was quoted as saying the offer made to him was 'an insult', adding: 'The offer I have been made is so far short of what I think I am worth it is untrue and, for the first time in my life, I would consider leaving Spurs.' However, his goal in Brussels seemed to break down the impasse and he was soon offered the contract he was looking for.

It was not just Miller who was aggrieved at the board's alleged frugality. The second leg had attracted national interest and ITV chose to cover the game live, which would generate a decent fee for the club. When Steve Perryman learned that the club would not honour a 12-year-old agreement first put in place by Bill Nicholson to pass on some of that income to the players, he called an urgent meeting with Irving Scholar.

Perryman remembers the episode clearly:

I'd been part of the squad in 1972 when Bill Nicholson had negotiated the bonus for us and it had remained within our contracts since. Bill's rationale back in 1972 had been that 'if the club earns money, then you should earn, too'. This had been going on throughout several rounds but now came to a head ahead of the second leg. I urged Scholar to speak with Bill, whose office was just along the corridor. He refused to speak with him and it rang alarm bells with me. Why wouldn't he speak with the fairest man in the world, who could have clarified the situation? It added to the distrust I had for him.

Perryman's disdain for the chairman continued through until the second leg itself. When he was interviewed before the game by ITV and when sitting on the bench during the game, TV viewers saw that Perryman had chosen to wear an adidas-branded tracksuit top instead of one made by the club's kit manufacturer, Le Coq Sportif!

Eventually, the PFA became involved in the financial dispute and Scholar backed down. In Scholar's book, *Behind Closed Doors*, he put the blame squarely on Paul Bobroff for, without his knowledge or consent, removing the bonuses, citing the profit projections made for the flotation.

Spurs had ten days to prepare for the second leg and the gap allowed Ossie Ardiles to play twice in friendly matches. The first, for a Spurs staff XI at Orient, saw the Argentine come through unscathed but that was not the case for Irving Scholar, who ruptured an Achilles tendon, meaning he would attend the second leg at White Hart Lane in a wheelchair.

There was further bad news for the Spurs owner when, on the day of the game, the *Daily Mirror* ran a back-page story that much-coveted Aberdeen manager Alex Ferguson had turned down the opportunity to join Spurs. Reports had circulated since early April that the Scot was Scholar's first choice and the pair had spoken and met on several occasions. Ferguson, however, remained happy in Aberdeen.

With Perryman suspended, Roberts took on the captaincy. There was a buoyant mood in the dressing room and the players were additionally motivated to win the game as a send-off for Burkinshaw. Speaking to ITV ahead of the game, Roberts said: 'Keith has looked after me a lot. He bought me from non-league. So, tonight, I'll be giving 120 per cent. We're all looking forward to it and to win it for Keith.'

Burkinshaw's final selection dilemma centred around the fitness of Ardiles and Mabbutt. Neither were capable of lasting 90 minutes and, of course, there was also the potential for extra time. It was decided on the day of the game that Mabbutt would start and Ardiles would be on the bench. Roberts dropped back into defence to partner Miller – the successful central defensive partnership of 1981. Ally Dick and Mark Bowen replaced Cooke and Culverhouse on the bench.

The ground was predictably a sell-out, with fans keenly aware of Spurs' formidable European record at White Hart Lane. Going into the game, Spurs were yet to be beaten at home.

Darryl Telles was an exiled Spurs fan studying at the University of Warwick. He found an innovative way of attending the game:

> There were a few of us Spurs fans at Warwick and we'd quite frequently attend games during my three years but, as a student, it was expensive buying return train tickets. This was a midweek game and obviously we just had to be there. The university had minibuses but they were only made available to cultural societies … so the North London Society was established! It actually included a couple of mates who were Arsenal fans who used the opportunity to have 24 hours at home. We found someone prepared to drive the bus and drove down expectantly on the morning of the game.
>
> Back then, you could still get tickets, even as a non-member, as long as you were prepared to queue, sometimes for hours, and that's exactly what we did. I know at some point it sold out but we got our tickets for my preferred place on The Shelf. It proved to be the most electric night of my Spurs-supporting life!

Players and fans alike who were at White Hart Lane speak of the incredible atmosphere of the evening and this comes across on the television footage. Spurs had, perhaps, caught Anderlecht on a slightly off-night in Brussels but the Belgians hit top form in north London. The first half was an evenly contested game that failed to produce any clear chances. A tense but enjoyable half ended goalless.

After the break, the visitors looked to quell the enthusiasm of the crowd and found a breakthrough on the hour. The exceptional Olsen strode forward from sweeper and slipped a ball through for the on-rushing Czerniatynski, who deftly flicked the ball over Parks and into the net to stun the Paxton Road End.

Despite the high stakes, the second leg didn't feature the same violent challenges seen in the first meeting. However, Spurs did begin to show their frustration and Miller kicked out at Scifo, earning a yellow card which sparked a reaction from Roberts. Spurs needed to keep their composure.

With the home side struggling to build any momentum, Burkinshaw knew that his one trump card was Ardiles but he couldn't afford to gamble too soon. Each team was allowed to make two substitutions but it was a surprise when, on 73 minutes, Ally Dick replaced Mabbutt. Unknown to anyone at the time, including the player, Dick ruptured knee ligaments shortly after coming on but managed to play on. The injury no doubt impacted the remainder of his career.

Four minutes later, the sight of Ardiles making his way to the touchline generated a huge roar inside the stadium. He replaced Miller, with Stevens dropping into defence, and had an immediate impact, with Spurs starting to gain more possession inside the Anderlecht half. The canny Belgians looked to run the clock down but, as the minutes ticked down, they couldn't quell the momentum of the home team.

With six minutes remaining, Archibald's shot was saved by Jacky Munaron. From the resulting corner, Falco's mishit shot landed for Ardiles underneath the crossbar. Somehow, Ardiles's left-foot shot cannoned off the crossbar and was scrambled away. Hazard retrieved the ball from the right-hand side and sent in a cross and – showing sheer determination – Roberts controlled the ball, held off an Anderlecht defender and slotted a shot into the corner.

Roberts credited his youth career as a striker for the composure that he found at the crucial moment. He told *The Boys from White Hart Lane*: 'Mark Falco did fantastic for me; he pushed the lad in front of him. Mark was going to head it but I shouted 'My ball' and went through. You just think to yourself

'Keep cool, keep cool'. The noise that greeted the goal – my word, I've never heard anything like it.'

Jill Lewis was in the crowd and contributed to that noise:

> It was Roberts's defining moment as a Spurs player. In that moment, he was like Dave Mackay – he showed his indomitable desire to win.

The adrenalinee pushed Spurs on; Galvin had the beating of his full-back but couldn't force another meaningful chance. Anderlecht created opportunities in what became a stretched final few minutes but the final whistle signalled extra time.

For much of the second half, Tony Parks had been a spectator. He has his own take on how the game unfolded:

> You've got to say it was just an incredible football match played between two outstanding teams. We should have won away, so were confident that we'd complete the job at home. I remember that we created lots of chances but Munaron made some incredible saves. They scored and suddenly it all became very tense. Ossie coming on changed the game. They decided to go man-to-man on him but he was so intelligent and a step ahead. He just took his marker all over the pitch into places he didn't want to go. It opened up spaces we hadn't previously found and that's what led to the equaliser.

With momentum behind them, Spurs had the better of the first half of extra time. Archibald almost capitalised on a mistake by Munaron and Galvin had a shot from range saved. Fatigue set in as the game approached its conclusion and the final 15 minutes passed without any further notable incident or, crucially, goals. For the first time in a competitive game, Spurs would be participating in a penalty shoot-out.

The concept of a penalty shoot-out was relatively new. As recently as 1968, the European Championship semi-final between Italy and the USSR had been decided by the drawing of lots after the game ended in stalemate. Penalties were first used to determine the winner in a European knockout competition when Everton beat Borussia Mönchengladbach in 1970. The novelty of a shoot-out was sufficient to cause confusion, however. In 1973, the referee of a game between Panathinaikos and CSKA Sofia ended the shoot-out prematurely and the result was annulled with the whole tie having to be replayed!

Spurs had some experience of penalties, having lost a shoot-out 3-1 to FC Köln in a pre-season tournament in 1982 in Amsterdam. This time, when it really mattered, they had home advantage.

Jason McGovern, a co-host of the *Last Word On Spurs* podcast, was at White Hart Lane and recalls his emotions as the club went into a penalty shoot-out in a competitive match for the first time:

> By the 90s and into the 2000s, we'd be scarred by both England and Spurs losing in penalty shoot-outs but, in 1984, it was a real novelty. Thinking back, I can't recall any sort of trepidation or anxiety. I think we were all caught up in the emotion of what was an incredible evening. That said, you looked at our players still on the pitch – Roberts, Falco, Archibald, Hazard – and fancied that they'd all score. If anything, it was Parks in goal whom we'd have been more unsure about.

The shoot-out took place at the Paxton Road End. Captain Roberts stepped up first and drove the ball into the roof of the net to give Spurs the lead.

Anderlecht captain Morten Olsen took their first. Perhaps the most accomplished player in the Belgian side, the Dane had Parks to beat. The preparation for taking or facing a penalty was nowhere near as scientific as it has become in the 21st century, as Parks explains:

> Keith had asked in the lead-up to the game who would fancy one but that was about it. We hadn't done any explicit

penalty shoot-out preparation but ever since the youth team days, a group of us – me as keeper, Brookey, Ian Crook, Mark Bowen – would routinely go out early to training or stay after to practice penalties.

All the stuff you see now – with keepers looking at iPads, notes on bottles – is all just kidology. It's utter nonsense. Saving a penalty is great for a keeper's profile but it comes down to how well the ball is struck. If the player gets the right amount of power and hits the corner, they're gonna score. Therefore, as a keeper, you need a bit of luck. The fella taking it needs to get a poor contact and then you have to guess the right way.

That was exactly what happened. Olsen hit a weak shot and Parks correctly threw himself to his left and pushed it away, sparking jubilation from fans behind him and around the stadium.

Spurs had an immediate advantage. Falco, Stevens and Archibald all scored their kicks, as did each of the corresponding Anderlecht players, which meant that Danny Thomas had the chance to win the UEFA Cup with Spurs' fifth penalty.

Talking to the official club website in 2020 about that moment, Thomas revealed: 'I wasn't down to be one of the five penalty-takers. We had five earmarked but my good friend, Micky Hazard, couldn't even walk, let alone take a penalty!'

Thomas was a popular figure among his team-mates and with the crowd. He had enjoyed a positive first season at White Hart Lane but was not known for his goalscoring. His run-up lacked conviction and Munaron correctly dived to his right, making a comfortable save.

Having been denied the euphoria of a win, the crowd could have shown their frustration but, instead, the instant reaction was one of solidarity. As Thomas returned, crestfallen, to the halfway line, he was serenaded with chants of 'There's only one Danny Thomas'.

Several players, including Perryman and Mabbutt, have later reflected that that was the moment they knew Spurs would win.

Over a number of years and decades, the White Hart Lane crowd have been labelled fickle but, on this occasion, they played their part in getting the team over the line.

Icelandic international Arnór Guðjohnsen (whose son, Eiður, would briefly play for Spurs in 2010) now had the opportunity to level the shoot-out and take it to sudden death.

Parks was one save away from glory.

I was still on a high from saving the first one, to be honest. For kicks two, three and four, I went the same way and didn't get near any of them. I honestly think that the crowd reaction to Danny Thomas spooked Anderlecht. Usually, when a kick is missed at that stage of a shoot-out, it shifts momentum and that's what they expected to happen.

I don't know whether Guðjohnsen had clocked that I'd been diving to the left or not but I'd decided I'd go the other way this time. I knew the instant that he struck the ball he hadn't hit it sweetly enough and I got across to it.

Brian Moore, commentating for ITV, exclaimed: 'He's saved it.' He hadn't just saved it; he'd also won it!

Graham Roberts led his team across the familiar turf in front of the West Stand to lift the UEFA Cup – Spurs' third major European competition. Keith Burkinshaw's eight-year reign had the fairytale finish he deserved.

Celebrations went on until the early hours, with the players enjoying the facilities in the West Stand, and many of the fans just didn't go home, remaining on or around the High Road until the morning. It was a rare opportunity to win a major trophy at your home stadium and is, therefore, remembered as one of the great nights for Spurs supporters.

Jill Lewis recalls the emotional rollercoaster of the evening:

I'd been there in 72 but, looking back, that doesn't seem as special as that amazing night in 84. It was the manner of it. Everything was against us – Perryman suspended, Hoddle injured. Ossie said later that he should never have played, either. It proved to be the most emotionally intense experience I've ever had at a football match. The pain of seeing Danny Thomas's penalty saved contrasted with the sheer elation of Parks's save and the realisation that we'd won. I was never a post-match drinker but even if I had been, I couldn't have gone out afterwards to celebrate – I was knackered! The adrenalinee was still pumping through me for days!

Steve Perryman feels that the make-up of the team that night deserved special recognition:

With Glenn and I not playing that night, it meant that none of the team Keith inherited and that had gone down and then come up again were involved in the final. Look at the names of some of those who did play. Parks, Miller, Hughton, Hazard, Falco and Ally Dick all came through the youth team. Danny Thomas, Roberts, Stevens, Mabbutt and Galvin – all relatively unknown when Keith signed them. Archibald and Ossie the only ones who'd cost any money or were high profile. It was credit to Keith that he gelled this team together. I think Scholar always had a thing for big names and I just don't think he got what we'd achieved.

As the dust settled on one of the most iconic nights in the club's history, Irving Scholar now had the seismic task of trying to replace the second-most successful manager in the club's 102-year history. Theo Delaney describes Burkinshaw's impact:

Looking back now, I still can't work out exactly why Scholar wanted to replace him but you never know what the personal relationships are like behind closed doors. Maybe he was a little too forthright and direct?
There was no pressure on him or talk of him needing to be replaced and that was before the UEFA final. I'd started watching Spurs properly in the mid-70s and we were really

ordinary. We'd fallen behind other clubs, largely because the board weren't putting in enough money. That's probably why they went for Burkinshaw, who was then assistant, in the first place. It seems absurd now that, having been relegated, he stayed on but thank goodness he did.

He completed the turnaround. He was responsible for our rise from mediocrity to being a real force in England and Europe. It seemed utter madness to replace him.

Burkinshaw was now effectively unemployed, one of more than 3m jobless in the country in what was a politically charged landscape.

On a micro-level, politics had played a huge role in his departure and his parting with the club will forever be immortalised by a quote he didn't actually say. It transpires that journalist Ken Jones mentioned to him an old Frank Sinatra song titled 'There Used To Be A Ballpark', which referenced Ebbets Field, a baseball stadium which was pulled down once the Brooklyn Dodgers left New York to relocate to Los Angeles.

Burkinshaw is said to have nodded, recognising the relevance of the comparison. It has since been wrongly attributed to him but the feeling that the club's owners had taken the football club well away from its primary function has never gone away.

League position	Eighth
Average home league attendance	28,753
Most appearances	Perryman (59)
Top goalscorer	Archibald (28)
League winners	Liverpool
FA Cup winners	Everton
League Cup winners	Liverpool

84/85 – THE HAND OF NEV

CLEMENCE
STEVENS PERRYMAN MILLER HUGHTON
CHIEDOZIE ROBERTS HODDLE GALVIN
FALCO CROOKS

WHILE THE most pressing issue in the haze of the 1984 UEFA Cup success was the appointment of a new manager, the now 'old manager' Keith Burkinshaw was announced as the next manager of the Bahrain national team. He would take up the role in August, taking Spurs' youth team coach Robbie Stepney with him, but received a fitting send-off before the end of May in a testimonial match at White Hart Lane against an England XI led by Bobby Robson.

Alex Ferguson had been Scholar's first choice to replace Burkinshaw. They had shaken hands on a deal during a spring meeting in Paris but the Scot, who would go on to join Manchester United in 1986, reneged. Scholar, who had now been elected chairman of the football club (as opposed to the plc), had pursued other options. Always keen to try and emulate a more continental approach to football, he later revealed in *Behind Closed Doors* that he was impressed with 36-year-old Swedish coach Sven-Göran Eriksson, who had performed wonders with Benfica, and there was some speculation linking Argentine World Cup-winning manager César Luis Menotti.

When Scholar spoke with the players (which he did far more frequently than his predecessors) the one name that kept coming back to him was Peter Shreeve. With such a large number of players in the squad having worked with Shreeve in the youth team, he was revered. Throughout the off-season,

Shreeve took on managerial and administrative tasks on the club's behalf. Along with the chairman, Shreeve represented the club at their FA hearing into fielding the under-strength team at Southampton in May. Despite the very legitimate mitigation that the game had been scheduled to take place just 48 hours ahead of the UEFA Cup Final first leg, the panel found Spurs guilty and issued a fine of £7,500.

Shreeve also led the team on their second successive summer post-season tour to Swaziland. In the summer of 1983, Spurs had toured with Manchester United, even joining forces to take on the national XI. Several of the players have spoken of their camaraderie with their Old Trafford peers. In 1984, it was European and English League champions Liverpool accompanying Spurs to southern Africa but the relationship between the teams was not as cordial.

The Liverpool players kept themselves to themselves and didn't mix with the Spurs players, despite staying in the same resort. The teams played each other twice, Liverpool winning the first game 5-2 before a 1-1 draw in the second. Spurs' shirts were sponsored by Black Cat – the deal with Holsten didn't extend to post-season tours – and images of these shirts occasionally surface on social media.

As had occurred the year before, the two clubs then fielded a mixed team against a Swaziland XI.

One player who was disappointed to be in Swaziland was midfielder Micky Hazard. During the lengthy absences of Hoddle and Ardiles the previous season, Hazard had shone in midfield and deservedly earned an England call-up at the end of the season. Hazard told *The Spurs Show* podcast how he'd been named on the bench for the Home International fixture against Scotland. At half-time England manager Bobby Robson had told Hazard to warm up and that he would be coming on.

Throughout the second half, he ran along the touchline and did stretching exercises but, to his dismay, the anticipated call never came. He was told that he'd definitely get a game the following weekend at Wembley against the USSR but, by that point, Spurs had insisted that, without injured pair Hoddle and

Ardiles and Roberts, who was starting for England, Hazard would have to travel with them to play in Swaziland. Hazard would never win a senior England cap!

On 25 June, a board meeting confirmed the appointment of Peter Shreeve as manager on a two-year contract. Internal appointments had been successful – Nicholson and Burkinshaw had both been assistants before being promoted to the top job.

Steve Perryman spoke for a number of players over his delight at Shreeve's appointment:

> Peter had been instrumental in our success. Firstly, as the youth team coach and then when he stepped up as assistant manager to Keith. The first-team squad was full of players Peter had worked with. Not just the older lads like Glenn, 'Maxi' [Paul Miller] and Hazard – we had a new crop like Bowen, Culverhouse and Crook, too. Peter was a good foil for Keith. He was a bit more streetwise and he understood the mentality of some of the London boys a bit better than Keith did. We were all really keen for him to get the job and delighted when he was appointed.

Shreeve appointed a familiar face to be his assistant. John Pratt had returned to the club, initially as youth team manager, and would now step up to work alongside Shreeve with the first team. Keith Blunt took on the role that Pratt vacated to support the conveyor belt of talent that continued to come through the ranks.

David Harris was one of the first Spurs fans able to put questions to Shreeve about his priorities:

> There had been strong rumours about Alex Ferguson coming in and Scottish managers had been very successful in England, so it was disappointing that didn't happen in the end. Another sliding doors moment for Spurs but Shreeve felt like a good continuity appointment and we knew he was well liked by the players.

Not long after he'd got the job, he appeared on LBC Radio for a phone-in and I successfully dialled in to speak with him on air. I asked him what he was going to do with Garth Crooks and whether he was going to pick Tony Parks in goal but then, when he asked me whether I'd be coming along to games, I told him that season tickets were now far too expensive. My dad and brother were listening from downstairs and roared in laughter!

Among Shreeve's priorities were the high-profile players whose contracts were due to expire at the end of June. The headline was Hoddle, who had signed a further one-year extension the previous summer but was now being heavily courted by others and it was well known that Hoddle had been offered lucrative deals on the continent. Much to the relief of all Spurs fans, Hoddle did re-sign with his boyhood club, keeping him at White Hart Lane until 1987. Galvin also signed an extension.

The most high-profile managerial change of the summer saw Terry Venables appointed by Barcelona. Venables, quickly dubbed 'El Tel', arrived in the same summer that Diego Maradona left the Camp Nou for Napoli. There was huge fanfare at the airport as Maradona left Barcelona for the final time as a Barca player but little was known of a shy-looking and scruffy fair-haired Scot making his way through the arrivals gate.

Steve Archibald's relationship with Burkinshaw had never recovered since their fall-out at the start of the 1983/84 season, despite having finished the season as top scorer with 28 goals. He revealed a terse conversation with Scholar at the end of the season in which the owner greeted him by asking whether 'he was coming to see him to ask for more money' – a legacy of the dispute with Burkinshaw from 1981.

Archibald's fellow Scot, Alan Brazil, also left to join Manchester United. Though he'd scored goals, Brazil had never quite looked right in lilywhite and failed to replicate the form and goalscoring he produced at Ipswich. It was later revealed that he'd developed a chronic back injury – a condition which would force him to retire in 1988 when he was still in his 20s.

Having become peripheral members of the squad, Paul Price and Gary O'Reilly also left in the summer.

At least Garth Crooks was still about – though he had just one year left on his contract and had been shipped out on loan to Manchester United the previous season. Falco now had a chance to establish himself as a first-choice striker but, with two strikers leaving, it was no surprise that Shreeve wanted to find a new centre-forward.

Just as Archibald wasn't the only Scot leaving Spurs, Maradona wasn't the only Argentine leaving Spain. Mario Kempes, best known to the international football audience for his two goals in the 1978 World Cup Final, was now aged 30 and was available for transfer. Utilising their Argentinian link, Spurs invited him for a trial on their pre-season tour of Scandinavia. He joined the squad at Cheshunt – with Ardiles acting as interpreter – though Shreeve hinted that the former World Cup winner's lack of match fitness and previous injuries might be an issue.

Kempes's first act in a Spurs shirt was to score a hat-trick against the Norwegian outfit St Jordal Blick in a 9-0 win. He featured in the next two Scandinavian games alongside Ardiles and Hoddle but didn't score. The trial was extended to two further pre-season games – a 7-0 win at Enfield and a 2-2 draw in Nice – but doubts over his fitness didn't subside and a deal wasn't pursued.

Some players are destined to play for particular clubs. Fate played its part in dissuading Shreeve from signing Kempes but the decision paved the way for Clive Allen to become a Spurs player.

Having suffered a significant ankle injury while playing against Spurs in the 1982 FA Cup Final, Allen returned to fitness and scored goals consistently over the next two seasons in Division One. In 1983/84, Allen played his part in helping QPR finish fifth – above Spurs – in the top flight, which put him on the radar of the country's biggest clubs. For Allen, the attraction of following in his father's footsteps was significant. He recalls the conversations that sealed his move to White Hart Lane:

Alan Mullery was the new QPR manager and he brought in Gary Bannister from Coventry. When I asked him about his plans and that I wanted to go, he made it abundantly clear that I wasn't going anywhere. While I took the train home from QPR back home to Dagenham, unbeknown to me there were conversations going on between Spurs and QPR. The instant I walked through the front door, I had a phone call. It was Peter Shreeve, who I knew from when I'd trained with Spurs as a schoolboy. He simply said to me 'Clivey, you know where the stadium is. I'll see you tomorrow'. It was good enough for me!

I guess you'd say it was destiny. After all, I'd been at Wembley for the 1961 FA Cup Final to watch Dad and for us to win the double – albeit I was still in Mum's tum at the time! I'd trained with Spurs as a kid and also played on the pitch at White Hart Lane for London Schoolboys (against Gary Mabbutt, who happened to be playing for Bristol!). I grew up on stories of the great Spurs teams over the years, so they were always our team.

I was excited to link up with Mark Falco again – we'd known each other for years and played together in schoolboy football. There was never a conversation about which of us or Garth Crooks would start up front but I remember Peter telling me about the heightened level of expectation on a Spurs player. I was joining an excellent group and we believed we'd do really well that season.

On the same day, Spurs also signed John Chiedozie from Notts County. The Nigerian winger had impressed, particularly against Spurs when he scored in both games in the 1982/83 season. His arrival added a different option for Shreeve in midfield. Both featured in the remaining three pre-season fixtures (Allen scored four times) ahead of the opening day of the Football League season, which saw Spurs travel to Goodison Park to meet Everton.

Having won the FA Cup in 1984, Everton now appeared to be the main league challengers to Liverpool. The Merseyside clubs were embarking on a fiercely competitive football rivalry and the two had met in the Charity Shield, with Howard Kendall's team running out 1-0 winners.

Spurs' abysmal record at Anfield was well documented but going into the opening game of the 1984/85 season, they hadn't won a league game at Goodison since 1968 (they had won in an FA Cup replay in 1972). The dismal run dated back to before Steve Perryman had even made his debut.

Having signed a new contract, Hoddle was still recovering from his Achilles injury and so missed pre-season but he was now joined at the club by his younger brother, Carl, who had been promoted from the youth team into the reserves. Ardiles was out indefinitely, having aggravated his leg injury in pre-season.

Shreeve's first big selection decision was who to start in goal. Parks had performed heroics in the UEFA Cup Final while Clemence had returned in pre-season, following a spell of injuries and poor performances, more determined than ever to win back his place. Had that magical night in May had an adverse effect on the young keeper?

> I had a difficult summer. Maybe I was too young and not mature enough. For the first time in my career, I started to believe my own hype; I wasn't focused and got up to some really daft things. Meanwhile, Clem did the complete opposite and knuckled down and got himself in top condition ahead of pre-season. I spoke to him a few years before he passed away and he told me that, for the first time in his career, he thought his place was under threat, so was determined he'd get it back. By the start of the season, it was an easy decision for Peter to make. I only had myself to blame and spent the next three and a half years out of the first team.

Clemence was recalled and was protected by a back four of Stevens, Perryman, Miller and Hughton, with Chiedozie, Roberts, Hazard and Galvin in midfield. Falco partnered Allen in attack, with Mabbutt named as the substitute.

Ahead of the game, Everton paraded the FA Cup trophy they had won in May and the feelgood factor in Goodison extended into the opening stages when Adrian Heath put the home side ahead from the penalty spot. But from that point on, Spurs took control. Falco equalised and then Spurs blitzed Everton either side of half-time. Both new boys, Allen, with two, and Chiedozie scored to give Spurs a 4-1 lead before the hour mark. It was Spurs' biggest and most emphatic opening day victory since Bill Nicholson's first full season in charge, when Les Allen had played in a 5-1 win at Newcastle.

On Bank Holiday Monday, Leicester frustrated Spurs at White Hart Lane, claiming a 2-2 draw. Four days later, though, another City, this time Norwich, couldn't stop Spurs, who ran out 3-1 victors – Chiedozie scoring his first White Hart Lane goal for Spurs.

Up next came an historic game, but for the wrong reasons, at Sunderland. Graham Roberts saw red in the first half for an off-the-ball incident and, with Spurs trailing 1-0, the night got even worse when Clive Allen received a second caution and joined Roberts for the proverbial 'early bath'. It was the first time in the club's history that they'd had two players sent off in a game.

When Spurs then lost again, this time at newly promoted Sheffield Wednesday, they were down in tenth position, with the win at Everton suddenly feeling a long time ago. September, though, turned out to be a very good month.

Allen scored his first White Hart Lane goals for his new club in a 5-0 rout of his old club, QPR. There were further league wins over Aston Villa and Luton and the defence of the UEFA Cup got off to a great start with a 3-0 away leg win over the Portuguese outfit Braga. There was also room for a 5-1 win at Halifax in the League Cup, with Crooks, in for the suspended Allen, bagging a hat-trick. October began in much the same manner as Spurs thumped Braga 6-0, with Crooks notching another hat-trick, to complete a 9-0 aggregate win.

Shreeve must have wished his team had saved some of those 24 goals scored in just six games for the next league fixture, away at Southampton, where Spurs were beaten 1-0.

Next up, at White Hart Lane, were Liverpool. On this occasion, just one goal was enough for Spurs. Crooks scored it and, by virtue of the fact that the game was played on a Friday night after being chosen by the BBC as a live TV game, the victory sent Spurs top for a few hours. The game also marked Steve Perryman's 600th league appearance. Now aged 33, Perryman remained Spurs' beating heart.

Having beaten both Merseyside clubs, Spurs' next test came against Manchester United at Old Trafford. United manager Ron Atkinson was under pressure, having spent big in the summer on the acquisitions of Gordon Strachan, Jesper Olsen and Alan Brazil. United had started the season with four successive draws but clicked into gear winning four of the next five, which included a big win over West Ham.

It was, therefore, very much a clash of the challengers but the game was decided in favour of the home team, with powerful 21-year-old striker Mark Hughes scoring the only goal of the game. Hoddle made his long-awaited comeback as a second-half sub. It meant that since the opening day victory at Everton, Spurs had now lost four of five away league games; winning away from home was something that championship-winning teams just had to do.

Four days later, Spurs lost on their travels again – this time in an event-filled UEFA Cup first leg away to Club Brugge. With the Belgians already leading 1-0 after an early goal, they were awarded a penalty, which their goalkeeper, Birger Jensen, came forward to convert! Perhaps still in a state of elation, the keeper then conceded a vital away goal when Clive Allen pulled one back. Spurs ended the game with ten men, however, when Hoddle, again coming on as a sub, was sent off for a second bookable offence.

Hoddle was able to start in the next league game and Spurs found their shooting boots again with a 4-0 victory over Stoke at White Hart Lane. Spurs' fine home form continued in the League Cup, with Liverpool beaten for a second time in 19 days.

Spurs would then have gone back to the top of the table but for bogey team West Brom recording a 3-2 win. It was now six league encounters since Spurs had beaten the Baggies at home.

That defeat proved to be an outlier in what was fast becoming a very promising early winter. Having dispatched Club Brugge back at White Hart Lane and then beaten the very physical Czechoslovakian outfit Bohemians, Spurs went unbeaten in six league games.

The only blemish was their League Cup exit at the hands of Sunderland. Having drawn 0-0 at Roker Park, Spurs were confident they would get the job done at home. Sunderland proved to hold the hoodoo over Spurs and, in particular, Roberts and Allen. Just three months earlier, the pair were infamously sent off and, in the replay, more misfortune followed. Roberts missed a decisive penalty (having scored once already from the spot) and Allen hobbled off with a groin injury that effectively ended his season. Sunderland goalkeeper Chris Turner was inspired, repelling shot after shot, and he was able to watch from afar as his team-mates scored from virtually their only two attacks to record an unlikely 2-1 win.

Back in the league, Spurs won at Watford and then travelled to Norwich on 22 December knowing that a win could send them to the top at Christmas for the first time since 1960. With Hoddle temporarily out injured again, it was Chiedozie who proved to be the key man as his pace terrorised Norwich full-back Greg Downs. Though the winger didn't score, he was named man of the match in a hard-fought 2-1 victory. Other results went Spurs' way – Everton were beaten at home by Chelsea and Arsenal could only draw with Watford. It was the perfect early Christmas present!

Spurs fan and author Adam Powley (who co-wrote *The Boys from White Hart Lane)* recalls:

Going top was a seminal moment and, as we came to terms with the fact we might actually be in with a chance of winning the league, it made us reconsider our priorities as to what we hoped our club could achieve. As Spurs fans, we'd often taken a snobbish view of what winning the league meant. We were Spurs – we were about playing with style and with a swagger that lent itself to winning cups – but now we went into Christmas top of the table. Was this going to be the year we became champions? The evidence on the field was that it could be. The team was evolving and we had greater depth. We still had the flair and flamboyance but perhaps we had the attributes of a league-winning team now?

Band Aid topped the Christmas charts with 'Do They Know It's Christmas' but, more importantly, Spurs sat at the top of the football charts! They retained top spot despite a home draw with West Ham on Boxing Day and beat Sunderland in the final game of the calendar year. George Orwell may have prophesised about a dystopian 1984 but for Spurs, with a UEFA Cup win and now top of the league, it might just have been the perfect year.

Nineteen-eighty-five couldn't have started any better. It could barely have begun any earlier, either, with the north London derby at Highbury kicking off at 11.30am. Arsenal took a first-half lead but Spurs grew in confidence after the break, scoring twice in front of the North Bank through Crooks and Falco. Roberts endeared himself to the home fans by flicking the 'V' sign towards the West Stand in celebration of the winning goal – or perhaps, as he subsequently explained in *The Boys from White Hart Lane*, he was just reminding them how many goals Spurs had scored!

In 1982, a combination of bad weather and over-exertions in the cup competitions had cost Spurs the league title. By January 1985, both factors again threatened Spurs' momentum. Although already out of the League Cup, Spurs battled with Charlton, of Division Two, in the FA Cup and could only draw the first tie at White Hart Lane.

A cold snap was forecast and it duly arrived, forcing the replay at The Valley to be postponed. Only grounds with undersoil heating were able to stage games the following weekend. By virtue of QPR's plastic pitch, however, Spurs were able to fulfil their fixture in west London. In what proved to be a seminal day in the season's title race, Spurs were held to an entertaining 2-2 draw while Everton thumped Newcastle to regain top spot.

In a hotly anticipated game, Spurs were then due to host Everton at White Hart Lane the following weekend but, with the pitch covered by a blanket of snow, the game had to be rearranged for later in the season.

The FA Cup replay against Charlton at The Valley was eventually played, with Spurs winning 2-1. Falco scored his 20th of the season as he and Crooks enjoyed a purple patch in front of goal. The pair had scored 35 between them, which mitigated the impact of the injury to Allen.

Having won at Charlton, Spurs then travelled to Liverpool in the fourth round, searching for that elusive away win at Anfield. The game had been selected for live coverage by ITV on the Sunday afternoon and that may have hardened efforts to ensure that the game could be played. The game was played in freezing conditions and large sections of the pitch were covered in snow.

The match was defined by two key moments inside the first 20 minutes. Perryman appeared to be tripped inside the Liverpool area but his fierce protests were waved away by referee Keith Hackett. At the other end, Rush evaded the challenge of Roberts and lifted the ball past Clemence for what proved to be the only goal of the game.

Out of both domestic cups by the end of January, it was now just the UEFA Cup that provided a distraction to league title ambitions.

The weather continued to play havoc throughout February. Spurs could only draw at Luton in a game with a crazy ending. Luton led 1-0 until Falco equalised, only for Luton to go straight up the other end and score what looked like being the winner. Roberts once again demonstrated his never-say-die attitude by thumping in a stoppage-time leveller. After the game, Luton manager David Pleat paid tribute to the Spurs performance, stating: 'If I was a football fan, I would go and watch Tottenham. I see them play more than any other side in the league because

I like what they do and the way they play.' Within 18 months, Pleat would get to watch them play even more closely!

The next two weeks were lost to the weather, although Spurs did then record back-to-back wins over West Brom and Stoke – both away from home. Spurs had now played six on the spin away from White Hart Lane. Everton hit full throttle, embarking on a six-game winning streak in the league and even a draw at third-placed Manchester United meant that they kept Spurs at arm's length going into March. There was a five-point gap now between Spurs in second, with Manchester United in third.

Spurs' defence of the UEFA Cup had seen them progress to the quarter-finals and they had their first-ever competitive fixture against Real Madrid to look forward to. Spurs boasted a proud European record at White Hart Lane, where they were still yet to be beaten since first treading the continental stage in 1961. Domestically, Real Madrid were about to be usurped in the league by Terry Venables's Barcelona. Venables commented ahead of the tie that he didn't see Madrid scoring over the two legs.

To an extent he was right. No Real Madrid player scored a goal but, sadly for Spurs, Steve Perryman did bundle the ball into his own net for the only goal at White Hart Lane. Spurs matched their illustrious opponents in both games and were mightily hard done by when Falco's goal in the Bernabéu was disallowed for no obvious reason. To add to his personal nightmare following the first-leg own goal, Perryman was sent off in Madrid. His pending suspension was irrelevant, though, as, unbeknown to anyone, this would be Spurs' last European tie of the decade.

In between the two Madrid games, Spurs faced two season-defining league fixtures. The first was in midweek at home to Manchester United. A crowd of more than 42,000, comfortably the largest at White Hart Lane so far that season, packed in but were left disappointed by a 2-1 defeat – Spurs' first in the league since November. To compound matters, Gary Stevens suffered a knee injury that kept him out for the rest of the season. Everton were now two points ahead, having played a game less.

The main football story of the week, however, also became front page and TV headline news. The following night, Luton and Millwall fans fought each other before, during and after their FA Cup tie at Kenilworth Road. Amid growing tensions in and around many football grounds, this was undoubtedly the ugliest reported incident of hooliganism in England. It wasn't just Millwall fans. Hooligans from a variety of London clubs travelled to the game to cause trouble in a coordinated act.

The scenes would have ramifications for all match-going fans across the country. It fuelled the Thatcher government to explore the use of football supporter ID cards and made some clubs consider the introduction of electric fencing to prevent hooligans entering the pitchside area.

Amid a tense atmosphere for any travelling fans on the trains, in city centres and at motorway service stations that weekend, Spurs made the familiar and so often fruitless trip to Merseyside for their league game with Liverpool. It was now 43 games and 73 years since they had won at Liverpool – it seemed all football fans and reporters could quote the fact that Spurs hadn't won at Anfield since 1912, the year the Titanic sank.

Spurs had often given a good account of themselves at Anfield, despite the results going against them, and this time around they again gave as good as they got. With Spurs attacking The Kop end in the second half, the much-awaited moment finally occurred in the 70th minute. Falco's header across goal was met by Hazard, who hit a sweet volley that Bruce Grobbelaar scrambled to push away. He could only parry the ball and quickest to the rebound was Crooks, who converted from close range.

The scenes at the final whistle were of jubilation, with players and fans celebrating just as vociferously as they had for any of the cup final wins.

The best line from anyone in the Spurs camp came, unsurprisingly, from Paul Miller. When interviewed later that evening, he remarked that 'they'll be shitting themselves on the QE2 tonight!'

Steve Perryman had played for Spurs at Anfield more than anyone else and the result meant a lot to him:

> Winning at Anfield was such a relief. I'd played there in just my third first-team appearance in 1969. We drew 0-0 that day and Greavsie came within a lick of paint of giving us a win that would have ended all this nonsense years ago!

Even better news followed when it emerged that Everton had conceded a late equaliser at Aston Villa. It was now level at the top, albeit that Everton had a slightly superior goal difference and had also played a game less.

Jason McGovern was one of around 5,000 Spurs fans at Anfield for what felt like a momentous victory:

> On a personal level, this result in itself was as sweet as anything I'd enjoyed that season. I'd been at Anfield for the first time when we lost 7-0 in 1978 and cried all the way home. I have despised Liverpool ever since and was so desperate for us to finally win there. Everyone in the media had kept reminding us about the Titanic sinking, so it was great to finally get that off our backs, too. But, having won at Liverpool, we definitely felt that the title was in our grasp.
>
> We were out of both the domestic cups and only had the second leg with Real Madrid as a distraction. Our away form had been magnificent but to look at the fixture list to see that we had 13 games remaining, of which nine were at home, made us all believe the league championship was on its way. What could possibly go wrong?

Defeat in Madrid didn't dampen enthusiasm and hopes for the rest of the league season grew the following weekend when Southampton were thumped 5-1 at White Hart Lane. Ardiles returned to the starting XI to play alongside Hoddle in midfield for the first time in more than a year.

To go back to the top, Spurs required a favour from Arsenal but they were beaten 2-0 at Everton. It was still neck and neck but the goal difference deficit had been reduced to just one.

However, owing to the number of upcoming home games, Spurs were perceived to have the advantage. Everton were still in both the FA Cup and European Cup Winners' Cup but looked relentless, unbeaten since Christmas, and showed no signs of losing momentum or focus.

Spurs needed to be perfect and had to hope that Everton would slip up. They had the game against the Toffees fast approaching but, first, Aston Villa travelled to north London on the final weekend of March. Preparations weren't aided by a string of injuries. Stevens, Mabbutt and Allen were out long-term and Chiedozie and Hughton were now added to the injury list. On top of that, Roberts was suspended. It meant that Mark Bowen was selected at full-back and fellow youth team graduate Ian Crook was named as substitute. Ardiles was able to start but was a long way off full fitness.

It proved to be a thoroughly dispiriting afternoon. Villa were able to break through Spurs' usually efficient offside trap and scored twice without reply. Everton won 2-1 at Southampton and there was now daylight between the two teams.

Steve Perryman remembers:

> People will talk about the Everton game but it was the Aston Villa result that really hurt us. Villa were one of our 'bop' teams. You can't really explain how or why but they could cause us problems and they did on this occasion.

Roberts returned to the starting XI against Everton but otherwise the same team that had been so disjointed against Villa took to the field.

Excitement soon led to a nervous tension as the visitors took an early lead, taking the wind out of the home crowd. Miller's misplaced header landed kindly for Andy Gray, who struck a powerful half-volley that beat Clemence from range. The anxiety on and off the field only increased as Everton's brawn got the better of Spurs' flair. Hoddle came closest to equalising but dragged his shot wide of the far post.

With Spurs chasing the game, they opened themselves up at the back and the inexperience of Bowen was shown up when Trevor Steven robbed him of the ball and rounded Clemence to slot into an open net just after the hour.

Spurs were staring into the abyss but kept attacking and built momentum after Roberts's piledriver from 25 yards screamed into the top corner. Spurs had 17 minutes to turn around the game – and their season – but found Everton to be well-organised and robust. With only minutes remaining, Hoddle worked the ball on to his left foot and crossed to where Falco had, for once, evaded the attention of Kevin Ratcliffe and he made a great contact with his head.

The ball seemed destined to crash into the back of the net to set up a blockbuster ending to the game but Everton goalkeeper Neville Southall instinctively threw himself acrobatically upwards and, from point-blank range, deflected the ball into the Paxton Road lower tier for a corner. There was a moment of disbelief within the stadium; 100 yards away, Ray Clemence dropped to his knees but applauded the save that his opposite number had made.

Adam Powley was on his usual spot in The Shelf:

The Villa defeat left us behind the eight ball, so we just had to win. The attendance figure was officially 49,000 but it felt like a lot more; their fans took the whole Park Lane End and I'd never seen anything quite like the electricity from that end when they scored the second goal.

We looked like we might get back into it at 2-1 and when Hoddle's cross landed on Falco's head, the whole of The Shelf surged forward in anticipation that we'd equalised.

There was disbelief when Southall saved it. You had to be there in the moment to appreciate the physicality of the moment. I've watched the save back and, yes, it's a great save but TV really doesn't do it justice. There were probably a few minutes left; had that gone in, we may well have gone on to win the game and who knows what would have happened beyond that? At the time, it felt like watching a sliding doors moment for both clubs.

It proved to be Spurs' last chance and the final whistle was met euphorically by Everton's players and supporters. Shreeve failed to concede the title, telling reporters: 'If I conceded it was over, my players would kick me from here to Merseyside … we have ten games to play and 30 points to play for.' The bookies didn't share his optimism – Everton were installed as 1/5 favourites with Spurs now out to 6/1.

Spurs had little time to recover, mentally or physically. Three days later, they travelled across London to play West Ham but could only come away with a draw. Just one point from three games dropped Spurs down to third. A last-minute win at Leicester kept Spurs vaguely in the hunt but Everton showed no sign of relenting.

In the end, it was a familiar foe who finally nailed the coffin on Spurs' title dreams. At White Hart Lane on a fine spring evening, Arsenal won 2-0 with a goal in either half. Charlie Nicholas was becoming quite the menace and he scored his fifth goal in five north London derbies. Roberts had the chance to equalise but saw his penalty smash against the crossbar and then Brian Talbot added the fatal second.

Ipswich completed a miserable few days for Spurs when they won 3-2 at White Hart Lane to boost their survival hopes. On a personal note, it was a memorable afternoon for striker David Leworthy, who scored both Spurs goals. The forward, signed from Fareham Town the previous summer, had spent the season in the reserves but was drafted in following an injury to Crooks at Leicester.

With the title now gone, Spurs did at least enjoy a mini-revival, with two wins and a draw from their next three. The third of those games, a 3-2 win at Newcastle, showcased the dribbling skills of Chris Waddle, who had recently gained his first England cap. Talk of a move to Spurs was rife, with some media outlets reporting that a deal had already been agreed to bring the winger to White Hart Lane.

While Spurs entertained on the pitch, the environment for supporters attending games became increasingly bleak. At Stamford Bridge, Chelsea chairman Ken Bates installed an electric fence around the perimeter of the pitch ahead of the Spurs game in April. Though it wasn't actually turned on, the deterrent was clear. Bates had held an audience with MPs to discuss football and society's challenge of hooliganism.

While hooliganism continued to be rife, the bigger crime was the conditions that many clubs and the authorities felt appropriate for spectators coming to games. Tragically, this was demonstrated on Saturday, 11 May when a fire engulfed the old wooden main stand at Valley Parade during Bradford's Third Division game against Lincoln. The home side had just secured promotion and a party atmosphere was anticipated, with regional TV crews attending the game. Instead of joy, the scenes turned to horror and were broadcast across the afternoon and evening news. Tragically, 56 supporters died and more than 250 were injured.

On the same fateful day, a 15-year-old was killed following clashes between Birmingham and Leeds fans in scenes that resembled a warzone.

Of far less significance, Spurs suffered a humiliating 5-1 home defeat to Watford. It seemed to be the culmination of an incredibly frustrating period of the season that, in six weeks since the historic victory at Anfield, had completely unravelled. With Spurs seemingly on the brink of signing Waddle, it was another England winger, John Barnes, who took all the plaudits, scoring once and assisting once, but Spurs' defensive errors were catastrophic.

Only 15,669 turned up for the penultimate home game of the season – a 2-0 win over Sheffield Wednesday. That attendance was less than a third of the gate for the Everton game. Victory in the final game of the season, at home to Nottingham Forest, saw Spurs leapfrog above Manchester United into second but

Liverpool went on to make it a Merseyside one-two with a strong end to the season.

It was a bitterly disappointing end to a season that had, for so long, promised to deliver the elusive league championship that felt like the natural evolution for this Spurs side. Unlike 1982, there wasn't the cup commitments or even the ridiculous fixture congestion, so why did the title slip away?

Steve Perryman felt that the demands on the team to entertain was ultimately what prevented Spurs from winning the league that season:

> On the way home from Anfield, we'd have looked at the fixture list and fancied our chances but, thinking back to the FA Cup successes, it took us two games to beat Manchester City and QPR and also Wolves [in the semi-final]. Given two opportunities, we were capable of beating all those sides but, in a title run-in, you don't have that luxury. I don't think we were ever pragmatic enough when it mattered. While I was a Spurs player, no one ever told me to kick the ball into the corner flag, to go down injured or waste time if we were winning. It just wasn't the way we were encouraged to play. Peter thought much the same as Keith.
>
> Everton were different to us. We'd beaten them 4-1 on the opening day of the season but they were consistent after that. They had a great player in midfield, Kevin Richardson, who went on to win the league with Arsenal as well. He had graft and tenacity but he wouldn't have got into our midfield ahead of Glenn, Ricky, Ossie or Micky Hazard. Liverpool were the same – they had the likes of Sammy Lee, McDermott and Ronnie Whelan. To win a league, it was easier to build a team of destroyers who could defend than one that could create and attack.

Twelve away wins was the most Spurs had achieved in a league campaign since they'd won it but the seven home defeats (plus the League Cup exit to Sunderland and first-ever European loss on home soil) told of the inconsistency that undermined Spurs.

Everton were denied a domestic double when Manchester United beat them in the FA Cup Final but they did end the season with a second trophy after defeating Rapid Vienna in the European Cup Winners' Cup Final.

By finishing third, Spurs should have qualified for the following season's UEFA Cup – a competition they would have fancied winning – but tragedy again struck when Liverpool fans clashed with their Juventus counterparts before the European Cup Final at the Heysel Stadium in Brussels. Again covered live on television, this time across the continent, the ugly scenes culminated in the deaths of 39 people.

The game eventually went ahead and was played against a chaotic and disturbing backdrop. The result felt irrelevant – Juventus won 1-0 – but the outcome of the night's events was far-reaching. The tragedy culminated in the FA, under pressure from the government, unilaterally deciding to withdraw all English clubs from European football, with UEFA soon formalising this into an indefinite ban. Football was shamed and all supporters risked social exile through association.

A hastily put-together government inquiry – the Popplewell Inquiry into Safety at Sports Grounds – gave a further nod towards the introduction of football supporter ID cards and proposed the installation of CCTV cameras. There was strong condemnation for the condition of stadiums. It was decided that stands, like the one at Bradford, with a wooden structure could be subject to local authority inspections and could be shut down in part or completely.

An article in *The Times* summed up how many people felt about football circa 1985. The game was described as 'a slum sport played in slum stadiums increasingly watched by slum people, who deter decent folk from turning up'.

Darryl Telles, who was by now about to graduate at Warwick University, remembers watching the Heysel tragedy unfold on TV:

Coming so soon after the Luton pitch riots and the Bradford fire, I thought I was watching the death of football. I'd already given up going to games. It was just toxic wherever you went – the violence, the overt discrimination and the dilapidated facilities. Why would anyone want to go? I'd come out as gay but that felt far more socially acceptable than admitting to being a football supporter. Being a football supporter at this time made you feel like a social pariah.

I went for many job interviews that summer but when it came to talking about my former enjoyment of going to watch football or that I supported a team, I stayed well and truly in the closet!

League position	Third
Average home league attendance	28,934
Most appearances	Clemence, Perryman (58)
Top goalscorer	Falco (29)
League winners	Everton
FA Cup winners	Manchester United
League Cup winners	Norwich City

85/86 – THE MAGIC OF THE (SCREENSPORT SUPER) CUP

CLEMENCE

PERRYMAN ROBERTS MILLER HUGHTON

STEVENS HODDLE MABBUTT P. ALLEN

FALCO WADDLE

THE INQUEST into Spurs' title near-miss began even before the season had ended.

Throughout spring, media talk speculated that Newcastle's flamboyant winger Chris Waddle, who earned his first England senior cap, would be making the journey south to London. Waddle had impressed during the meeting at White Hart Lane before Christmas and scored the opening goal with a trademark jinking dribble and finish. With the player into the last few months of his contract, Spurs had attempted to sign him before the transfer deadline in March – a transfer that Scholar reckoned might have been the impetus Spurs needed to win the league. Newcastle dug in their heels and refused to sell amid huge interest in the player, with Chelsea prepared to outbid anything Spurs offered.

However, Waddle was determined to join Spurs. He had already forged a relationship with Hoddle while on England duty. Waddle had idolised Hoddle in his teen years and also admired the way Spurs played.

The deal was eventually completed immediately after the season, with a tribunal determining that Spurs should pay £590,000. -Another opposition player who had impressed at White Hart Lane that season was West Ham's high-energy and versatile midfielder Paul Allen. His contract was due to run out at Upton Park and, despite being heavily courted by Liverpool, had his heart set on joining cousin Clive across London.

It was in defence that Shreeve felt Spurs most needed reinforcements. At home, in particular, Spurs had conceded too many goals. The high line and offside trap had been exposed far too often, which led Shreeve to consider a more continental approach, deploying a sweeper. Anderlecht's Danish captain, Morten Olsen, who was well known at White Hart Lane for his involvement in the 1984 UEFA Cup Final, was available and was initially keen on a move to north London.

This was the sort of signing that piqued Scholar's interest. Olsen was a sophisticated and classy footballer with international pedigree whom the chairman felt matched his vision for the club.

Scholar and Shreeve flew to Copenhagen to meet Olsen and the Dane was ready to agree to a deal until he realised that his two beloved dogs would have to remain in quarantine for up to six months! It proved a 'red line' for Olsen and the transfer never materialised.

Steve Perryman was philosophical about what the proposed transfer meant for him:

> Two years earlier, when Stevens and Danny Thomas joined, 'Maxi' told me he thought they were going to take our places. I told him I wasn't going to let that happen but, by 1985, I knew that my days were coming to an end, so it didn't surprise me that the club was looking to bring in new defenders but I was concerned for 'Robbo' and 'Maxi'.
>
> Olsen had been a fantastic player and Scholar liked big-name, high calibre players. It's easy to pick out style over effectiveness and those two had been as effective for us as anyone. Scholar reckoned he knew a classy player but he'd never been 'down in the trenches' to understand what attributes were needed. I could see the direction Scholar wanted to go in.

Spurs jetted off for a post-season tour to the Far East and Australia before the end of May in another lucrative deal that would see them play Hong Kong and Australian opposition before a four-game tournament involving the Italian side Udinese and Brazilian outfit Vasco De Gama. A strong squad flew out, bar Hoddle, Stevens and Waddle, who were selected for England's tour to Mexico and the USA, and Steve Perryman, who required a cartilage operation.

With the tour under way, it was following the game against the Australian Soccer Federation that, back in Europe, the Heysel tragedy occurred. Initially, Spurs officials still expected the club would be competing in the following season's UEFA Cup. However, these hopes were dashed when the FA announced it would be barring English clubs from European competition the following season, with UEFA then imposing an indefinite ban. FIFA soon extended this ban worldwide, meaning that, in theory, Spurs would not be allowed to play their forthcoming tour games against Udinese and Vasco De Gama.

While the fallout of Heysel rumbled on in Europe, Spurs were eventually told that FIFA would offer a temporary exemption for them to fulfil their fixtures without fear of disciplinary action. The Udinese game was, understandably, a tense affair, being against Italian opposition, and Spurs made a symbolic gesture of handing each of their counterparts a bouquet of flowers ahead of the game.

By the time Spurs returned to the UK, it was clear that the ban on all English clubs would be upheld. The club initially joined forces with Everton, Manchester United, Southampton and Norwich – who had all qualified for Europe – in threatening to appeal the case at the High Court but this action did not go ahead. It didn't help when a member of UEFA's executive committee listed Spurs, when interviewed by a reporter, as one of four English clubs who had been specifically identified as having particularly troublesome fans, suggesting that an extended ban could be applied.

The summer of 1985 was a particularly bleak one for English football. Not only was hooliganism and its after-effects dominating the front and back pages but there was an increasing likelihood of a complete TV blackout on domestic football from the start of the following season.

The previous TV deal allowed for ten Division One games, shared between the BBC and ITV, to be screened live during the season. The television companies, seemingly now working in a cartel, had opened negotiations in February, requesting to screen 16 live league matches, plus three League Cup ties (including the final) with an option for additional live regional games throughout the divisions. Most club chairmen were fearful, particularly against a backdrop of dwindling attendances, of what this would do for gate receipts. This offer was treated with derision and, by the summer, a stalemate had set in.

Irving Scholar had already established himself as a leading figure within the Football League circuit of chairmen and – alongside Chelsea's Ken Bates and Robert Maxwell, then of Oxford – was co-opted on to a committee representing the clubs.

Scholar, on behalf of the management committee, commissioned Saatchi & Saatchi to analyse the worth of football to the television companies. It highlighted that football was being short-changed and undervalued in relation to the advertising revenue generated for ITV. However, the TV companies were unwilling to budge and refused to negotiate. For them, football was dying. Many sections of society had become increasingly anti-football and it was an association the TV companies didn't want. Besides, earlier that year, the iconic World Snooker Championship Final between Dennis Taylor and Steve Davis had become the best live sporting spectacle of the year.

The impasse was not resolved before the new season kicked off and there was a total football blackout on TV in England. Even the *Match of the Day* highlights show was taken off air, though cameras were still present at most grounds so that games could be watched in other parts of the world, particularly Scandinavia, where English football remained popular.

Armchair fans would at least be able to enjoy the insightful and often irreverent takes of Spurs-legend-cum-TV-star Jimmy

Greaves, in partnership with Ian St John, who got their own standalone show, *Saint & Greavsie*. This was first aired in October when ITV scrapped its long-running *World of Sport* programme.

* * *

Back at the Spurs training ground, new recruits Chris Waddle and Paul Allen joined their new team-mates for the start of pre-season and embarked on a six-game schedule, playing only against English opposition as a result of the post-Heysel ban.

Hoddle, still managing his troublesome Achilles injury, only appeared once before his testimonial game against Arsenal at White Hart Lane on 3 August. Scottish champions Aberdeen had initially been lined up but the FIFA ban prevented English clubs meeting 'foreign' opposition. A somewhat disappointing crowd of just over 13,000 came out in the heavy rain to pay their respects to Hoddle.

It was quite common for the two north London rivals to meet for players' testimonials and benefit matches and it wasn't unheard of that players would cross the divide to appear for the other side in such fixtures.

In May of that year, Pat Jennings, the most recent example of a player who had crossed north London, was awarded a testimonial by Arsenal, having served them with dignity since arriving in 1977. His contract was due to expire in the summer. Spurs had sent a strong team to Highbury that evening, winning 3-2. Jennings was now looking for a new club to keep him active for the season and he hoped to play for Northern Ireland in the following summer's World Cup finals.

Parks was well out of favour and Jennings jumped at the opportunity to return to White Hart Lane, agreeing a one-year contract. He would appear mostly in the reserves but would benefit from working alongside Clemence on a daily basis.

While one legend returned, another left. Garth Crooks knew that his game time was going to be limited, especially with Waddle's arrival, and was allowed to leave, joining West Brom for £100,000. Crooks told local reporters in the West Midlands:

'Spurs have one of the biggest squads in the country of over 20 top quality players, so it is possible to be playing reasonably well and not get a look in.'

Not helped by injuries, Crooks had only appeared in 22 league games in 1984/85 but still scored 18 goals in all competitions. Overall, he had found the net 75 times in 183 appearances and, beyond the numbers, his partnership with Archibald will forever be remembered as one of the great Spurs strikeforces.

After the tired end to the previous season, there appeared to be a freshness about Spurs, not least because of their new kit. The contract with Le Coq Sportif, worth £75,000 per season, had come to an end and Scholar decided to go with the Danish sportswear manufacturer Hummel. The first kit Hummel designed proved to be an iconic one. It featured a distinctive chevron pattern and also included white shorts – usually only worn in European competition.

The deal with Hummel was worth considerably more on a like-for-like basis but, ever the opportunist, Scholar also agreed to take over Hummel's UK distribution across all their football deals, which included the Wales national team and Norwich and, in time, would add Aston Villa, Coventry and Southampton. As a result, Hummel UK was formed – a new subsidiary in the Tottenham Hotspur plc portfolio. The deal, according to Scholar, would provide a guarantee of £1m per year and was in keeping with the company's status as a 'broadly based leisure company'. Around the same time, a women's clothing company was also added to the portfolio.

It was now just under three years since Scholar and Bobroff had taken over the club. Alan Fisher seeks to summarise the impact on supporters:

More than just the Tottenham chairman, Irving Scholar, a man with an ego the size of the East Stand, saw himself as a mover and shaker in the world of football, an innovator dragging a moribund club into the modern world. Coming from a business background, his response to these financial problems was to maximise income from commercial sources, rather than rely solely on gate receipts. These days, this feels a normal part of the game. Back then, the club shop was a glorified market stall.

By treating football as a business, Scholar realised the potential income from club merchandising. He trademarked a freshly created club badge for an endless variety of new branded products, created an electronic ticketing system and booked television advertising for matches. In 1983, Spurs became the first English club to float on the Stock Exchange and also bought a couple of sports clothing businesses, including Hummel, all with the aim of raising funds. This was heady stuff, unheard of in the game. Scholar also recognised the potential for club owners to make a personal profit, following a change in the FA rules for dividend payments.

Most fans were excited by these developments, even if our experience of watching games at the Lane didn't change very much. It felt like we were part of a club moving forward. We know now that Scholar over-reached himself.

The opening day of the season saw Watford return to White Hart Lane just three months after they had embarrassed Spurs at the tail end of the 84/85 season. Paul Allen and Chris Waddle made their debuts, though Hoddle headlined a list of injured absentees that included Graham Roberts, Clive Allen, Gary Mabbutt and Gary Stevens.

Seeking a first home win over troublesome Watford since they had been promoted to Division One, Spurs were majestic in front of a crowd of nearly 30,000. Both debutants scored – Waddle twice – in a 4-0 victory that seemed to justify the bookies' predictions that Spurs could mount a title challenge.

The following day, newspaper reports salivated at the impact of Waddle and Allen. It was a rare good news story in English football on an opening day when attendances were down 50,000 on the corresponding weekend in 1984.

In midweek, an unchanged team struggled against Oxford, who were playing their first-ever home game in the top flight. Spurs led through Danny Thomas but conceded three minutes from the end.

Spurs' unbeaten away run in the league now extended to 16 games but came to an abrupt end in the next game at Ipswich. Spurs had an off-day and the 1-0 deficit would have been worse had it not been for a Clemence penalty save.

Worse was to follow when Everton, returning as league champions, won again at White Hart Lane on Bank Holiday Monday and then Manchester City, back in the top flight, beat Spurs 2-1 at Maine Road, with Clemence again saving a penalty in vain. With one win, a draw and three defeats, Spurs languished in 16th by the end of August.

In those three defeats, Spurs only scored once and that was through a defender – Paul Miller. After the game, Shreeve conceded that City had been the better team and that the lack of goals by his forwards was a worry.

Talk of a crisis was averted for the time being with emphatic back-to-back wins over Chelsea and Newcastle at White Hart Lane.

The game against Chelsea, on 4 September, had high potential for crowd trouble, with the game scheduled, much to the anxiety of all involved, for a midweek fixture. Over the summer, Spurs had spent £75,000 on additional surveillance cameras around the stadium. The Chelsea fixture was always one that risked heightened trouble in and around the ground.

As it turned out, the notable aggression and violence took place on the pitch, with four players cautioned and Chelsea captain Colin Pates sent off in the first half. Danny Thomas had to be withdrawn following a clash with Paul Canoville. Spurs ran out 4-1 winners, with Hoddle, in his third game back from injury, beginning to show his class again in midfield.

Hoddle again starred in the 5-1 win over Newcastle, scoring the fourth goal, but it proved to be a bittersweet afternoon for the scorer of the fifth goal, Micky Hazard. The midfielder, coming on as a sub, had started the opening three games of the season and still appeared to be a vital part of Shreeve's squad. However, after the game, he was summoned by Shreeve, who advised him that the club had accepted an offer from Chelsea and that he should go and talk to their manager, John Hollins. Talking to *The Spurs Show* podcast in September 2018, Hazard revealed that he was fuming and had no intention of leaving. He met with Hollins the following day and the Chelsea manager explained that they had agreed a record fee, would offer a substantial wage increase and wanted to build the team around him. But it wasn't until he was offered a signing-on fee of £100,000 that he agreed to move. By his own admission, it was the worst decision he ever made and he vowed never to be persuaded by money again.

Hazard recalled that he knew he'd made a huge error by the time he arrived for his first Chelsea training session on the Monday morning. He asked to return the signing-on fee and cancel the transfer but it was too late.

Without Hazard, Spurs continued their revival, winning their next two league games against Nottingham Forest and Sheffield Wednesday; the latter was another 5-1 home victory, with Hoddle and Waddle both scoring twice. Spurs had now scored 14 goals in three home games but no more than 23,000 had turned up.

What had otherwise been an enjoyable month turned sour, though, when lower-division neighbours Orient stunned a full-strength Spurs side with a 2-0 League Cup first-leg win at Brisbane Road. At least Spurs managed to overturn the deficit, winning 4-0 at home the following week. In between, normal service resumed at Anfield after the previous season's win when Liverpool comfortably beat Spurs 4-1.

Having been denied the opportunity for glory in Europe and the revenue it could generate, Spurs were among a number of clubs involved in a new competition designed to alleviate the financial loss.

The Football League created a three-tiered tertiary competition. 'Full' members – those in the top two divisions who had full voting rights – were invited to enter the Full Members'

Cup while teams in the lower two divisions competed in the Associate Members' Cup (which had existed in a different guise for the two previous seasons). The six clubs who should have qualified for Europe – champions Everton, FA Cup winners Manchester United, Spurs, Southampton and League Cup winners Norwich – were entered into a new competition initially titled the Super Cup.

In a clunky looking format, the teams were divided into two groups of three, with home and away fixtures, before the two top teams in each group progressed to a semi-final and final (both over two legs). It guaranteed four home matches, with the possibility of two more. Spurs were drawn with Southampton and Liverpool and the fixtures were slotted into midweeks around league and League Cup schedules. Unlike the Full Members and Associate Members competitions, which were both scheduled to culminate in a one-off Wembley final, the Super Cup would conclude with a two-legged home and away final.

Spurs' opening game of the as-yet unsponsored competition was at home to Southampton on 2 October and only 11,549 turned up to see a Falco-inspired 2-1 win.

On 1 October, shock news leaked in the national newspapers of a proposed breakaway led by Irving Scholar and the chairmen of Arsenal, Everton, Liverpool and Manchester United – now referred to as the 'Big Five'. The ongoing confusion over the present and future of TV coverage had prompted the forward-thinking Spurs owner to question the very structure and commercial set-up of the entire English football pyramid.

In Scholar's words, the top clubs 'had to break out of the straitjacket we were in'. Scholar also had support from a number of other Division One club chairmen and looked to overturn the existing convention that all sponsorship and potential TV income be shared equally between all 92 clubs. A central pot made up of a voluntary four per cent contribution of all clubs' home gate receipts was also shared equally among all member clubs. Scholar cited a weekend when home games at Highbury, Old Trafford and Anfield alone attracted a total of 100,000 more spectators than all other 43 home gates combined.

Additionally, it was written into Football League rules that for any motion to be passed, 75 per cent of all 92 clubs had to vote in favour. Scholar argued this meant that clubs in the lower divisions held the power to veto anything that might appear to be only favourable to the clubs in Division One.

Essentially, Scholar and the rest of the 'Big Five' wanted more lucrative commercial deals that they felt they could better generate without a bloated Football League pyramid of 92 clubs.

There was renewed talk of Scottish giants Celtic and Rangers being part of a British league but, unsurprisingly, the concept was met with stony faces and derision from the majority of club chairmen. The plans did not progress at this point but sowed the seeds for what would, in 1992, become the Premier League.

The breakaway threat caused an obvious rift between the 'Big Five', along with most other Division One clubs, against their contemporaries in the lower divisions and this rumbled on throughout the rest of 1985. Eventually, a compromise of sorts was reached in December in what became known as the 'Ten-Point Plan'. It was agreed that Division One would be reduced to 20 teams by the start of the 1988/89 season, that a promotion play-off system would be introduced and that clubs in the top division would have increased voting powers and a bigger cut of distributed money.

Mihir Bose, a financial journalist who would later go on to co-write *Behind Closed Doors*, offers his take on the Spurs chairman's role:

Irving was a visionary. He was fed up with the way that television was undervaluing football and the authorities, and other clubs, seemed equally entrenched in an archaic way of thinking. Football needed modernising and he was now in a position, as chairman of Tottenham, to affect much-needed change. He understood the romance of football and recognised the value of the pyramid but, first and foremost, he was Tottenham chairman and needed to look after their interests. It so happened that what was good for Tottenham was also true of the other 'Big Five' and, indeed, most aspirational First Division clubs. The outcome of the Ten-Point Plan wasn't perfect and diluted many of the changes he wanted to make but it was a compromise and a significant step in the modernisation of English football that culminated in the launch of the Premier League in the 90s.

Spurs' league form meandered throughout autumn while Manchester United embarked on a ten-game winning streak that saw them set the early pace. In October and November, Spurs won two, drew two and lost three, keeping them planted around mid-table.

Mabbutt and Clive Allen returned from long-term injuries but were unable to help build any momentum. Waddle may have scored six goals by early December but, by his own admission, was playing well below his capabilities. He told *The Spurs Show* podcast in December 2018 that he and his wife were struggling to settle. He even broached the subject of being sold but was talked out of it by Shreeve and Hoddle.

Spurs' participation in the League Cup came to a disappointing end at the fourth-round stage with a loss to second-tier Portsmouth after two replays. Spurs failed to score against their lower-division opponents in 300 minutes of football.

Shreeve stated publicly that he felt the team had 'let their standards slip' and it was hard to argue against his assessment. A year previously, Spurs were mounting a credible title challenge but, as the winter of 1985 set in, they dropped into the bottom half of the league and were out of the League Cup.

The end to 1985 was marginally better. Another 5-1 home win, this time over Oxford, provided glimpses of the early-season promise but only 17,698 attended. Ipswich and West Ham were also put to the sword at White Hart Lane but this was another false dawn as, at the start of 1986, Spurs endured a six-game league streak without a goal and just one point.

That single point came at Highbury on New Year's Day. The game has entered folklore for Graham Roberts's 'challenge' on Arsenal fan favourite Charlie Nicholas. The game was at real risk of postponement due to the freezing conditions in north London. Highbury had undersoil heating but it didn't extend effectively to the touchlines.

Roberts was a pantomime villain at Highbury at the best of times. The home crowd hadn't forgotten that he'd flicked them the 'V' sign and they had taken particular joy at his missed penalty against them at White Hart Lane.

Now, with Spurs defending a corner in front of the North Bank, the ball was cleared and was chased by Nicholas and Roberts as it bobbled towards the touchline in front of the dugouts. A combination of Roberts's ferocity and the slippery conditions meant that he crashed into the Arsenal forward, sending Nicholas over the touchline, across the gravel and over the fence designed to separate the crowd from the playing surface.

A melee ensued, with the Arsenal physio giving Roberts a right hook! Somehow, Roberts escaped with just a booking but neither player or the fans in attendance have forgotten the incident, which became immortalised in a chant quickly developed by Spurs fans!

By January 1986, a temporary solution to the TV blackout was reached between the broadcasters and the Football League, with five games scheduled to be covered live before the end of the season. However, Spurs' mid-table existence meant that their games were of little interest in comparison to the three-way battle between Manchester United and the Merseyside pair at the top of the league.

The FA Cup, under the auspices of the Football Association, continued to be covered, with a highlights package available on *Match of the Day*. The competition, barring the Super Cup, now provided Spurs' best hopes of success for the rest of the season. The third-round draw sent Spurs to Oxford, where they drew 1-1. Back at White Hart Lane, it took extra time for Clive Allen to score the winner.

In the fourth round, Spurs were fortunate to escape from Notts County with a draw. Ray Clemence made a fine last-minute save to preserve a 1-1 draw after Clive Allen had given

Spurs an early lead. In the replay, Spurs' class shone through in an emphatic 5-0 win but they already knew that the next round would see another visit from Everton.

There was, of course, the Super Cup! Spurs had finished second in their group, having lost twice to Liverpool but beaten Southampton home and away. About the only thing of note in these fixtures was Pat Jennings's inclusion for the home defeat to Liverpool on 14 January – his first Spurs first-team appearance since May 1977.

The competition failed to capture the imagination of fans but managers continued to field strong teams. Some of the games were available to watch live via the fledgling Screensport as satellite TV made an early foray into English football.

Having qualified for the semi-finals, Spurs were scheduled to play Group B winners Everton over two legs. The first game at White Hart Lane on 5 February attracted a crowd of just 7,548 – the smallest crowd ever attending a competitive home game since wartime conditions restricted the number of spectators allowed in!

The gate wasn't helped by a freezing wind and fog that engulfed White Hart Lane. The 0-0 draw did little to raise enthusiasm. Everton won the second leg in mid-March, meaning they would go on to play Liverpool in the two-legged final, although both games had to be put back to the following season due to fixture congestion. By the time the final was played, Screensport had agreed to sponsor the competition and, so, it retrospectively became known as the Screensport Super Cup.

Alan Fisher was one of the 7,548 at White Hart Lane for that semi-final against Everton.

I wonder what sort of self-deluded sense of loyalty led me to go to the semi-final, one of a crowd of just 7,548. I confess I don't remember anything about the football and my only recollection is the crowd – or lack of it. Even sharing the results conveys a degree of undeserved credibility to an ersatz competition that nobody cared about – not even the organisers.

At the time, football and football fans did not fully appreciate how much of a blow the European ban was. English football had outdated, inflated ideas of its own importance and ability. Being out of Europe enhanced that sense of isolation. Football on the continent moved on and, for years, we struggled to keep up.

Looking back, if the Screensport Super Cup holds any lasting significance, it was the start of fans picking and choosing games in a crowded fixture calendar; of saying 'Actually, the football authorities have cynically created too many games and this one's not worth my while. No one cares about the trophy and, even if we put out a strong team on paper, the players aren't going to be flat out. I'm staying home!'

Unsurprisingly, the competition was dropped, though the seed of satellite television's relationship with English football had been sown. The Full Members – later sponsored by Simod and then Zenith Data Systems – continued through until 1992, although Spurs never entered (Everton were the only one of the 'Big Five' who did). The Associate Members exists to this day, providing a Wembley day out for teams in the third and fourth tiers.

Spurs' league form was so poor that unwanted attendance records continued to be broken at White Hart Lane. When Coventry visited on 8 February, coming away with another 1-0 win, a measly 13,135 arrived through the turnstiles, breaking a 50-year low for a Saturday league game.

For Spurs' next league game at Sheffield Wednesday, Shreeve turned to youth team striker David Howells to answer the lack of goals and fit strikers. It was a dream start for the 18-year-old and the perfect tonic for Shreeve. The fixture was one of very few to survive the cold weather but the pitch was still covered in snow. Spurs trailed at half-time but Paul Allen, filling in at right-back, helped turn around the game with assists for Chiedozie and then debutant Howells, who pounced to fire Spurs into the lead.

It proved to be the winner, not only snapping a dismal six-game goalless and winless streak but helping to lift the pressure on Shreeve, who was now hotly tipped in the press to lose his job. His case wasn't helped by the half-year financial accounts that showed a £528,000 loss – largely due to falling gate receipts.

Howells returned to the reserve team for the remainder of the season, where he rejoined a far more successful squad. Midfielders Vinny Samways and John Moncur were impressing and looked on the verge of a call-up to the first team. Reserve team home games were regularly played at White Hart Lane on Saturday afternoons when the first team were away. It was a great way for fans to see those promising players or the experienced first-teamers, like Jennings.

If Spurs could look to the future, they were about to say goodbye to experience as it emerged that Steve Perryman was about to leave the club.

Perryman made what proved to be his final league appearance for Spurs at home against Liverpool on 2 March but his final appearance came in an anticlimactic FA Cup home defeat to Everton two days later, ending any hopes of a dream finale to his career. Nobody, including Perryman, knew at that time it would be his 854th and final game for Spurs. He'd made his debut on 26 September 1969, lining up alongside Alan Mullery, Jimmy Greaves and Alan Gilzean. It was a quite remarkable career but could have been extended even further.

Steve Perryman reminisces:

I could have stayed on. I maybe wasn't ready to become a coach yet but I'd have held my own. Ultimately, if I'd taken the assistant manager role it would have been at John Pratt's expense and I wasn't prepared to do that. It said everything about Scholar that he had even considered doing that. However, I could have fulfilled a vital role of acting as a buffer between the club and the players. It wasn't just about acting on behalf of the players but making sure that they understood the wider perspective.

Perryman joined Oxford for the remainder of the season but was appointed player-manager of Brentford in early 1987. He did return to Spurs in 1993 as Ossie Ardiles's assistant manager and took the team as caretaker for one game at Blackburn the following year. It seems unlikely that anyone will ever surpass him as the club's all-time leading appearances-maker.

With Perryman gone and Shreeve's impending departure quickly becoming football's worst kept secret, the remainder of the season had an 'end of days' feel.

March saw a thumping 5-0 win over West Brom and a welcome 1-0 home victory over Arsenal. The Gunners were, themselves, in a state of transition, having just parted company with Don Howe.

Unusually, it was neither Spurs nor Arsenal who ended the season as London's top club. West Ham had been the season's surprise package, with their strike partnership of Frank McAvennie and Tony Cottee both scoring against Spurs in a 2-1 win on Easter Monday. The pair scored 54 goals between them and contributed to West Ham's third-place finish behind the Merseyside duo, with Liverpool reclaiming the title from Everton.

Defeat at West Ham proved to be the final loss of the season and in April, far from suffering fixture congestion that had dogged them in previous years, Spurs actually looked for additional games! Just 24 hours after beating Leicester 4-1 at Filbert Street, they travelled to Glasgow to play a friendly at Ibrox and then, two days later, contributed eight players to an England XI who formed the opposition to play at Luton for midfielder Ricky Hill's testimonial.

Spurs returned to play on the 'plastic' pitch at Kenilworth Road the following weekend for a league game for which, officially, there were no away fans. Following the riot at Luton's game against Millwall the previous March, Hatters chairman David Evans banned all away fans from their ground.

One player not involved was Graham Roberts, who was serving a two-match suspension. Roberts had been summoned to an FA disciplinary hearing at the start of the month, having accumulated 41 penalty points for the season. It was the second time in his Spurs career that he had passed the points threshold and meant that he would face suspension for the 13th time in six years.

While Spurs ended the season with something of a flourish, a mid-table finish was a certainty. However, a few key personnel developments that would have significance for the future were taking place. Gary Mabbutt performed well in a new central defensive role, Clive Allen looked to have regained his fitness and sharpness – ending the season with six goals in six games – and Chris Waddle looked far more settled.

Spurs' final three league games saw them record 5-2, 4-2 and 5-3 victories against QPR, Aston Villa and Southampton respectively. In between, the QPR and Aston Villa games, Ossie Ardiles was rewarded for his nine years' service to the club with a benefit match at White Hart Lane against Inter Milan.

That, in itself, was something of a coup but it paled into insignificance amid speculation that none other than Diego Maradona, Ardiles's international team-mate and good friend, was going to appear for Spurs for one night only.

Now established as a demigod in Naples, Maradona was considered the best and most recognised player in the world. His appearance in London came amid a hectic end-of-season campaign for Napoli ahead of the 1986 World Cup in Mexico.

Clive Allen revealed that Maradona's involvement was not confirmed to the players until just before kick-off:

> There had been a lot of speculation about Maradona playing but whenever any of us asked Ossie, he just told us that 'he knows nothing!' There was a huge crowd, who must have been expecting that he'd be there, but we didn't know for sure until about 90 minutes before kick-off when Ossie arrived in the changing room with a huge grin on his face and, sure enough, the best player on the planet walked in behind him. We couldn't believe it! He couldn't speak any English, so Ossie translated, but he was very down to earth. He was still in the middle of a really hectic schedule with Napoli and they still had vital games to play. I remember vividly seeing our physio strapping up his ankles ahead of

the game – they were the size of footballs due to the number of kicks he'd taken and you could bet Inter Milan weren't going to go easy on him!

It turned out that he hadn't brought his own boots, so Ossie asked whether any of us had a spare pair of six and a halfs. That was my size and, as ever, I had two pairs. One were the boots that I'd worn all season, so were well worn in but comfortable, and the other were a fresh pair I hadn't yet played in. Through Ossie as an interpreter, Maradona initially wanted to take my worn ones but, somehow, I managed to convince him to put on the fresh ones instead! After the game, he signed them for me and they still sit proudly on my mantelpiece!

Maradona helped to draw a crowd of more than 30,000 to White Hart Lane and attracted television and media to a football ground for positive reasons. His arrival generated huge intrigue and Scholar wrote that there were very provisional conversations about what a deal to bring Maradona to White Hart Lane would look like. He was quickly put off by the astronomical finances required.

Maradona wore the No.10 shirt for both club and country and Hoddle, recognising the magnitude of the occasion, was happy to wear No.11 for the evening. Straight away from kick-off, Hoddle passed to Maradona who, in turn, played the ball to Ardiles, which generated a huge roar from the crowd.

Falco and Clive Allen scored Spurs' goals in a 2-1 win, though it was Maradona who stole the headlines, as Clive Allen remembers:

I scored the winner in the end. It was from a Maradona cross but it was the only game I've ever played in where I was a spectator just mesmerised by what he could do. He and Glenn were just on a different planet to anyone else. It was an honour to have played alongside the pair of them.

Spurs' temporary star was hounded afterwards by the media, desperate for just a few words with him, via Ardiles, about his thoughts on the upcoming World Cup. The reaction to him wouldn't be quite so cordial before the end of summer!

One name on the team sheet that evening that not so many fans were familiar with was that of Vinny Samways. The 17-year-old midfielder had progressed that season from the youth team into the reserves and had formed a bond with Ossie Ardiles, as Samways explains:

> Peter Shreeve would often invite three or four young players to train with the first team. Ossie seemed to take a shine to me and took me under his wing. The day before his benefit game, I was stunned to see my name on the team sheet. Because I hadn't spent much time in and around the first team, I had no idea about the Maradona speculation, so the first I knew anything was when he arrived in the dressing room with Ossie. I was completely shocked. It was a privilege to be on the pitch with him for the second half.

The feelgood factor after Maradona's appearance and the swashbuckling end to the league season couldn't mask the fact it had turned out to be a really underwhelming campaign. The final position of tenth was the lowest since 1981 but the lack of any substantial cup run meant that the 85/86 season had really hurt.

Steve Perryman felt that the buy-in from the players just wasn't the same:

> Peter had still been the same Peter and the players all played for him but he wasn't allowed to manage properly. The lack of trust in Scholar and the ownership festered down into the subconscious. I think that impacted our results and performances that season. It was clear Tottenham was changing and the club, not Peter, didn't fancy the likes of me, 'Robbo' and 'Maxi'.

Mark Falco had been Spurs' most consistent performer, scoring 25 goals – his best goalscoring season. However, as the season ended, he was subject of a police investigation and the possibility of a criminal charge. This related to a gesture he was alleged to have made to Aston Villa fans after scoring against them in the penultimate game of the season. Eventually, the police decided to refer the matter to the FA and the striker was fined £1,500 and banned for one game the following season.

Paul Allen earned plaudits for his versatility, having played across midfield and at right-back. However, Hoddle was still the jewel in the crown and his future, once again, seemed uncertain. Scholar had promised him that he would be able to leave after the World Cup.

While the senior side's season had gone stale, there was optimism generated by the success of the youth team, who had won the South East Counties League for the first time since 1981. Howells and Samways both appeared regularly but several other members of that team, coached by Keith Blunt and Keith Waldon, would go on to appear in the first team over the coming years.

Shreeve, who had begun his journey at Spurs as youth team coach, finally learned of his fate on 13 May in a short meeting at the stadium with Scholar. Shreeve knew what was coming but remains philosophical. He told Adam Powley and Martin Cloake in *The Boys from White Hart Lane*: 'The posse catches you up. In a John Wayne film, the cowboys get together and go off and hunt the villain as a posse. It doesn't matter who you are, how good you are, the posse catches up with you. It's one of my sayings. Circumstances come together and they get you.'

In truth, Scholar had probably always wanted to make a more high-profile appointment in the first place but fate two years earlier, with a strong steer from senior players, had led him to promote Shreeve to the top job.

Rumours were rife over various candidates' credentials but both the vacant positions in north London were available. Terry Venables had been touted for both jobs and Watford's Graham Taylor and Millwall's George Graham were linked with Highbury, in particular. However, Scholar had seemingly made up his mind and, by the middle of May, had offered the job to David Pleat, who willingly accepted. Pleat told *The Spurs Show* that he'd been sounded out via an intermediary in 1984 and again in 1985, though Scholar decided to stick with Shreeve for a second season.

Pleat grew up in the Midlands but had been mesmerised by Bill Nicholson's great Spurs team when he saw them hammer Nottingham Forest in 1960. Pleat developed an affection for Spurs and the way that they had played left a mark on him that he had adopted into his own coaching and football ideals.

He had achieved wonders at Luton, taking them from Division Two and then establishing them in the top division. On the final day of the 82/83 season, Luton won at Manchester City, which saw Pleat's team avoid relegation at the Maine Road club's expense. He was famously seen skipping in jubilation across the pitch, wearing a beige suit and slip-on shoes, to celebrate with his players and the away supporters. In 1985, Luton had been agonisingly beaten by all-conquering Everton in the FA Cup semi-finals, which got the wider football audience talking about Pleat.

His eventual departure from Luton became an acrimonious one. Owner David Evans pleaded with his manager to stay but, having been told with certainty by Pleat that he wished to take the Spurs job, chillingly told him: 'You'll pay for this.' The tone of Evans's warning never left Pleat.

Writing in the *Sunday Times*, esteemed football journalist Brian Glanville reckoned that Spurs had 'won the managerial derby' over Arsenal, who appointed George Graham. Incidentally, one of Graham's final acts as Millwall manager had been to sell his highly promising 17-year-old defender Neil Ruddock to Spurs on transfer deadline day in March. Spurs had scouted Ruddock in Millwall's reserves and offered a fee of £70,000, potentially rising to £300,000. Millwall needed the money and Graham personally drove Ruddock to meet Shreeve at White Hart Lane, even acting as his agent to negotiate a contract and car!

Having joined Spurs in mid-May, Pleat had precious little time to speak with or meet with his new players before travelling to Mexico as an ITV co-commentator for the World Cup. It's fair to say that Pleat divided opinion while making first impressions.

Having been a Spurs enthusiast since his visit to watch the double team play in Nottingham, Pleat viewed Bill Nicholson with high reverence and was keen to seek his thoughts on the current squad. Pleat revealed in his 2024 autobiography, *Just One More Goal*, that Nicholson had asked him whether he'd noticed how many fouls Spurs' central defenders had committed? It made him question whether Roberts and Miller needed to be replaced.

Roberts explained in *The Boys from White Hart Lane* how he received an abrupt phone call at home from Pleat, who told him that he was going to sell him as soon as he got the right offer. Roberts's response to his new manager was similarly curt.

Roberts may not formally have been captain but he was certainly a leader and a dominant personality in the dressing room and he was just the first of the old guard whom Pleat would quickly move on to stamp his own mark on the squad.

In contrast, Clive Allen took to Pleat instantly after their first dialogue:

I'd got back to somewhere near full fitness towards the end of the season and my intention was to work as hard as I could all through summer so that I could hit the ground running when the new season started. David rang me shortly after he'd been appointed and asked me what my plan was. When I told him, he was adamant that I needed to have a proper break and that a holiday would do me the world of good. It was great management and I put a lot of my success that following season down to the way David managed me from the off.

It was immediately clear that David had a real affection for the traditions of the club and he wanted us to continue playing exciting football. His football ideals were a perfect match for the club.

Three Spurs players – Hoddle, Waddle and Stevens – had been selected by England for Mexico 86. ITV arranged for Pleat to conduct an interview with Hoddle at the England camp for TV but the pair continued talking afterwards. Hoddle revealed in *Playmaker* that he was seeking a new challenge and was desperate to play on the continent. He had come very close to joining FC Köln and Napoli at the start of the decade and, despite his love for Spurs, wanted to test himself and broaden his professional and personal horizons.

As recently as 1984, Scholar had offered a new five-year contract that Hoddle signed, in part through pragmatism because of concerns over his Achilles injuries. There was, however, always a sense that Hoddle would want to leave sooner or later and Scholar was resigned to that fact.

Having initially told Pleat that he wanted to leave that summer, the new manager was able to convince Hoddle to give the club one more season.

One midfielder who did leave the club was Ian Crook, who followed a familiar trading route to Norwich, where he would team up with fellow former Spurs players Garry Brooke and Ian Culverhouse.

The other news to emerge in June was that the club had agreed a £4.9m deal to sell the training ground in Cheshunt. The money would help manage the club's cash flow, though they would remain there as a base for a further 12 months and it would be the headquarters from which Pleat would create one of the most entertaining Spurs teams in living memory.

League position	Tenth
Average home league attendance	20,862
Most appearances	Clemence (58)
Top goalscorer	Falco (25)
League winners	Liverpool
FA Cup winners	Liverpool
League Cup winners	Oxford United

86/87 – FANTASTIC
DISAPPOINTMENT

CLEMENCE
STEVENS   GOUGH   MABBUTT   M. THOMAS
CLAESEN   P. ALLEN   ARDILES   WADDLE
HODDLE
C. ALLEN

THE DRAMA of the 1986 World Cup tournament, in which Maradona became immortalised for his brilliance and also by casting himself as the ultimate hero and villain (the latter from an England perspective), was on the whole a great advert for football. The added advantage of the competition taking place as far away as Mexico was that there was no English hooliganism to speak of, either.

By spending three weeks at the tournament for TV, David Pleat was able to carry out scouting missions and Irving Scholar joined him. They both spotted the potential of Belgium forward Nico Claesen, who joined Spurs later in the year.

Pleat's first signing was rather more familiar to him. He returned to his old club, Luton, to sign full-back Mitchell Thomas in a move that further aggravated their chairman, David Evans. Thomas's contract had expired, so a fee of £275,000 was agreed by a tribunal. It was standard practice for a new manager to return to their old club to buy players but the transfer was also a reminder that Pleat was only the second external managerial appointment, after Terry Neill, since the 1950s.

This was evident through Pleat's appointment of trusted assistant manager Trevor Hartley and physiotherapist John

Sheridan, thus making stalwarts John Pratt and Mike Varney redundant. Pleat was making his own mark on the club.

Spurs' pre-season began later than usual (owing to the World Cup) on 21 July and was overseen by Trevor Hartley. Many players have spoken of how hard pre-season was, with an intention of getting the squad up to very high levels of fitness in the five weeks before the season began.

Ray Clemence had been named as club captain when Perryman left the previous season and, having just turned 38, was undoubtedly the senior player in the squad. That didn't mean Spurs lacked experience, though. Seven players – Ardiles, Hoddle, Hughton, Miller, Roberts, Falco and Galvin – had been around since the start of the decade and were big characters in the dressing room.

The first pre-season fixture saw Glasgow Rangers visit White Hart Lane for Paul Miller's testimonial. It was ten years since Miller had signed his first professional contract at Spurs but, by this point, he knew that his days at Spurs were numbered. In *The Boys from White Hart Lane,* Miller revealed that, like his defensive partner, Roberts, he had been told by Pleat that he was looking to move him on.

Stephen Peace wrote the 2023 book *Fantastic Disappointment* – an in-depth account of the 86/87 season – and he was able to speak with Pleat, as well as several players:

> That conversation he had with Bill Nicholson about the fouls that Roberts and Miller committed definitely had an impact on David. He saw Mabbutt as a central defender now and was looking to get a partner for him in.

Unsurprisingly, Miller didn't take to Pleat and never felt he had the right credentials to manage Spurs, given the sort of strong characters he inherited – players who had enjoyed so much success at the club. Miller reasoned: 'He was like a small-time shopkeeper who'd come to run Harrods ... he sold most of the characters in the team ... and not to the benefit of the club.'

Miller may have been unappreciated by his new manager but he still drew a crowd of just under 17,000 for the visit of Rangers on 2 August. Miller started alongside Roberts in central defence in a 1-1 draw that saw Clive Allen score Spurs' equaliser. Miller was brought off to a standing ovation in the second half to be replaced by Neil Ruddock, who made his first appearance in the first team. There were a few isolated crowd disturbances, both inside and outside the ground – a reminder that football was still battling hooliganism. These scenes were, sadly, followed by trouble on a cross-channel ferry as fans of Manchester United and West Ham clashed en route to a pre-season tournament in the Netherlands, with UEFA having relaxed restrictions to allow English clubs to play non-competitive matches against foreign opposition.

The summer had already seen two big English-based exports, with Everton's Gary Lineker and Manchester United's Mark Hughes both joining Barcelona. With English clubs still banned from European competition, not only were good English-based players moving to the continent, even Scotland was able to offer the attraction of European club football. Glasgow Rangers, now managed by Graeme Souness, began to take players north of the border.

Two of England's Mexico 86 squad, Norwich goalkeeper Chris Woods and Ipswich defender Terry Butcher, both joined Rangers. Spurs had been long-time admirers of Butcher and Pleat had made him his first-choice target. A deal for £750,000 was agreed but Scholar insisted that Spurs should, instead, pursue a deal for the Scottish defender Richard Gough, who had been part of the highly successful Dundee United side that had won the league championship in 1983 and reached the following season's European Cup semi-finals.

At 24 years old, Gough was three years younger than Butcher and Scholar felt he was a better investment, especially as the two clubs agreed a fee of £650,000. Butcher subsequently signed for Rangers, who had also been interested in Gough – although Dundee United's chairman was reluctant to sell domestically.

Having believed the deal for Gough was done, Pleat and Scholar were stunned to learn that Chelsea had 'gazumped'

Spurs with a bid of £750,000 and Gough was now on his way south to *west* London. Scholar had to intervene quickly and submitted a counter-offer to match that made by Chelsea. Pleat had to drive to the airport and intercept the player to bring him to a meeting with Scholar, where personal terms were quickly agreed. It's safe to say that Chelsea chairman Ken Bates was far from amused!

Gough was now a Spurs player. Scholar believed he had signed the outstanding central defender Spurs had lacked since Mike England and referenced the conviction in the player's handshake as an indicator of a true winner who would become a future Spurs captain. He signed a five-year contract and, before long, became captain.

Spurs' pre-season concluded with a four-team tournament in Barcelona. It served as a reminder of the glamour of continental football that Spurs would be deprived of in a competitive sense for a still indefinite period. They played against PSV Eindhoven, losing 4-3 on penalties after a 1-1 draw. The following evening, they met AC Milan, who had lost to hosts Barcelona in their semi-final. Spurs won that game 2-1, with goals from Falco and Mabbutt.

A column by Brian Glanville in *The Times* the following week made reference to the tournament and how it was a reminder that, with the European football ban intact, English football risked becoming even more insular and less progressive than continental clubs. This was something Scholar had been concerned about even before the ban.

Commercially, the summer's World Cup had been a success, not least on television, and it sparked optimism that football and TV might be able to work together. A two-year extension deal was signed off by the Football League clubs, allowing the BBC and ITV to continue to broadcast a small number of live games each season, alongside the return of edited highlights shows.

The league itself was under new sponsorship – fledgling daily newspaper *Today* replaced Canon in a one-season deal.

Scholar had also been busy during the summer of 1986 increasing Spurs' own commercial opportunities. The club shop, largely untouched since it was first opened in the early 70s, was redesigned and expanded to include a greater variety of stock and merchandise. By the start of the season, mail order catalogues were incorporated into matchday programmes.

Pining for European football, Scholar personally led a project to produce a hardcover illustrated book titled *The Glory, Glory Nights* that provided detailed accounts of all Spurs' European matches to date. This was published later that year by a newly formed company, Cockerel Books & Videos, that sat within the plc portfolio. The book was soon followed by a VHS of Spurs' greatest European games, with Scholar himself painstakingly sitting through hours of footage during the editing.

Both were huge hits in the club shop and encouraged Scholar to create a *Best of the 80s* series, which was presented by Jimmy Greaves. Cockerel Books & Videos also produced Arsenal, Everton, Liverpool and Manchester United versions to be sold to their supporters, with those clubs receiving a percentage of royalties.

Roberts featured in each of Spurs' pre-season fixtures. He and Pleat weren't on speaking terms but he had made it his personal mission to get himself into the best physical condition of his career and get himself back in favour. Pleat's assistant, Trevor Hartley, was keen for Roberts to play in midfield and that was where he lined up for the opening fixture at Aston Villa.

Pleat's first starting XI for a competitive game was: Clemence, Stevens, Gough, Mabbutt, M. Thomas, Waddle, Roberts, Hoddle, Galvin, Falco, C. Allen (substitute P. Allen).

Gough's value and class were highlighted within five minutes. His interception and quick pass to Hoddle started the move that ended with Clive Allen converting Galvin's cross. It was the start of a perfect afternoon in the sun at Villa Park. Allen scored twice more to complete a hat-trick in a 3-0 win.

After a home draw with Newcastle, Manchester City were the next opposition at White Hart Lane. Falco's suspension for his crowd gesture kicked in and he was replaced by Chiedozie, though not as a striker. Instead, Spurs lined up with five midfielders – a precursor of a significant tactical innovation that would follow later that season. Spurs dominated possession against a City side set up to defend deep and in numbers and Roberts, with a trademark buccaneering run and powerful shot, scored the only goal of the game.

It turned out to be Chiedozie's final game for Spurs. He dropped out of the starting XI for Falco and then picked up a series of frustrating injuries and eventually left White Hart Lane in 1988.

With only three games played, Spurs were top. It didn't last long, though. Spurs travelled to Southampton on a luxurious new coach wrapped in the livery of sponsors Holsten. New physiotherapist John Sheridan was awe-struck, not just by the coach but by the opulence at White Hart Lane compared to what he was used to at Luton. He wrote in his 2021 autobiography, *The Limping Physio*: 'As I sat down in the leather seats on the luxurious coach, I was surprised but delighted when a steward presented me with a menu and asked for my dinner order for the journey home ... the meal on the trip back to London was similar to dining at a top restaurant – the tables were laid, we had solid silver cutlery, three courses and unlimited drinks.'

Sheridan explained that post-match meals during his time at Luton involved pulling over and ordering 20 fish and chip suppers out of chip paper to be eaten with a wooden fork!

The luxury that the players travelled in made little difference to the match at The Dell. Spurs hadn't scored in any of their last three league visits there and once again failed to do so in a 2-0 defeat.

There wasn't time for a three-course meal on the way to or from the next away game, as Spurs made the short journey to Highbury on 6 September. Pleat named an unchanged XI but did finally have Ardiles available from the bench. The little maestro had undergone further surgery in the summer in a bid to finally overcome the lower-leg injury that had affected him for well over three years.

It was the first of five games that season between the two north London rivals but the first under new management. There had been little between the two teams the previous season and this encounter proved no different, a 0-0 draw lacking any real excitement. Pleat turned to Ardiles in the second half and he was responsible for the best moments in the game. Pleat commented post-match that if he'd started Ardiles, the outcome might have been different. He made a phased return to full fitness, only featuring sporadically as a sub until November.

Spurs had another derby up next, with Chelsea visiting White Hart Lane. It was a first return to Spurs for Micky Hazard, who had made the move across London almost exactly a year beforehand. Hazard revealed candidly on *The Spurs Show* podcast how he had yearned to return to Spurs and that, just four weeks after he had left, Peter Shreeve had tried to re-sign him.

Although the Chelsea fans had taken Hazard to heart, his affections remained with Spurs. Typically, the afternoon belonged to Hazard, who scored twice, the first a penalty, in a miserable 3-1 home defeat. Hazard was, predictably, the main talking point after the game and, when asked by a reporter how it felt to have scored twice, he responded that he felt as though he'd scored two own goals!

Having begun the month at the top of the table, Spurs were now down to 12th. Pleat made changes for the following game at Leicester. Paul Allen replaced Galvin and Danny Thomas returned to the starting XI at the expense of Falco, who was dropped to the reserves. Those personnel changes sparked several positional moves, with Stevens moving to central defence alongside Gough, Mabbutt playing in midfield alongside Roberts and Hoddle operating in a free role behind Clive Allen.

Against a poor Leicester side, Spurs struggled to find any rhythm but found a way to win with two goals from Allen, who continued his remarkable start to the season. The win was welcome, even if the performance wasn't great.

It did end a spell of three games without a win and they were able to follow up with a League Cup (now sponsored by Littlewoods) second-round first-leg victory at Barnsley. Miller replaced the injured Stevens and, for the first time in domestic football, a second substitute was permitted, which allowed Falco to come back into the matchday squad.

The Yorkshire outfit found themselves 2-1 ahead midway through the second half but Spurs avoided an upset with late goals from Roberts and Allen to win 3-2. They completed the job at home the following month with an entertaining 5-3 victory in which youngster Shaun Close scored on his first-team debut.

Part of the 1986 South East Counties-winning youth team, Close was another prospect. That he was given his opportunity for the second leg was a result of Falco's departure at the start of October.

Falco's final appearance in lilywhite came as a second-half sub in a 2-0 home win over Everton. Clive Allen's two goals meant that he had scored nine of Spurs' ten league goals. It ended a run of five home games without a win against Everton.

Pleat had received an agreeable bid from Watford for Falco, who was deemed surplus to requirements. Falco's departure was fast-tracked once Scholar and Pleat agreed a fee with Standard Liège for Nico Claesen. The 24-year-old had impressed for Belgium in the World Cup and, unlike Falco and Clive Allen, was quicker and more comfortable making runs in behind defences. A deal for £600,000 brought Claesen to White Hart Lane, where he was still just one of very few foreign players playing in English football.

Claesen was presented to the crowd ahead of the home game with Luton, though he was unavailable until his work permit was signed off. Crucially, with Falco gone and Claesen unavailable, Clive Allen picked up a niggling injury that kept him out for a week. David Howells returned to the starting XI.

The afternoon was a tense one. It was the first time the two sides had met since Pleat's acrimonious departure in the summer and flames were fuelled higher due to an unfortunate typo in the matchday programme. Pleat insisted on writing his own notes for the manager's page but his unfortunate and unintentional omission of a comma between the words 'hooligan' and 'chairman' when writing about his desire for the game to be remembered for the football and not the all-too-common sideshows didn't help the strained relationships.

Scholar had, however, gone to great lengths to try and thaw the bad feeling. Having already created a 'family' area in the stadium, he also provided complimentary tickets for young Luton fans to come to the game. It was another example of trying to create a far more friendly and welcoming environment at a football ground. As it was, the game was unmemorable for any football reasons, ending goalless.

If Spurs were to reinvigorate their title hopes, the following weekend's game at Anfield would be pivotal to creating some positive momentum.

Allen had missed the historic victory at Anfield in 1985 but he continued his phenomenal form with the only goal of the game, having come on just after half-time. Claesen's tireless running into the channels had been effective and helped occupy Liverpool's defenders, though it was Gough who was singled out for praise after another commanding performance to keep Ian Rush and Kenny Dalglish at bay. It was now two wins at Anfield in 75 years!

Two years earlier, victory at Anfield had provided a very short-lived belief that the title was Spurs' for the taking. It was early days this time but Spurs were up to third above both Merseyside clubs. There was growing expectation now but inconsistency was Spurs' biggest enemy. A draw with Sheffield Wednesday and three successive defeats at the hands of QPR, Division One new boys Wimbledon and Norwich meant Spurs were back in mid-table by the start of November.

The home game against Wimbledon on 1 November was the first league meeting between the two London clubs. They had met twice previously in the League Cup but Wimbledon were one of the feelgood stories of English football. While Swansea and Watford had previously made remarkable ascents from the foot of the Football League into the top division, Wimbledon's story was even greater, as they had existed exclusively outside the Football League until 1977.

Their rise through the divisions was rapid. Their shanty stadium, Plough Lane, was dilapidated and lent itself to the rough and tumble style of football under manager Dave Bassett.

While the club's story was admired, their playing style wasn't. However, the criticism they faced, something which was magnified when they became a First Division club, only served to create a siege mentality and encouraged them to double down on their ultra-aggressive tactics.

Spurs didn't play well but created chances, even after Wimbledon had taken a 13th-minute lead. The away side were able to drag their more illustrious opponents down to their level and, after the break, the game descended into a series of violent brawls. Gary Stevens was knocked unconscious by the elbow of John Fashanu who, in the same movement, was able to bundle the ball past Clemence to give Wimbledon a 2-0 lead. The Spurs players remonstrated with ferocity but the goal was awarded and Stevens left the pitch on a stretcher.

It was a busy afternoon for the stretcher-bearers. Lawrie Sanchez kicked Roberts in the shin with such might that the Spurs man, never one to want to show any weakness, had to leave on a stretcher, too. Sanchez was sent off but so was Roberts, supposedly for instigating the clash.

Despite Mitchell Thomas's bundled consolation goal, Wimbledon held on to win 2-1. Pleat, usually magnanimous in defeat, couldn't hide his fury and felt that the second goal should have been disallowed. He revealed that Roberts had had an X-ray and, although this revealed no broken bones he had left the ground on crutches. Jill Lewis was so disgusted with Wimbledon's approach that she left early:

> I've never felt like that at a game, not even when Barca were absolutely filthy against us. It wasn't just dirty, it was going out deliberately to hurt, to injure, to damage the opposition. Nowadays, the game would have been abandoned, as they'd have had so many red cards. I was so disgusted I just walked out around half-time and walked up to the North Circular and got a bus home! I couldn't bear what I was seeing!

The defeat at Norwich was headlined by Hoddle being dropped to the bench. The shock news was revealed in the morning newspapers, with David Pleat giving an exclusive interview to *The Times* in which he explained that the midfield balance wasn't right and that he needed to seek a new solution.

Stephen Peace remembers the early days of Pleat's reign:

> Results were inconsistent as Pleat tried to find the right formula. The wins at Villa and Anfield were impressive but the joys were short-lived, with underwhelming performances against Chelsea, Wimbledon and now Norwich. He had a vision for the way that he wanted to play but needed to make some quite drastic changes, both in terms of personnel and tactics.

Spurs' 2-1 defeat by Norwich sparked further speculation about Hoddle's future and, to make matters worse, the best player on the pitch was former Spurs midfielder Ian Crook, who scored one and assisted the other. For once, Hoddle felt more appreciated at international level than with his club. In the midweek against Yugoslavia, Hoddle played for the 21st time in the last 22 England games and created a goal for Mabbutt, who had been picked in midfield.

Hoddle returned to the Spurs starting XI for a narrow 1-0 win over Coventry in which young defender John Polston made his debut at the expense of Miller, who had made a rare cameo at Norwich. Hughton became the latest right-back to pick up an injury and, early in the game, had to be replaced by Ardiles, with Paul Allen dropping into defence.

Ahead of the next game at Oxford on 22 November, Pleat called a team meeting and announced that he was going to try a new formation with only one outright striker (Clive Allen) and a midfield five that would include Hoddle in a free role.

It was a formation devised to play to the strengths of the best players in the squad. Clearly, Hoddle would be the chief benefactor of the sort of role that contemporaries like Platini and Scifo enjoyed on the continent. Waddle had all the attributes to become a goalscoring winger and Claesen had the pace to be effective on the other side. With Ardiles fit and available to start, the midfield balance was designed to ensure Spurs had plenty of the ball.

During the team meeting, there was scepticism, particularly from Ray Clemence, who had seen Liverpool trial a similar approach and quickly abandoned it. Pleat stuck to his guns and selected the following team: Clemence, P. Allen, Gough, Polston, M. Thomas, Claesen, Ardiles, Mabbutt, Waddle, Hoddle, C. Allen.

Oxford may have scored first but Spurs ran out 4-2 winners in a fluent performance, with two goals apiece from Waddle and Clive Allen. The tactical tweak was barely noticed by any of the attending media but it provided a blueprint for what was to come.

Having played Oxford, Spurs then travelled to Cambridge for a League Cup fourth-round tie. Spurs won again, deploying the same shape, with Shaun Close, in for the injured Claesen, scoring one of the three goals. The month concluded with another entertaining afternoon but Nottingham Forest, going well in second place, won 3-2 at White Hart Lane, despite Clive Allen's two goals.

The new system seemed to be a good fit for Clive Allen:

Far from feeling alone up front, I never felt isolated, as the wide players and midfielders were encouraged to link up with me. Having that extra player in midfield really suited us and got the best out of everyone. I was disappointed that Mark Falco had left the club but Nico Claesen offered a totally different threat, predominantly in a wide position. I never felt that David received the credit that he deserved for what was, at the time, a completely new way of setting up a team.

Allen had now scored 21 goals in just 20 games and there was talk of the records he might break. Jimmy Greaves, Spurs' leading all-time scorer at that point, had once netted 44 goals in a season. That still stood as a club record, as he and Ian St John discussed on an episode of *Saint & Greavsie*.

Defeat against Forest left Spurs in tenth but the build-up to Christmas saw some outstanding performances and results.

First up were Manchester United, who, having suffered an abysmal start to the season, had sacked Ron Atkinson and replaced him with Alex Ferguson, whom Scholar had been so keen to appoint in 1984. Ferguson's first game in charge was a horrendous defeat at Oxford and United had won just one of four games ahead of the live televised game against Spurs.

It proved to be a thriller. United went 2-0 ahead, Spurs fought back to lead 3-2 but the home side equalised from the penalty spot with two minutes remaining.

The home game with Watford the following weekend marked Graham Roberts's final appearance for Spurs. Pleat received an agreeable offer from Glasgow Rangers and Roberts told *The Spurs Show* how, in the early hours of the morning of the away game at Chelsea, a game he had anticipated playing in, he received another curt call from Pleat advising him that he'd been sold.

As Spurs beat Chelsea 2-0 at Stamford Bridge, Roberts travelled to Glasgow and met with Graeme Souness to agree personal terms. By Sunday evening, he was no longer a Spurs player. On Monday morning, he made the familiar journey to the training ground to collect his belongings and say goodbye to his team-mates and members of club staff, only to be denied entry. His boots and kit had been left in a bin bag at the front gate.

The acrimony between Pleat and Roberts played out in the national press when the manager commented in the *Daily Telegraph* that 'he [Roberts] has kicked a few people in England and perhaps he will kick a few more in Scotland. We will live without him and I'm sure the referees won't miss him. I am happy with my central defensive partnership, with Gough and Mabbutt'. The article also included Roberts's response, which was: 'If that's what they think of me after seven years, then I am glad that I'm going.'

Sadly, Spurs' history is littered with examples of legendary players leaving the club acrimoniously – both Greaves and

Jennings have spoken of similar frustrations at the way their exits were handled under previous managers and owners. Roberts had given the best years of his career to Spurs and had many a physical scar to show for it. He should always be remembered for his goal, scored through sheer determination, willpower and a composed finish, in the crucial moment of the UEFA Cup Final.

His good mate, Paul Miller, had also played his final game for the club and was sold to Charlton in the new year. Nineteen-eighty-six had been a transformative calendar year; Perryman, Miller and Roberts had been the heartbeat of the great 81 and 82 teams and, with Shreeve also having left the club, there was a very different feel to the changing-room dynamic, with several new characters.

One of those new characters was Steve Hodge, who completed his transfer from Aston Villa just before Christmas. Hodge, an England international who had enjoyed a successful World Cup after replacing the injured Bryan Robson, was a left-footer and, so, added some balance to the midfield. He was signed just in time to make his debut on Boxing Day against West Ham.

In the days well before Sky Sports News and social media, fans traditionally relied on the newspapers or matchday programmes for club news. In December, Scholar unveiled another new innovation designed to ensure that fans could hear the latest and most exclusive news directly from the club … at a cost! News of Hodge's arrival was among the first stories covered by Spursline.

The premium rate phone line (0898 100 500) that supporters could call at any time of the day was regularly updated and in-time voiced by John Motson, who would present and lead exclusive interviews with players.

Many Spurs fans (and parents!) experienced the horror of receiving the monthly phone bill to discover astronomical amounts spent dialling Spursline. It generated immediate commercial success and the club had to increase the number of phone lines available to cope with demand.

Against West Ham on Boxing Day morning, Spurs were majestic and put in one of their best free-flowing performances since they'd taken apart Feyenoord in 1983. Hodge fitted into midfield effortlessly and was among the scorers in a 4-0 victory that could have been even more emphatic.

Spurs played again the following day, away at Coventry in a game that would provide several omens for what would happen at the end of the season.

Spurs were told during the referee's pre-match meeting that both their lilywhite home shirt and sky blue away shirt clashed with Coventry's home kit. Having not brought their alternative navy blue jerseys, Spurs were forced to play in Coventry's change yellow shirts. At least they weren't red!

In the game itself, Spurs attacked with fluency and scored goals – three times on this occasion – but, at the other end, were undone by the tricky wing play of Dave Bennett and aerial prowess of journeyman striker Keith Houchen. In a ding-dong encounter, Coventry scored four, with the winner coming in stoppage time.

Spurs ended 1986 in sixth, ten points behind Arsenal, who had built a seven-point lead over Everton and Liverpool.

The north London derby was the first game at White Hart Lane in 1987 – Spurs had opened the calendar year with a New Year's Day win at Charlton – and the game was selected for live TV transmission.

It was a particularly special occasion, as it was the 100th league meeting between the two clubs. Of the previous 99 encounters, Spurs had won 38 and Arsenal 40, with 21 draws, highlighting just how closely matched the two clubs had been over the last century. Legends from both clubs, including Bill Nicholson and Danny Blanchflower, formed a guard of honour to welcome both sets of players on to the pitch.

Julie Welch describes the north London dynamic going into 1987:

For the first time since the 60s, we felt superior to Arsenal. The 80s had been our decade – on the pitch we'd won three cups, challenged for league titles and played the most sophisticated style of football. Arsenal had won nothing since 1979 and descended into a period of mediocrity, playing dull and defensive football. Off the field, we appeared to be well ahead of them. One of the biggest triumphs of the West Stand rebuild had been that it was the first to incorporate executive boxes; the Arsenal board had tried but failed to gain planning permission to incorporate them into the East and West stands at Highbury, as they were listed buildings. That said, you could see that George Graham was starting to make things happen for them and they'd started the season really well but we were looking pretty good under David Pleat, too, so we had great confidence that we'd continue to be the dominant force in north London going into 1987 and beyond.

It was Pleat's first home north London derby but George Graham was no stranger to the fixture, having appeared 13 times as a player between 1967 and 1972 – most famously in the 1971 game at White Hart Lane which secured the title and the first half of their double.

Upon his arrival, Arsenal were £500,000 in debt, so signing a raft of new players wasn't on the agenda. However, Graham inherited a fine crop of young players. Tony Adams, Paul Davis, Michael Thomas, David Rocastle and Paul Merson had all now made their first-team debuts.

Going into 1987, Arsenal were top of Division One, by a margin. They hadn't been a serious league side since the early 70s but were now favourites to end the Merseyside dominance of English football.

While they were scoring goals (37 from 23 games) it was defensively that they excelled. They boasted by far the meanest defence in the league, having conceded just 12 times. Having beaten Wimbledon on New Year's Day, they had recorded a club record 18 games without defeat.

This new Arsenal was embodied by 20-year-old central defender Tony Adams. Born in Romford, Adams had broken into the first team at just 17 and, while initially labelled a 'donkey' after some shaky performances, was now being spoken of as a captain and his England debut was imminent.

After just five minutes, it was Adams who scored his first north London derby goal to put the leaders ahead. Spurs huffed and puffed and contributed to a physical encounter, with Hoddle going into the book early on for a late challenge on Steve Williams. Mitchell Thomas was equally impetuous in challenging Martin Hayes illegally on the edge of his own area. He avoided a red card but Spurs paid the price when Paul Davis converted the free kick.

Seemingly out of the game, Spurs did pull one back just before half-time when Thomas used the wet conditions to his advantage by sliding in across the mud to convert from close range. Arsenal, playing with the confidence of a team who were top of the league and on a long unbeaten run, kept Spurs at arm's length throughout the second half and extended their lead at the top of the division.

The defeat ended any faint hopes Spurs had of joining the title race; having won just five of 12 home league games, they were simply too inconsistent. Even if Arsenal suffered a lapse, Spurs knew there was also the might of Merseyside to overcome. Therefore, the cups once again appeared Spurs' best pathway to glory.

Three of Spurs' remaining games in January were cup matches. They overcame Scunthorpe at White Hart Lane in the FA Cup third round, which set up a tie against Crystal Palace, which they won 4-0. Before that, Spurs visited West Ham for a League Cup quarter-final at Upton Park.

Games against West Ham were always tense but both teams wanted to play football and, so, it was an excellent game, combining technical skill and endeavour. Fittingly, the game ended 1-1, requiring a replay at White Hart Lane.

Spurs had beaten West Ham 4-0 on Boxing Day at White Hart Lane and could have scored more. On this night, they did, putting five past the Hammers, including a Clive Allen hat-trick to take him beyond the 30-goal mark for the season.

Though Clive took the headlines, cousin Paul enjoyed perhaps his best individual performance in lilywhite.

Spurs fans left White Hart Lane purring after that performance and result. West Ham may not have been the side that had finished third the year before but to have put nine past a local rival in such style in the space of just over a month was unforgettable.

Mihir Bose, who had followed the club since 1961, both as a supporter and reporter, still remembers this performance:

Normally at Spurs, like in all football grounds, I was in the press box. But this time I had gone as a fan, having secured two tickets. This meant I did not have to take notes about what was happening or worry about filing my report. I could just savour it as a fan – and what a match to savour! I had gone with my friend, Jeff Randall, a fervent West Ham supporter. Jeff and I had worked together in *Financial Weekly* and he played for my cricket team. I was worried how Spurs would play and more worried that, if West Ham did well, Jeff would give me a hard time.

But Spurs dominated West Ham from the kick-off, playing some silky, one-touch football, with Hoddle the supremo in the midfield and Clive Allen looking like he would score every time he got in the box. In a normal match, when the opposition have the ball, you fear. In this one, I did not, as I felt when Spurs had the ball they would score. As Spurs demolished West Ham, and demolished is not too strong a word, watching Jeff react was interesting. With Spurs 4-0 ahead, Jeff shouted out encouragement to West Ham as one of their midfielders got into the Spurs half. He said something like 'Come on Hammers, do something'. It was a plea to show they could also play. But Spurs soon won the ball back and launched another attack and scored.

It made you realise the contrast in emotions between victory and defeat generated in fans. This was a match which lived up to what Irving Scholar defined as the cigar time match. In those days, you could smoke in the grounds and he defined cigar time as when your team is leading 4-0, there are 20 minutes to go, you are sure victory is assured, although with the present Spurs team, you cannot be sure, and you light up a cigar, turn to your neighbour and ask him what he is doing after the match.

Depending on whether it is afternoon or evening. If afternoon, 'Is he going to the cinema?'. If evening, 'Where is he going to dine?' In those days, I was also the Indian food critic of *Time Out* and asked Jeff which Indian restaurant he would like to go to. I wanted to take him to the best.

David Pleat revealed on *The Spurs Show* that West Ham manager John Lyall had written to him afterwards congratulating him, and his team, for such stunning football.

The draw for the semi-final had already been made ahead of the replay. Having beaten one local rival, it would be another who Spurs would face, with a date at Wembley to play for. Spurs had met Arsenal five times in cup competitions, in addition to the 100 league encounters. In 1968, they'd faced each other at the same stage of the League Cup, with Arsenal narrowly progressing over two legs.

Once again, in 1987, the first leg was at Highbury. Following their league win at White Hart Lane on 4 January, Arsenal dropped points against Coventry and Manchester United. The League Cup semi-finals had enough prestige that they were staged on weekends and the north London derby was selected for live television. As a result, Everton, who had won their league match on the Saturday, leapfrogged Arsenal to go top.

Arsenal were unbeaten at Highbury all season and had only conceded seven goals. If anyone was going to breach the Arsenal defence it was Clive Allen and he duly did so to score the opening goal of the tie in the 39th minute.

Having played in so many European ties in the 80s, Spurs were well accustomed to the dynamic of a two-legged tie. Away goals were not a factor in the League Cup, so Spurs knew holding on to their lead was important to give them a huge psychological advantage ahead of the second game at White Hart Lane.

Defensively, Spurs were starting to look more balanced and assured. Mabbutt and Gough looked as natural a partnership as Roberts and Miller had at the start of the decade. The Scot had also assumed captaincy responsibilities, wearing the armband for the first time at Charlton on New Year's Day.

The balance of the five-man midfield, which now saw Hodge operate on the left and Allen centrally, plugged any gaps behind them, while allowing Ardiles and Hoddle to dictate play.

They comfortably saw out the second half and even came closest to adding a second. Hoddle's through ball found Clive Allen marginally offside, denying him and Spurs a goal that may have ended the tie. It was three weeks until the second leg and Wembley seemed within reach.

February 1987 was to become the peak of this Pleat side. Having dismantled West Ham and cannily beaten Arsenal at Highbury, Spurs proceeded to win their next three games without conceding a goal. Southampton and Leicester were beaten in the league – the latter another midweek 5-0 superlative showing.

In the FA Cup, Newcastle were beaten 1-0 in a game low on incident and Spurs progressed to the quarter-finals, where they would face Wimbledon away in mid-March.

Not only had February been glorious for Spurs but it had been bitterly disappointing for Arsenal. They'd failed to beat Oxford and Sheffield Wednesday and now trailed Everton and Liverpool in the title race. Going into the League Cup semi-final second leg, momentum seemed to be with Spurs, who had a sell-out crowd buoyantly behind them.

Having appeared for Aston Villa in the competition earlier in the season, Steve Hodge was cup-tied, which was a huge loss, even though Spurs had performed well enough without him at Highbury. Ahead of the game, Pleat urged the fans to 'enjoy the game if you can but it's going to be a tense one'.

It was just as tense as Pleat had predicted but when Clive Allen scored inside 20 minutes, Spurs had a two-goal advantage.

They went in at half-time a goal ahead on the afternoon and 2-0 ahead on aggregate. In the ten-minute half-time interval, an infamous Tannoy announcement from Willie Morgan may have impacted the outcome of the game ... and the destiny of both clubs for a generation:

> Before the game, the club secretary, Peter Barnes, and ticket office manager, Chris Belt, told me that I needed to read out the details for cup final tickets. They were concerned that we didn't have many home games between now and the final to provide this information to fans and so needed to share the arrangements at half-time. I felt really uncomfortable reading it out, with the game so tightly poised, but reluctantly did what I was told. I made a point of saying 'In the event of a Spurs win' before giving the details of where and when tickets could be purchased. In later years, I got to know Kenny Sansom, who was Arsenal captain that day, and he told me their players heard it in the dressing room and that it galvanised them for the rest of the tie!

Kicking towards the Paxton Road, the visitors were level on the day within three minutes of the restart. Viv Anderson scrambled the ball over the line after a long throw had caused confusion. Midway through the second half, they were 2-1 ahead. Waddle's shot was saved by John Lukic before Arsenal went straight down the other end and scored when Niall Quinn slid in from close range to silence the home crowd.

Pleat had spoken pre-game about the possible tense afternoon that lay ahead. The final 23 minutes of normal time were as tense as anyone could remember since the Anderlecht game three years earlier. No further goals were scored, so a replay was required. Perhaps this is where Spurs could have benefitted from the experience that Roberts, Miller and Perryman would have provided. After all, they had negotiated extra time in the successful 81, 82 and 84 finals.

A coin toss decided that the venue for the replay would be White Hart Lane. That should have been an advantage but

Arsenal had now beaten Spurs twice in N17 since the turn of the year. The replay, just three days later, generated a crowd of 41,005 – more than had attended the previous game.

Much like the first two games, Spurs started better and Arsenal had Lukic to thank for two great saves to deny Claesen and Waddle. At the other end, Spurs were incensed when Quinn collided with Ray Clemence, who had already gathered the ball cleanly. The tension levels had been turned up again and several other skirmishes occurred in a goalless first half.

The tie was now becoming an epic and Clive Allen broke the deadlock, latching on to Gough's knockdown and firing past Lukic from close range. It was his 13th goal in the League Cup that season – a new competition record.

Allen was Spurs' talisman and their hopes should have been boosted further when Arsenal's star striker, Charlie Nicholas, hobbled off with 15 minutes remaining. Nicholas had been a regular thorn in the side for Spurs but had been ineffective so far in the tie. He was replaced by the workmanlike Ian Allinson.

With just eight minutes remaining, it was Allinson who scored the equaliser. Gough made a rare mistake, over-running the ball, giving the Arsenal substitute the chance to control the ball and fire in a shot that beat Clemence at the near post.

The goal shifted momentum. Suddenly, Spurs looked panicked and, with extra time looming, Rocastle rode through a challenge inside the Spurs area and slid the ball under Clemence into the net in front of the Arsenal fans. In nearly 300 minutes of football played in the tie, Arsenal had led for little over one of them.

Spurs barely had time to kick off again and it was Arsenal who progressed to the Littlewoods Cup Final where they would play, and beat, Liverpool.

Clive Allen, having set a new goals record for the competition, was handed two bottles of champagne as he walked off the pitch:

I hadn't given that record any thought at all and, as I walked off the pitch feeling absolutely dejected, someone from the cup sponsor handed me these bottles of champagne and asked me to smile to the camera. I walked back into the dressing room with them still under my arm. It was totally at odds with the scenes of sheer devastation on everyone's faces. I've never seen a more subdued dressing room. The worst thing that happened to us was Charlie Nicholas's injury. He'd been our best player that night and there's no way George Graham would have taken him off had it not been for the injury. Of course, it was Allinson who equalised and then Nicholas ending up scoring both goals for them to win the final!

The emotion among Spurs fans was of disconsolation but if the raw emotion of the defeat wasn't bad enough, it proved to be a seminal moment in both clubs' developments and the north London dynamic, as Julie Welch discusses:

Just everything about the night was utterly sickening. That it was a semi-final, it was against them and that we'd led in each game. I'd been at the 5-0 loss in 1978 but this was worse. We didn't know it at the time but, looking back, this was the point that they overtook us. The belief they took helped them beat Liverpool in the final and set the tone for their league championships in 89 and 91 and subsequent success under George Graham. It took until the mid-2010s for us to achieve any sustainable superiority over them. If only we'd held on to the lead when we had it at White Hart Lane, history might have been very different.

There was little time for the Spurs players to lick their wounds before QPR arrived at White Hart Lane for a league encounter three days later. Hoddle remained out but Hodge was available again. He replaced Ardiles, whose playing time was being carefully managed.

Prior to the two back-to-back games with Arsenal, Spurs had gone six games without conceding. A vital component of this success was the full-backs – the two Thomases, who had started in each of those games. Tragically, this would be the final occasion Danny would take to the field as a professional player.

In a challenge with QPR defender Gavin Maguire, Thomas was caught just above the knee while his foot was planted in the ground. The QPR player had a reputation for tough tackles but this one was disgraceful. Yet, incredibly, he avoided any disciplinary action.

John Sheridan knew instantly from the dugout that it was a serious injury and, after lengthy on-field treatment, Thomas was carefully placed on to a spinal stretcher before being brought back to the dressing room for an injection to numb the pain.

When his team-mates returned at half-time, they were visibly shaken by the condition of his leg. Thomas told them that his 'knee had gone' and it had. He was never able to play again but was sufficiently inspired through his rehabilitation that he trained to become a physiotherapist himself.

The rest of the game was played with a solemn tone, Spurs winning 1-0 with a Clive Allen penalty.

Spurs sat fourth, eight points behind leaders Liverpool, but the FA Cup was opening up nicely. Liverpool, Manchester United and Everton had all been knocked out in the early rounds and the day before Spurs travelled to Wimbledon for their quarter-final, the biggest shock of the round saw Watford win 3-1 at Arsenal.

Memories of the battle with Wimbledon at White Hart Lane in November were still fresh as Spurs travelled to Plough Lane. That sense of injustice was channelled perfectly as Spurs matched Wimbledon's physicality, allowing their superior technical quality to make the difference. Second-half goals by Waddle and Hoddle gave Spurs the win. Stevens played at right-back and Neil Ruddock made his first senior Spurs appearance, coming on a as sub to help subdue Fashanu. Interviewed post-match, Hoddle dedicated his goal to Danny Thomas.

The semi-final draw was made that evening. Spurs were drawn against Watford, with Coventry facing Second Division Leeds.

Spurs were live on TV again the following Sunday when league leaders Liverpool travelled to White Hart Lane. The title now looked to be a two-way shoot-out between the two Merseyside clubs, though Spurs had so many games in hand they couldn't be ruled out. A season-high league crowd of just under 40,000 turned up and were rewarded with a first-half Waddle winner. There was a 14-point gap to Liverpool but Spurs had five games in hand!

The first of those came at Newcastle. Hoddle gave Spurs an early lead but the home team, inspired by teenage midfield sensation Paul Gascoigne, scored a second-half equaliser. The point actually moved Spurs up into fourth but failing to win was a big dent in their faint title hopes.

Those hopes were well and truly extinguished on Luton's artificial pitch in the next game. Spurs were well beaten 3-1 but the story was in the boardroom and dugout. Whipped up by David Evans's rhetoric, many Luton fans brought placards describing Pleat as a 'Judas' for leaving them. There were several vile anti-Semitic comments directed at Scholar and Pleat (both Jewish). After the game, Scholar confronted Evans in the boardroom and promptly departed without accepting the hospitality usually afforded to directors of the visiting club.

April began well when Norwich were beaten 3-0 at White Hart Lane. Clive Allen had endured a frustrating afternoon until the 75th minute when, somewhat against the run of play, he put Spurs ahead. Within nine minutes, he'd completed a hat-trick. The following day he was named PFA players' player of the season. It was the ultimate individual accolade to receive the plaudits of your fellow professionals and Allen became only the second Spurs player, after Pat Jennings in 1976, to win the award. Hoddle came second and both featured in the PFA Division One team of the season.

Allen was now just one goal behind Greaves's club record of 44 goals in a single season.

He didn't have to wait long to level it. His was the only goal as Spurs won 1-0 at Sheffield Wednesday. That win pushed Spurs up ahead of Arsenal, who had hit a league slump, into third place but Everton were now seven points ahead with just nine games left to play.

That gap would increase to ten points as Everton thrashed West Ham on the same day that Spurs met Watford in the FA Cup semi-finals at Villa Park. Spurs were boosted by the news that not just one but two Watford goalkeepers were unavailable. Usual custodian Tony Coton was out and back-up Steve Sherwood had broken his finger and was extremely doubtful. The season's transfer deadline had passed, meaning Watford either had to promote their youth team goalkeeper, 16-year-old David James, or find a free agent. Pleat revealed in *Just One More Goal* that both Pat Jennings and former Arsenal double-winner Bob Wilson (now a 45-year-old TV presenter) were approached but turned down the opportunity.

Enter into folklore, Gary Plumley. The 31-year-old had enjoyed a respectable career during the 70s with Newport County in Division Four but then spent much of the 80s as a back-up goalkeeper at Hereford, Cardiff and various Welsh non-league clubs. He had subsequently retired but was training with Newport on a non-contract basis. His father, Eddie, worked for Watford FC and called his son, explaining the situation and asking him to stand by.

When Sherwood failed a fitness test, Plumley was signed on a short-term basis in time to play against Spurs.

Spurred on by Watford's defensive frailties, Spurs settled immediately, seeking to expose their opponents' obvious weakness. Clive Allen's 11th-minute low shot from range was well struck but it should have been easily gathered. Plumley spilled it and Hodge slid in to give Spurs the lead.

Within two minutes, it was two. Allen, encouraged by the first goal, shot from range and benefitted from a wicked deflection that wrong-footed the hapless Plumley. That goal was Allen's 45th of the season. He had overtaken Greaves's record.

It was three before half-time. Paul Allen made room for himself and struck a powerful shot that beat Plumley at his near post. After the exertions of the League Cup semi-final, this was a breeze. Played to a backdrop of constant singing from the Spurs fans, Hodge added a fourth in the second half before Watford scored a late consolation.

Spurs' opponents for the final were confirmed the following day. Coventry had trailed Leeds at half-time but won 3-2 in extra time. It was their first-ever major cup final.

Nominally, the league title was still up for grabs but, realistically, Everton were too far ahead of Spurs with just a few games, including the league encounter at Goodison between the two sides, to play. Spurs remained third throughout April winning two, drawing two and losing one of their next five.

Speculation about Hoddle's future was rampant. Scholar had promised that he'd be able to leave before his contract expired and, even though Pleat had persuaded him to stay for another year when he took charge, the writing was now on the wall that he'd be leaving at the end of the season. The FA Cup Final seemed a suitable swansong.

Speaking of songs, Hoddle made the showbiz news when he and Waddle were talked into recording a song titled 'Diamond Lights'. The pair were good friends and had agreed to help out a friend, Pat Mitchell, who supplied them with sponsored cars, by attending a social function, ironically in Coventry. After a few drinks, the pair were persuaded to sing on stage with the band. By all accounts, they were well received and Mitchell, who had a song-writing friend, pestered them to record 'Diamond Lights'.

The record and a video were recorded and, six weeks later, Hoddle and Waddle were invited to perform it on *Top of the Pops*. Of all the things both achieved in their decorated football careers, it is a certainty that they'll be asked about 'Diamond Lights'.

It was not the only song they recorded that month, either. Chas & Dave were again called upon to record an FA Cup record and they duly obliged with the very catchy but, in hindsight, somewhat hubristic 'Hot Shot Tottenham' that reminded everyone that 'seven times we've won the cup now number eight is coming'.

The song begins with 'David Pleat and his blue and white army' before going on to describe Spurs as the 'football connoisseurs'. The names of every active member of the squad were included, with a special mention for Danny Thomas, for whom 'all the goals were going to be for'.

With Hoddle's departure imminent, he created one more truly iconic moment in his penultimate appearance at White Hart Lane. Against Oxford in late April and with Spurs 2-1 up approaching the final minute, Hoddle collected the ball just inside his own half. With three Oxford defenders closing in on him, he effortlessly flicked the ball past all of them and found himself bearing down on Peter Hucker. As Hoddle approached goal, he feinted to shoot, forcing the helpless keeper to drop to the ground. Hoddle nonchalantly dribbled around him and rolled the ball into the empty net. He wheeled away towards The Shelf, blowing a kiss to the adoring fans.

It proved to be Hoddle's 110th and final Spurs goal. Contrary to a popular myth, that game against Oxford wasn't his last game for Spurs at White Hart Lane. His final home appearance came in a 4-0 win over Manchester United on 4 May. The *Daily Mirror* ran an exclusive story that morning, revealing that Hoddle would definitely be leaving after the FA Cup Final. The interview quoted Hoddle:

> The perfect script has already been written with my goodbye at Wembley and I've got that to look forward to but playing my last game at White Hart Lane will still be a very emotional experience ... I am seeking new horizons. It [wanting to leave] has nothing to do with my affection for Spurs.

Pleat played it safe for the final four league games, drafting in a host of youth and reserve-team players to give his seniors rest ahead of the cup final. Vinny Samways, Phil Gray, John Moncur, Paul Moran and Mark Stimson all made their debuts and there were rare outings for Parks, Polston and Ruddock. Despite losing three of those four games, Spurs held on to third position, which matched their finish in 1985.

Although it had been five years since Spurs' last FA Cup Final appearance, there was a familiarity about the build-up.

Spurs had the enviable record of having won each of the seven FA Cup Finals that they had appeared in.

Coventry were rank outsiders but had, by their standards, enjoyed a decent league season, for once avoiding their perennial relegation battle. They were workmanlike but, as they had demonstrated when beating Spurs 4-3 in December, possessed threats going forward. Dave Bennett's tricky dribbling on the wing had been a feature all season and Cyrille Regis, top scorer with 16 goals, was their talisman but his fellow striker, Keith Houchen, had really taken to the FA Cup – he had only scored twice in 20 league games but had netted five in five in the FA Cup.

David Pleat's starting XI was relatively straightforward to pick. Since Danny Thomas's injury, Hughton had re-established himself at right-back. He, Ardiles and Hoddle were the veterans of the 81 FA Cup Final. Galvin, the other remaining member of that squad, had been injured for most of the season.

Spurs would be wearing a new kit for the game. Hummel had already created the 87/88 strip – a smart plain lilywhite design. The kits had been delivered to club secretary Peter Day several weeks before the final. The batch included two sets of long-sleeved shirts and two sets of short-sleeved shirts. One of each was for the first team and the others for the youth team, though, unbeknown to anyone, only one of each set had the name of sponsor Holsten printed on them.

Kitman and long-time club servant Johnny Wallis had taken them to Wembley and followed his usual routine of folding them with the numbers showing so that he knew where to hang them. Nobody had thought to check the front.

As it was such a hot day, the players had warmed up in training T-shirts and only pulled on their match shirts shortly before kick-off. The players kept their tracksuit tops on as the teams were introduced to the royal dignitaries prior to kick-off. It was only when the players lined up for the start of the match that anyone noticed.

Barely anyone else had noticed before Clive Allen scored his 49th goal of the season inside two minutes. Waddle bamboozled his full-back and crossed low for Allen to stoop at the near post and head home. It was only as the players celebrated together that it was noticeable that some had Holsten on their shirts and others didn't!

The goal should have given Spurs the perfect platform to go on and record a comfortable win, just as they had in the semi-final, but Coventry had other ideas. Within seven minutes, they were level. Houchen won a flick-on and Bennett responded far quicker than Hodge to beat Clemence from close range.

The game ebbed and flowed. Clemence had a couple of shaky moments and Spurs were fortunate when referee Neil Midgley spotted a slight nudge by Houchen on Thomas before Regis looked to have headed Coventry ahead. Spurs managed to shift momentum and, five minutes before half-time, Gough caused confusion in the area from Hoddle's wide free kick, allowing Mabbutt to score from close range. It had been a brilliant spectacle of a first half and Spurs led 2-1.

The second half began with much the same tempo and tenacity and it was again from a wide position that the next goal came, with Coventry pulling level again. Bennett turned Thomas inside out and his cross was met powerfully by Houchen, who headed past Clemence for what was to become an iconic FA Cup Final goal.

There was still half an hour to go of an absorbing match. It was a particularly hot afternoon and the pace of the game got the better of the players, who were running purely on adrenalinee. Neither team could score again in the 90 minutes, meaning that extra time beckoned.

Six minutes into extra time, the crucial moment occurred. Paul Allen was dispossessed in midfield; the ball was quickly played into space behind Mitchell Thomas for Lloyd McGrath, whose role throughout the game had been to successfully man-mark and nullify Hoddle, to run on to. McGrath crossed, looking for Houchen, but Mabbutt had instinctively moved towards the front of the six-yard box and moved his knee to block the cross.

The next few seconds will live on in infamy for Spurs and Mabbutt. He has described it as a 'one in a thousand moment', with the ball ricocheting off his knee at precisely the right height, angle and speed to deflect it into the one spot that Clemence couldn't possibly have dealt with it, just under the crossbar and inches inside the far post.

Like Tommy Hutchison had done against Spurs six years earlier, Mabbutt had scored for both teams in an FA Cup Final. He dropped to his knees, not realising that he'd never have to buy a meal in the city of Coventry ever again!

Pleat's final throw of the dice was to bring Claesen on for Hughton but it was to no avail. Looking dejected and slightly resigned to their fate, Spurs were unable to create any clearcut chances for the remainder of the game and looked on in disbelief as Coventry claimed their first-ever major trophy.

On the BBC, John Motson described the game as the most exciting cup final he had ever commentated on. It was of little comfort, though, for Spurs who were on the wrong end of one of the greatest cup finals and upsets in the competition's history.

Clive Allen remains philosophical about the outcome:

We were confident going into the game, as we knew we were an excellent team, so didn't approach the final or Coventry any differently to other games. We had great respect for them and, having already been beaten by them earlier in the season, took them very seriously. There was no lack of focus or attention.

Looking back, there was a couple of things that make you think. At the PFA dinner on the Thursday night, I'd mentioned to David [Pleat] as I picked up my players' player of the season award that I hoped I wouldn't suffer the same fate as Gary Lineker had the year before when he'd won the same award, scored in the FA Cup Final but ended on the losing side. Why had that particular thought even occurred to me?

The day before the game, David had taken the warm-up, instead of Trevor Hartley. It was the first time that season he'd done that. Then there was the Holsten situation, too. None of these things affected the game whatsoever but they've all just played on my mind. I think it was just one of those days and nothing that we could have done would have prevented that outcome. Coventry's name was just on the cup that day.

For the first time, Spurs went to an FA Cup Final and came away with the runners-up medals, sportingly looking on and applauding the Coventry team, led by Brian Kilcline, who lifted the famous trophy.

David Pleat told *The Spurs Show* podcast in 2021 that he takes responsibility for not spotting earlier that Bennett was running Mitchell Thomas ragged. He also felt that a heavy challenge by Kilcline on Mabbutt in the second half should have been more severely punished. Writing in *Just One More Goal*, Pleat elaborated on Mabbutt's condition. To compound the injury sustained in the challenge from Kilcline, Mabbutt also felt the effects of his diabetes which, with the extreme heat, meant he suffered from a lack of circulation of blood through his legs. Pleat stated that the player couldn't feel his feet by extra time.

The club had arranged for the after-final party to take place in a marquee on the pitch at White Hart Lane. Willie Morgan had been asked to act as DJ:

As you can imagine, it was an incredibly glum atmosphere as players, their families and staff reluctantly made their way to the 'party'. Richard Gough took it particularly badly; he was very upset when he learned that he was the first captain in the club's history to lose an FA Cup Final. When I saw him go home shortly after he'd arrived, I realised just how badly the players were taking it. As DJ, I had to try and lift the mood and, having sifted through my collection, felt that 'C'est La Vie' by Robbie Nevill was an apt record to play. Soon after, Chas & Dave arrived and were encouraged to get up and perform as well. It broke the ice and I think everyone enjoyed themselves about as much as they possibly could for the rest of the evening.

The sense of undignified Hubris was extended when the team still completed their pre-planned bus parade tour, empty handed, the following morning along the High Road to Tottenham Town Hall. Needless to say it was not well attended.

For some Spurs fans, the scars of this afternoon have never left them. The prominent Spurs blogger, podcaster and philosopher 'Spooky' recalls:

I don't think I'll ever get over the 87 cup final. In all my years following this club, belonging to it, accepting every low because I know the highs will feel better for it, this one still gives me cold sweats in the depths of any given night. There was something mystical about Spurs back then. The 'Cup Kings'. Unbeaten in the grandest of them all – the FA Cup. Played seven, won seven.

I'll ignore the 82 League Cup defeat to Liverpool; minutes away from winning that, too, but no shame, just disappointment. What happened in 1987 was devastating but I think it's everything that followed that has compounded that moment to perhaps existing as a monument to my torment of wanting my football club to achieve great things.

I wasn't cocky about the Coventry game. I did not underestimate them. They were decent but not spectacular and never comparable to the glam of Spurs. I remember when Clive Allen scored and my uncle said the words 'too early'. Funny how often this is a staple of football match experiences, as though there's a quantifiable moment where scoring first won't be a detriment.

It was unfathomable that we would not go on to win this game. But football happened. 1987 was my first proper season at White Hart Lane following the team and it served as a template for the decades that followed. We stood on shoulders of giants in the 80s and this game set the benchmark for how relentless the heartbreak can be.

Waddle, Hoddle, Allen and the rest could not muster a comeback after Gary Mabbutt's own goal. It was not only a great FA Cup upset but also an iconic and entertaining game that history will never forget. And, with the game changing the way it has, this benchmark game grounded me to never take anything for granted. Tottenham lost that magical romanticised aura that day and I lost my football innocence.

The FA Cup Final encapsulates a season. Success in 1982 rescued what would have become a fruitless season but 86/87 had nothing tangible to show for what is still considered to be one of the most bittersweet seasons in Spurs' modern history.

League position	Third
Average home league attendance	25,910
Most appearances	Clemence, Gough (55)
Top goalscorer	Clive Allen (49)
League winners	Everton
FA Cup winners	Coventry City
League Cup winners	Arsenal

87/88 – 'IN LOVING MEMORY OF THE SHELF 1936–1988'

PARKS

STEVENS FAIRCLOUGH MABBUTT M. THOMAS

P. ALLEN ARDILES SAMWAYS HODGE

C. ALLEN WADDLE

THE 'FANTASTIC disappointment' of 86/87 is one of the most memorable seasons in a generation. The great team and their wonderful style of football are still fondly remembered more than 30 years later. The following season, by contrast, is one of the most unmemorable and is rarely discussed. That's not to say 87/88 didn't contain significant drama off the field.

Throughout 86/87, there was a sense that football was starting to win the battle against hooliganism. Attendances, across the league, had barely changed but the number of incidents inside and outside the grounds slowly reduced.

Sensing the turn in mood, the Football League announced plans to commemorate its 100th anniversary with an exhibition match, scheduled for Wembley at the start of the season, that would see a Football League side take on a 'world' team. Gough, Waddle, Ardiles and Clive Allen were selected from Spurs, while Maradona was paid £100,000 to play in the World XI.

The following summer's European Championships in West Germany were on the horizon and there were hopes that England would complete their qualification and that hooligan problems would subside sufficiently for English clubs to be readmitted into European competition sooner rather than later.

It was, therefore, vital that the whole football community worked hard to maintain an immaculate public image on and off the field. Following Spurs' harrowing FA Cup Final defeat, Scholar had two major issues to manage. Hoddle and Holsten.

Hoddle had said his goodbyes. There was no surprise that he left but his destination of Monaco rather than Paris Saint-Germain raised eyebrows.

The Parisian club had done all the groundwork with the player but dragged their heels at the last minute, allowing Monaco, managed by Arsène Wenger, to make a successful 11th-hour move. The deal included two friendly matches to be played between the two sides at White Hart Lane during the 87/88 and 88/89 seasons.

Pleat now had a huge creative hole to plug in midfield. Hoddle's departure presented the almost impossible question of how to replace him. To quote Steve Perryman several years earlier, Hoddle was 'the leader of the orchestra'.

Having spoken with Pleat, Stephen Peace reveals that, in hindsight, the solution may have been within the squad already:

> When I spoke to David for *Fantastic Disappointment*, he told me that he should have played Waddle in the more central role after Hoddle's departure. It would have been easier to try and replace him on the wing than the free role that Hoddle had occupied so well. Curiously, a few years later, Terry Venables did exactly that. Waddle was a revelation for Spurs in a more central role.

Later in the summer, Pleat did sign what he hoped would be a Hoddle replacement in Nottingham Forest's Dutch midfielder Johnny Metgod. The former Real Madrid player had spent three years in England, making more than 100 appearances under Brian Clough. He had international calibre but, unbeknown at the time, was carrying an injury that would ravage his Spurs career.

Tim Vickery felt Metgod was a good signing:

Metgod was a technically outstanding player who, like Hoddle, could also hit a brilliant long pass. He'd always played well against Spurs and scored a rocket of a free kick at the end of the previous season. Stylistically, Nottingham Forest were the closest to the way that Pleat wanted to play, so you could see the sense in the deal.

The inquest into the Holsten shirt episode cost club secretary Peter Day his job and kitman Johnny Wallis was demoted to the reserve team. Reports of the German company completely withdrawing sponsorship were well wide of the mark. Many believe that Holsten actually came out of it pretty well – the fact that it is still remembered now says much for the publicity received.

Another of the great 1981 team also left. Tony Galvin joined Sheffield Wednesday. In just under ten years, he made 277 appearances, scoring 31 goals, but, most importantly, his tireless energy and running provided a balance for Hoddle, Ardiles et al in midfield, meaning he was one of the most unsung heroes of a fabulous era. He was granted a testimonial, scheduled for October.

Clemence announced this would be his final season as a professional and with Ardiles fast approaching the end of his career, too, Spurs were in a period of significant transition. The five-man midfield had baffled opponents but it worked so well because of the personnel available and was centred around Hoddle's creative capabilities.

Mabbutt's contract situation was well documented throughout June. Now out of contract, clubs were free to speak with him. Arsenal and Manchester United had made contact but it was Liverpool who expressed most interest. Mabbutt met with Kenny Dalglish, who told him that he wanted to pair him with Alan Hansen in central defence and that he would be one of three big signings alongside John Barnes and Peter Beardsley as Liverpool looked to wrestle the title back across Stanley Park. The financial package was also good – more than he was on at Spurs.

Mabbutt would have been forgiven for leaving but turned down the move to stay with Spurs. On 20 June, it was confirmed that Mabbutt had signed a new contract. He told the press: 'It's a tremendous compliment being linked with clubs like Liverpool and United. They are among the biggest in the country … but so are Tottenham – and if you are already with the best in the business, why bother to change?'

Not only was it great news for Spurs but Mabbutt's story, as a type-1 diabetic, was exactly the sort of good news story that football needed. Since joining Spurs, he had continued his ambassadorial work to promote awareness of diabetes to such an extent that the club had appointed an extra secretary to handle all the letters he received specifically about his medical condition.

Spurs fan Danny Jarvis had particular reason to idolise Mabbutt:

> As someone with a disability (I have cerebral palsy), I was always drawn to Gary Mabbutt's work as a diabetes ambassador. He was a great source of inspiration to me for the way that he overcame significant barriers to become the superstar that he'd become at Spurs. Because of Gary, I pursued a career in sports coaching and have been working for Tottenham Hotspur Foundation and I've been able to meet him on a number of occasions through his role as a club ambassador.

As the news of Mabbutt's new contract broke, it also emerged that Richard Gough wanted to return to Scotland. While Gough was happy in north London, his wife gave him an ultimatum – his career or his marriage. It was an unsettling time for player, manager and chairman. No decision was made for the time being and Gough remained a Spurs player during pre-season.

At the same time, a new central defender was brought to the club. England Under-21 international Chris Fairclough joined from Nottingham Forest, with Spurs beating off competition from Liverpool and Manchester United. Fairclough would add pace that neither Mabbutt nor Gough possessed and was signed to add versatility and competition.

Pleat claimed that Metgod's signature, confirmed at the start of July, would likely be Spurs' last of the summer. He was half right, as no other senior player joined after that point, but Pleat did secure the signing of Exeter's talented central midfielder Mark Robson for £50,000.

The player turnover was a frustration but it was the sort of thing that football clubs were used to dealing with. However, a bigger issue materialised at the end of June when Pleat was approached on his doorstep by a journalist from *The Sun*, with the tabloid about to run a front-page story accusing him of kerb-crawling.

As Pleat discussed in *Just One More Goal*, the allegations emanated from a three-year-old Bedfordshire Police crackdown on kerb-crawling in the area immediately surrounding Luton's stadium. Pleat's car was one of many that had been clocked, with registration details kept on record, though no further action had been taken. Pleat vehemently denies any wrongdoing, describing the allegations as 'baseless fabrications'. In the incendiary allegations about to be released, one particular sex worker claimed that Pleat had paid her for sex, though there was absolutely no evidence to substantiate this.

The allegations were deeply upsetting to Pleat and his family. He sought support from Scholar and the pair spent the day working out their options. Scholar felt that they had no legal grounds to block the story being released and, so, the British public woke up to front-page news alleging that the Spurs manager had been caught kerb-crawling. Despite the fact he knew he hadn't done what he'd been accused of, the incident brought shame to Pleat, Spurs and to football. The story dominated the front and back pages for several days but did go away ... for the time being.

Pleat has spoken about how the incident affected him. He felt incredibly self-conscious in public and particularly when addressing his players in pre-season.

When pre-season did begin, it was at a new training base. Having used a couple of temporary bases, a deal was eventually struck with the London Borough of Camden to rent the Chase Lodge facility in Mill Hill, north-west London. The site contained four full-size pitches, which could host the first team, reserves and youth teams, but it was not exclusive to Spurs and local grassroots teams and schools would play there, too. The main building was a 19th-century Grade II-listed house that contained a rabbit warren of rooms and corridors that were repurposed to become changing rooms and offices.

There was not sufficient space for suitable medical facilities, so John Sheridan had to innovate. Writing in *The Limping Physio*, Sheridan explained that he purchased two old portable cabins directly from a North Sea oil rig. One was a treatment room and the other fulfilled the purpose of a very limited 'gym'.

The only space to locate them was in the corner of the car park, meaning no water or electricity could be provided. Sheridan purchased an old diesel generator to power them, so his first task each morning was to try and start them. Fortunately, he had an engineering background prior to becoming a physiotherapist.

Tony Parks felt the new training ground was an example of the direction the club was travelling in:

> Moving away from Cheshunt was a significant downgrade. As a footballer, you spend 90 per cent of your working life at the training ground. Cheshunt was fabulous as a base – it had great facilities and there was a real homely feel about the place. We lost a lot of our identity moving home to a council site. It was rubbish. I suspect the club needed the money but, however much they got for Cheshunt, it wasn't worth it. Look at the facilities that Daniel Levy has created now – he understands the importance of the working environment. It was scandalous that we ended up at Mill Hill.

Pre-season consisted of matches against Exeter and Bournemouth before a four-game tour of Scandinavia in which

Fairclough and Metgod were both involved. The final game of pre-season was Chris Hughton's testimonial against Arsenal. Since making his debut in 1979, Hughton had now racked up 358 first-team appearances. With Hoddle and Galvin now gone, he had outlasted all his contemporaries from the early 80s team.

For the first time in the league's 100-year history, the top division lacked the symmetry of having an even number of teams. Under the Ten-Point Plan agreed in 1985, the league was being reduced to 20 teams over a phased two-year period. For 87/88, Division One would comprise 21 teams, meaning 40 league games, with each team having two free weekends during the season.

Of all the opponents Spurs could have been given for the opening day, it just had to be Coventry away!

Eight of the XI who started the cup final made Pleat's team, though the Hoddle hole was palpable. Metgod was named as a sub, with Mabbutt playing in midfield to accommodate Fairclough and Gough in central defence. Claesen played in attack alongside Clive Allen. Stevens, the other sub at Wembley, started at full-back instead of Hughton.

In weather conditions reminiscent of the Wembley afternoon three months prior, the same outcome followed, although it was not quite as dramatic this time. Coventry took a two-goal lead before half-time before Gary Mabbutt, of all people, scored a late consolation with a deflected effort!

Another change that season saw two substitutes permitted for the first time. Metgod came on at half-time and Ardiles later became the first-ever player to be used as a second substitute for Spurs in a league match.

Metgod replaced Claesen for the next game, a 3-1 win over Newcastle in which Waddle was on top form against his old club. Metgod was overshadowed in central midfield by Newcastle's Paul Gascoigne, who once again impressed at White Hart Lane.

Claesen was clearly frustrated at his lack of game time. He had joined the club just before the 4-5-1 experiment that either saw him forced to play out wide or subservient to Clive Allen's excellence as the lone frontman. The Belgian issued a 'play me or sell-me' ultimatum to Pleat, who was still unsure about the best way forward with the new Hoddle-less side. Claesen came off the bench to score the only goal against Chelsea the following weekend – a game that Spurs had been second-best in for most of the afternoon – and would then go on to start in each of the next 13 league games.

Between Claesen and Clive Allen, they scored each of Spurs' next six goals and two wins and two draws saw Spurs climb into second place by mid-September.

Metgod made just eight league appearances, including six as a sub, at the start of the season before a long-standing groin injury resurfaced. That kept him out until the end of the season, when he managed just four more appearances before returning home to the Netherlands and Feyenoord.

His 14 appearances for Spurs make him one of the most easily forgotten Spurs players of the 80s. Undoubtedly a good technical player, he suffered from arriving at the wrong club at the wrong time.

On 19 September, when Spurs won a tight game at West Ham with a Chris Fairclough goal to stay in second place, all seemed well but they were about to undergo a tumultuous six-week period that rocked the foundations of the club.

A 1-0 League Cup second-round first-leg defeat at Torquay (Spurs won the return game 3-0 two weeks later) was a sign of what was to come. Reluctantly, Spurs allowed Richard Gough to leave at the end of September. He cited marital problems and that his wife would divorce him if he wasn't allowed to return to Scotland immediately. A deal with Rangersl worth £1.5m was quickly agreed, meaning Spurs had doubled their money in just over a year but at what cost to the team? Gough is still fondly remembered for his all-too-brief career in north London, as Jason McGovern explains:

> Gough was a Rolls-Royce of a defender. He possessed every attribute you want in a centre-half – he was tough, gritty, physically strong, quick enough, positionally superb, read the game exceptionally well and had a great calmness about

him, which made him a leader. It was a gut wrench to lose him so soon but his great legacy was Gary Mabbutt, who had converted to defence and settled into that position alongside Gough.

Two defeats in the next three league games saw Spurs drop down the table and, in the last of those, Clemence picked up an Achilles injury that proved to bring about the end of his playing career. He formally announced his retirement later in the season, by which time he'd begun his coaching career at the club. In 1992, Clemence became joint first-team head coach before joining the FA as a goalkeeping coach under Glenn Hoddle in the mid-90s.

Clemence had been club captain until the end of 1986 when Gough took over. Now Gough had departed, Mabbutt was named captain, a role he would hold until his retirement in 1998.

With Clemence injured, there was a recall for Tony Parks, who had spent much of the previous three years in the reserves. His return to first-team action came in the north London derby, televised live, at White Hart Lane on 18 October.

In the midweek beforehand, the UK had been battered by hurricane-force winds. The previous evening, weatherman Michael Fish infamously told viewers on the BBC News that they had nothing to be concerned about. The storms were particularly fierce in the south-east, with many households losing power. Schools and offices were shut the next morning. The force and impact of the storm was an ominous forebearer for what lay ahead for Pleat and Spurs.

Despite the literal and figurative clouds circling, Spurs came into the game in excellent home form – they'd won each of their 12 games at White Hart Lane since losing to Arsenal in such heartbreaking manner in March. In fact, of the 22 home games played in the calendar year, Spurs had won 19 and lost only three – all to Arsenal!

Meanwhile, Arsenal had built on the momentum of winning the League Cup and, with a young and improving side, were on a seven-game winning streak and sat in third place. ITV's

The Big Match anchor, Elton Welsby, led a discussion over the possibility of either north London side being able to put pressure on the Merseyside clubs. The already brief pre-match discussion was cut even shorter, however, by the game kicking off two minutes earlier than the 2.35pm scheduled start!

Anyone switching on at 2.35pm would have missed the quickest goal of the season when Claesen capitalised on a rare piece of slack Arsenal defending to give Spurs a first-minute lead.

The game then followed the pattern of the two League Cup semi-finals, with Arsenal coming from behind to win 2-1. The TV cameras were also able to capture images of several Arsenal fans wearing T-shirts that made reference to the latest allegations against David Pleat, which had surfaced earlier that week.

While driving into central London for a TV interview, Pleat had been stopped by a police officer who suggested he had been acting 'suspiciously'. His details were taken but no further action followed and nor was there any evidence to suggest that Pleat had done anything wrong.

Mischievously, the incident was leaked to the tabloid newspapers. Pleat has suggested that his previous chairman, David Evans, may have been responsible. The Luton chairman was, by this time, an MP and was well connected with both the Metropolitan Police and national media. Pleat alludes to the chilling passing shot Evans had given him when leaving Luton back in 1986 that he would 'pay for it'.

This time, there was no way back for Pleat and, following a lengthy meeting between him, Scholar and Douglas Alexiou, he reluctantly tendered his resignation, despite insisting that all the allegations were baseless. The episode had understandably broken Pleat.

Pleat revealed in *Just One More Goal* that he should have sought legal representation during these discussions and, in hindsight, should never have offered to resign. Eventually, Scholar offered him a payout of just £8,000. He was dissuaded from fighting a legal battle against *The Sun* for defamation owing to the huge initial costs involved.

The following morning's *Daily Mirror*, which had very close ties with the boardroom, ran a headline 'The man who disgraced Spurs' and vilified Pleat for his alleged behaviour at a time when English football was trying desperately hard to clean up its act. The article explained that Spurs were a 'family club' and – with a club membership of more than 31,000, including many thousand junior members – it was right they should want to distance themselves from such sleazy allegations.

The article did credit Pleat for his tactical innovations and for producing a highly entertaining style of football that had helped increase attendances by more than 20 per cent since the dark days of the mid-80s. It described Pleat as 'a nearly man', having come close to winning both domestic cups and overseeing a strong, if inconsistent, league campaign that briefly flirted with a title challenge.

Over time, Pleat has come to be remembered fondly for his first spell at the club as a manager who produced scintillating football. While Clive Allen speaks highly of him, there are others, big characters like Graham Roberts and Paul Miller, who remain critical. In *The Boys from White Hart Lane*, Paul Miller said: 'We could've won the treble with a decent manager … by then [autumn 86], we had the best squad … it was criminal he never won anything.'

A cynic may suggest the timing of Pleat's departure was convenient for Scholar, having learned of Terry Venables's availability. Pleat alludes to this theory in *Just One More Goal*:

> I had no other alternative at the time. The headlines were so strong, I couldn't resist them. It was too much to handle. Scholar was quite supportive at first but we'd fallen out over one or two things and, in the end, he turned the other way and I think it's because they'd spoken to Terry Venables and it semi-suited them.

Theo Delaney feels there was an air of convenience over the timing of Pleat's departure:

We all saw the headlines about Pleat and, initially, you assume there must be some truth in them, though now I'm very sceptical. It did feel very convenient that at exactly the same time that Terry Venables became available, the club decided to act with such haste. Scholar seemed besotted by Venables and with that sort of marquee signing.

What is without doubt, though, is that Pleat had the rug well and truly pulled from under him in the summer of 87. To lose Hoddle and Gough – and at a time when Clemence and Ardiles were approaching the end of their careers – was debilitating and required time to solve.

News of Pleat's departure broke on a Friday evening and Spurs had a game to play the following day at Nottingham Forest. Trevor Hartley and reserve-team manager Doug Livermore took charge and Spurs were emphatically beaten 3-0. It was the second defeat in a four-game losing streak that also saw Second Division Aston Villa knock Spurs out of the League Cup in the third round.

It wasn't the only knockout involving Spurs that October. On the same day as that Forest defeat, White Hart Lane staged Frank Bruno's heavyweight boxing bout against Joe Bugner.

While attending the bout, Scholar got talking to Hoddle's agent, Dennis Roach, who was also a close friend of Terry Venables, now a free agent. Roach suggested that Venables would be very interested in the vacancy at Spurs and also gave him contact details for Venables, who was on a family holiday in Florida. For all this, it is unimaginable that the idea of approaching Venables hadn't already crossed Scholar's mind.

Links between Venables and Spurs weren't new. Scholar had been minded to talk to him in 1984 but suggests that he was concerned about Venables's supposed lack of discipline and whether he would give his full attention to the job. After all, at QPR, Venables had not just been the manager but also a club director and was also well known for his various other business ventures.

Since then, the two had met socially on several occasions and while negotiating the Archibald transfer. When Scholar was invited by Venables to attend a European Cup tie at the Camp Nou in 1986, it was again reported that he might be coming to White Hart Lane.

Venables had initially achieved success in Catalonia, winning the club's first league title in 11 years in his first season and the following year he reached the European Cup Final, agonisingly losing in a penalty shoot-out.

He never recovered from that European setback and, after a disappointing 86/87 season and a poor start to the next campaign, he was sacked, with Johan Cruyff replacing him.

Scholar moved quickly after Pleat's resignation. By Monday morning, he had spoken with Venables at his Miami hotel by telephone and then flown out, under an alias to avoid any press leaks, to meet him. Venables greeted him at Miami airport and the pair had a detailed and lengthy conversation about the state of the team, talks which culminated in Venables agreeing to sign a three-year deal – though, at his request, he wished to commence his new role at the end of November so that he could fulfil his family break.

Writing in his 2014 autobiography, *Born to Manage*, Venables references the lure of returning to his former club, a factor which eventually persuaded him to cut short the 12-month sabbatical he had planned. Venables was impressed with the passion Scholar had for the club and his ambitions for the team.

The pair even agreed to record an interview on a portable tape recorder that they had to purchase from a local Florida supermarket. Led by Scholar, the interview was made exclusively available on Spursline by the end of the week. It was the first time that supporters could hear from their new manager ... at a cost of 50p per minute!

Scholar had also insisted on a photo of the pair shaking hands against a backdrop of palm trees and this image became the front page of the next matchday programme.

TERRY TAKES CHARGE was the headline of the November issue of *Spurs News*, which contained exclusive interviews with both the chairman and manager. Scholar was quoted as saying: 'He is the right man for the right club at the right time.' Scholar said elsewhere that Venables had been 'on a shortlist of one'.

When Venables and Scholar spoke during their initial conversation about team affairs, the chairman had been asked to write down the names of the existing Spurs players he believed could help them win the league. It struck Scholar at the time that he could only write down the names of four (unnamed) players. It was a reminder of how the quality had dropped in such a short space of time. Venables states that Scholar had promised £4m for new recruits – as long as half of that could be recouped through sales.

Trevor Hartley and Doug Livermore continued to lead the team and Spurs lost three and drew two of their next five prior to Venables's arrival. Back in Florida, Venables had been studying the squad he was due to inherit, acutely aware of the talent that had already left.

He was able to watch videos of previous games, going back to the FA Cup Final earlier that year. He wrote in his autobiography: 'The players I was left with were good but not gold and the departures meant the dressing room had lost some of its most influential characters.'

Behind the scenes, Venables brought his trusted assistant and long-term friend, Allan Harris, with him and Doug Livermore remained on the coaching team. Trevor Hartley departed.

To much fanfare, Venables took up the reins for the visit of Liverpool at the end of November. More than 47,000 turned up – nearly double the average gate that season. Venables's arrival had also captured national attention and the game was the main focus that day, helped by the fact that Liverpool were the league leaders and, now boosted by the arrival of Barnes and Beardsley, were already looking like champions-elect.

Venables's first challenges were to deal with poor form, low confidence and injuries. Over the previous six weeks, there had been various changes each week, with players like Mabbutt and Stevens operating in different positions to try and plug gaps. At least Waddle was able to return to the first team for the first time in six weeks.

Spurs had done the double over Liverpool the previous season but the game highlighted the journey both clubs had been on since. Overcoming the league leaders was going to be hard enough as it was but the task got even harder when Steve Hodge was sent off for lashing out at Houghton after just ten minutes. Spurs had looked bright until that point but succumbed to two second-half goals.

They lost the following match, too – against Charlton at home, with just over 20,000 attending. Spurs were languishing below mid-table at this stage, just three points above the relegation zone in a season in which four clubs would be going down. The 'R' word hadn't been heard at White Hart Lane since the late 70s. This was not the challenge that Venables had signed up for.

Results improved over Christmas, however. The team recorded their first win under the new manager at Derby, with Clive Allen and Claesen scoring, and then lost only once in the next five to at least get back into the top half.

Scholar had promised Venables money for new signings to help bring the glamour back to White Hart Lane. Venables's first signing broke a record but it wasn't a deal that was going to capture the imagination. Peter Guthrie became the first player to be sold by a non-league club for £100,000 when the Weymouth goalkeeper chose Spurs over his native Newcastle United. Guthrie was immediately loaned to Swansea for the rest of the season and only ever played for Spurs' first team in five pre-season games in the summer of 1988.

The next signing was, by relative standards, far more high-profile but the arrival of Terry Fenwick created little fanfare. Venables had worked with Fenwick at both Crystal Palace and QPR. He was a versatile player who could operate in defence or midfield. Whilst an accomplished England international, he was of a very similar profile to Stevens. It wasn't a signing that would excite the crowd but 25,000 turned up to see him make his debut on New Year's Day against Watford.

Spurs' first defeat in five came in late January at Newcastle, where Gascoigne ran the game, scoring twice. Newcastle were still a backwater of English football; after Waddle had left for Spurs and then Beardsley for Liverpool, Gascoigne was the star of the city and his presence was just about the only thing to keep the passionate home fans excited. Even the exotic Brazilian signing of Mirandinha had been eclipsed by Gascoigne's mercurial brilliance all season.

Crucially, it was the first time Venables had seen Gascoigne play live. After the game, Venables and Scholar discussed their admiration for the player and their ambition to bring him to White Hart Lane.

Since his arrival, Venables had given opportunities to Neil Ruddock, David Howells, Brian Statham and Paul Moran, while Vinny Samways had been in and around first-team matchday squads all season. Tony Parks retained his place in goal.

Venables had won the FA Cup as a Spurs player and this year's competition now offered an opportunity for quick success. In the third round, Spurs got past Oldham on their artificial pitch to set up a comfortable-looking fourth-round tie at Port Vale, who sat towards the bottom of Division Three.

Port Vale, located in Burslem, a suburb of Stoke-on-Trent, must have felt a world away from the palm trees of Florida where Venables had agreed to sign for Scholar. It proved to be a chastening afternoon for Venables and the most humiliating defeat for Spurs in the 80s as they went down to a 2-1 defeat. It was the first time since 1959 that Spurs had been knocked out of the FA Cup by third-tier opposition.

Venables did cite the poor condition of the pitch but conceded the second goal had been 'a disaster'. The scorer of that Port Vale second goal, Phil Sproson, told the media that 'Spurs had lacked heart'.

It was further humiliation for Spurs fans like 'Spooky':

This Port Vale game practically ruined my love for the FA Cup. It was our cup. Not only did 1987 see us dethroned (momentarily, as we made a comeback in 1991 and never again), this game made me fear every draw and the potential for an away day at a lowly club.

Magic of the cup? The stuff of nightmares.

Lower league opponent. Terrible pitch. Shanty stadium. Adverse weather conditions. Oh, and THFC thrown into the mix.

You'd still expect us to negotiate the early rounds and get past any given minnows. But, alas, no.

I didn't go to this game. I listened to it on the radio. Two-nil down at half-time, miserable there and miserable indoors as I started to contemplate the Monday at school. *Grandstand* confirmed the result and Spurs were pushed into the realm of memes long before the internet turned it into a culture.

Invincible cup kings to this. Eight months between the 87 final and now this. Mediocrity here we come. School was rubbish on the Monday and Spurs were just rubbish, full stop.

It was a humbling defeat and set in motion a mediocre end to the season. Spurs won one and drew three of the next five. The supporters continued to show their apathy. Only 15,000 showed up for the visit of Derby in March and they were 'rewarded' with a 0-0 draw.

A crowd of more than 21,000 did turn out on a cold February evening to welcome back Hoddle to White Hart Lane for the friendly arranged as part of his transfer. Monaco won 4-0 against a Spurs team featuring several youngsters.

Hoddle's was not the only flock of long blonde hair on display. In the days just before the game, striker Paul Walsh joined from Liverpool and he started against Monaco. The former Charlton and Luton striker was a proven goalscorer in Division One but was unable to dislodge Aldridge and Beardsley in Liverpool's attack. Walsh possessed pace but had missed several months due to an Achilles injury.

Walsh's arrival was welcome. Goals had become painfully hard to come by. Claesen was in and out of the team too sporadically to find any rhythm. Waddle was the sole creative force and, though Allen continued to score at a healthy rate, he couldn't possibly recapture his previous season's form. Additionally, Allen was out of contract at the end of the season and, having experienced the malaise setting in, had his eyes on following Hoddle to France:

> I knew Terry very well and he'd been a family friend since before I was a pro, so I was really excited that he came in. He knew me from our time at Palace and QPR and, in theory, it should have been the ideal situation for both of us. I'd always had ambitions to play on the continent but wasn't desperate to leave.
>
> Eventually, I was offered a new contract, which was very underwhelming. I think Terry was a little embarrassed about what they were offering and it helped make my mind up. Bordeaux came in and offered a decent fee, which the club took. It would be a wrench to leave Spurs but it felt like the right time, though I was desperate to finish the season well.

At the other end of the pitch, Venables bought a new goalkeeper, Bobby Mimms, to fill the void left by Clemence, who was persuaded to join the coaching team permanently. Parks had played throughout the winter months but wasn't able to convince Venables that he was any more than a stand-in and he promptly left to join Steve Perryman, who was now the Brentford manager. Parks will forever be remembered for his heroics in 1984 and did return to the club as a goalkeeping coach under Harry Redknapp in 2008.

As back-up keeper to the brilliant Neville Southall at Goodison Park, Mimms had watched on from the sidelines for two years and wanted regular first-team football. He'd made 28 appearances for the Toffees, which included the 1986 FA Cup Final against Liverpool when Southall had been injured. From afar, Mimms looked a good signing.

Both Mimms and Walsh made their league debuts at home to Manchester United on 23 February, with Clive Allen on the scoresheet in a 1-1 draw.

Walsh scored his first Spurs goal in a 2-1 win over Everton in March but there was very little else going on as Venables started to plan his first off-season and transfer targets. As he'd discussed, he'd need to sell players especially now that more than £2m had been spent on Mimms, Fenwick and Walsh.

On transfer deadline day, Ossie Ardiles joined ambitious Division Two club Blackburn, who had also signed Steve Archibald from Barcelona. Ardiles went on loan for the remainder of the season.

The loan period would take Ardiles to the end of his contract, so his appearance against Wimbledon on 19 March became his final one in a Spurs shirt. His arrival in 1978 stunned the football world. He will forever be immortalised for his role in the 1981 FA Cup Final, where his 'dream' came true. The second half of his Spurs career, following the Falklands interruption, had been beset by injuries but his class and ability still shone through.

Tim Vickery shared his thoughts about Ardiles' departure:

He'd probably had an injury too many by this time but I think Hoddle's departure really impacted on him. For ten years, the pair of them had formed an incredible relationship and synergy. We naturally think of Crooks and Archibald or Miller and Roberts as the great partnerships of the era but I'd argue that Ardiles and Hoddle in midfield was the most important and definitely the most durable. Ossie was a fetcher and carrier and provided the rhythm with short passes but without Hoddle to execute the long passes, the balance wasn't right and it nullified him, too.

For me, one of the biggest regrets of the decade, and going into the 90s, was that Spurs didn't build on this association with Argentinian midfielders. In many ways, Spurs were already pioneers and benefitted from the earlier days of importing global talent to England but they didn't follow through with it.

Clive Allen's final Spurs goal came in the televised north London derby defeat at Highbury in March. Allen remained a Spurs player until the end of the season before joining Bordeaux.

Allen was one of very few genuinely top-calibre players left at the club. Venables is said to have questioned 'where have all the players gone?' shortly after he arrived. He now had to hope that Mimms, Fenwick and Walsh might have an impact but the one shining star of the season was Waddle. At the start of the season, he had signed a new, improved five-year contract and seemed now to be the talisman within the squad, though he only had three goals to show for his efforts.

Results continued to be mediocre. Venables was trying to instil some of the tactics that had worked for him in Barcelona and persevered with a suicidal high line that the players just weren't equipped for and opponents found a lot of joy against.

The spring of 1988 also saw more than 20,000 attend Danny Thomas's benefit match, with a full-strength Manchester United side making up the opposition against a Spurs team that included Kenny Dalglish and John Barnes! It was an incredible gesture by Liverpool, who were closing in on the league title. Dalglish was player-manager and both he and Barnes had played in a hard-fought game against Wimbledon two days beforehand. Steve Archibald and Graham Roberts also returned to play in lilywhite. Roberts might even have returned on a more permanent basis. It has been speculated that Venables considered bringing him back from Rangers before deciding to sign Fenwick instead.

While Archibald and Roberts provided a look back to the past, there was a lot of room for optimism outside the first team.

The reserves won their second successive league title in the Football Combination and the youth team topped the South East Counties League for the third year in a row. The youth team also reached the semi-finals of the FA Youth Cup but came unstuck against Doncaster, largely due to a string of injuries at the crucial time. Guy Butters was a 17-year-old apprentice who had spent the season in both the youth team and reserves. He explains what made the junior teams so successful:

There were several things, really. Keith Blunt and Keith Waldon hammered home how important technique was. Keith Blunt always had this thing about continental teams having better technical ability than most English sides. We'd spend hours in the ball courts at the stadium but we were really fit, too. On Mondays, we'd attend college in the morning and then run around the outside of the pitch afterwards. I can still picture coming round the north-west corner and seeing our reflection in the West Stand executive box windows. We were brought up to be really competitive, too. On Fridays, we'd play young v old (first years v second years) and those games were really rough – you had to stand up for yourself or you'd get smashed. We won the South East Counties and should have gone further in the FA Youth Cup. From memory, we suffered a load of injuries before playing Doncaster in the semi. It was a really good set-up. We had great values instilled in us as apprentices. We'd clean boots, sweep the changing rooms but that taught us to be humble. We could also see so many of the older year groups settling in the first team – players like Polston, Statham, Samways and Moran had played, so we knew we had a chance.

Venables had been impressed with the youngsters, who regularly joined in training and often looked better than the senior team. Samways, Brian Statham, Paul Moran and John Moncur all appeared in the first team.

At the end of the season, Guy Butters was about to be awarded his first professional contract:

We had a really strong group that year. I'd completed my two-year apprenticeship on the old YTS programme. There were whispers going around that nearly all of us were going to get pro contracts. In fact, the only lad that didn't was unfortunate that there were lots of players in his position already. Keith Blunt got us together at the training ground and congratulated us. I then had to get showered and changed and go and meet Terry Venables at White Hart Lane. I still cringe now thinking about the limp handshake I gave him; he told me to go outside and come back again with a proper one! Terry was brilliant – he told me that he'd seen me playing in the reserves and that he thought I was better than anyone already in the England Under-21s. He told me that he had plans for me and I walked out of there feeling about 10ft tall.

The first team did at least end the season with a home win, when Luton were beaten 2-1 on 4 May. A paltry crowd of 15,437 watched Mabbutt and Hodge score (in what turned out to be the latter's final Spurs game ahead of a move back to Nottingham Forest) but many decided to stay on well after the final whistle. To understand why requires a brief jump back in time.

Having rebuilt the West Stand and generated income principally through the corporate hospitality facilities, the club owners began to consider the next stadium redevelopments. The other three sides of White Hart Lane were largely untouched since they'd first been built. The North and South stands, behind the goals, had seats installed into the upper sections during the 60s but the iconic section of the stadium had always been the East Stand which, unlike most grounds, provided a terrace that ran the whole length of the touchline, affording an incredible vantage point. The whole lower tier was known as The Shelf and was largely uncovered by the roof that only really offered protection from the elements to those sitting in the upper tier.

Around 17,000 could legally be accommodated on The Shelf. Over the years, those positioned there had unbelievable views of the great 'Push and Run' team of 1951, the double team a decade later and, in 1984, the incredible conclusion to the UEFA Cup Final. Quite simply, The Shelf was the heartbeat of White Hart Lane.

To replace the West Stand was one thing but to do anything to The Shelf risked an outcry. The problem that Scholar had was that the East Stand had barely had a lick of paint since he first stood there in the early 50s. The facilities were basic to say the least and, following the Popplewell Inquiry, there were risks that, at any time, the local authority might refuse to issue a safety certificate. Any potential East Stand rebuild was going to cost several million at a time when Scholar wanted to invest in the team. It was quite the conundrum, with no obvious solution that would suit all parties.

In 1985, Bobroff had submitted plans to Haringey Council to completely rebuild the East Stand. It was promptly rejected, as the new plans would have infringed on Worcester Avenue behind it. Word had got around and, unsurprisingly, it unsettled large sections of the supporter base.

Shelf regular Alan Fisher co-wrote *A People's History of Tottenham Hotspur* and dedicated a chapter to this episode. He reflects on the dynamic created by the design of the West Stand:

> The new West Stand symbolised Tottenham's attempt to present themselves as a thoroughly modern club. All-seater with a seam of 72 executive boxes masked behind smoked glass, it included upgraded facilities for entertaining, as well as an excellent, albeit expensive, view. Not that this mattered all that much to many of the box holders and their clients, where football was often a distraction, interrupting fine dining and schmoozing. With their own entrances and exclusive suites, they didn't have to mix with the hoi polloi like me on the terraces and, with the flick of a switch, they could even shut out the crowd noise.
>
> Spurs were responding to demand from a new and different breed of spectator, with money to spend and tired of the antiquated, shabby facilities that characterised English football clubs at the time. As such, it sat as part of chairman Irving Scholar's drive to maximise income, alongside higher ticket prices, expanded merchandising and the Stock Market flotation in 1983. Many boxes were taken by companies as part of their corporate client relations – this is football as conspicuous consumption, not supporting your team.

It sat uneasily with me, looking on from my spot on The Shelf opposite, the same as where I had stood for a decade or so. This was new and different and not necessarily in a good way. But, at the time, it felt as if the club, to be fair, had made these changes while still paying attention to the terrace fan, because we had exactly the same view, better than almost any other First Division ground, for a fraction of the price. More often than not, you could make out that many boxes were empty and those that weren't would often have a TV on in the background showing horse racing or something else that wasn't remotely related to Spurs. It created a 'them and us' dynamic but I'd much rather be jampacked on The Shelf with 'Knees Up Mother Brown'. More fool them if they wanted to watch football that way and, anyway, their money would help the team be more successful. Only it didn't, not in the long run, and it soon became clear the board was more 'them' than 'us'.

In February 1988, the *London Evening Standard* broke news of a new planning application that sought to rebuild the internal parameters of the East Stand within its original structure, thus not building back and on to Worcester Avenue. It required the complete demolition of the roof and the building of a replacement that would cover the very front of the lower tier, which no-one would be too upset about. Crucially, though, it included a row of 36 executive boxes at the expense of 11,700 standing places … on The Shelf.

The club was clearly very confident that their plans would be passed. They had arranged with the Football League that the final home game of the season would be brought forward into April, which would provide sufficient time to complete works in time for the start of the new season in August.

What they hadn't accounted for was the backlash from several thousand fans. When the Haringey planning committee met in April, the club chose not to send a single club representative to the meeting.

The committee was, therefore, stunned to find about 20 Spurs fans in attendance. They had been mobilised by the chair of the London Football Supporters' Association (FSA) who happened to work in local government and was also supporting Charlton fans who were seeking a return to their Valley stadium.

Like the club, the committee had not anticipated any objection to the plans and, so, decided to defer a decision, asking that the club engage with supporters before the committee reconvened in May. The group of supporters had, by this time, come up with the acronym LOTS (Left on The Shelf). Scholar felt the use of the word 'Left' had political connotations although the group always denied this.

On 20 April, fans were invited to the club for a consultation, which was led by Scholar and secretary Peter Barnes. Terry Venables also attended. At the meeting, Scholar outlined the rationale behind the plans, though he later conceded in *Behind Closed Doors* that he could have done more to consult with supporters much earlier in the process. He reckoned that the meeting had ended cordially, with fans pleased to be able to hear from Venables about his ambitions for the team.

The impasse remained, though. Those who felt converting The Shelf into executive boxes was sacrilege could not be appeased. Scholar did share plans to convert the Paxton Road Stand into a single-tier terrace that he believed would match the Anfield Kop and become the new home of Spurs fanatics.

Time was now against the club. They had hoped to begin work before the end of April but the deferred decision and the fact that Spurs had been forced to reschedule the home game against Luton back into May (because Luton had reached and won the League Cup Final, where they beat Arsenal in a rare moment of joy for Spurs fans that season) meant that, by the start of May, work was still far from even starting. The delay provided LOTS with time to galvanise support and, by the time of the Luton game, they had printed and distributed thousands of flyers encouraging a 'sit-in' at the end of the game.

By the late 80s, fans were able to share ideas through the publication of fanzines. Following the success of the national-level *When Saturday Comes* fanzine, first published in 1986, Stuart Mutler and Matt Stone created *The Spur,* a fanzine dedicated to Spurs. These were sold outside the ground and were the first of many other fan-led publications that emerged in the 90s.

David Harris was a regular reader:

> My reading habits changed throughout the 80s. From about 83 onwards, it was *Smash Hits* and then I'd get *Shoot!* or *Match* magazine but by the end of the 80s, it was all about *The Spur* fanzine. The writing was brilliant and always very funny. Fanzines then were what podcasts and YouTube channels are today. They were a great way of galvanising fans and allowed us to share thoughts about what was and wasn't going well.

Up to 5,000 fans sat in peaceful protest for up to 40 minutes following the final whistle against Luton before making their way around to the West Stand to build awareness of their cause. A wreath containing the words 'In Loving Memory of The Shelf 1936–1988' was placed on the gates of the stand.

The planning committee reconvened at Haringey Town Hall twice more in May. Even more fans attended while Spurs at least sent vice-chairman Douglas Alexiou to represent the club. Alexiou is said to have taken an abrasive stance, allegedly threatening to withdraw club funding to a local community pot if the plans were rejected.

In a compromise from the original plan, the club redrew the designs to allow a thin row of standing immediately in front of the new boxes, though Scholar states that Bobroff was against this. However, many fans who applied for a standing season ticket were promptly told that there was too little space to accommodate all of them, with most having to be relocated to the very front of the lower tier.

The plans were eventually passed, signalling the death of the iconic Shelf. The committee insisted that the proposed Paxton Road Kop be built within three years. Owing to the tragedy at Hillsborough the following year and the subsequent Taylor Report, this never materialised.

Construction work began the very next morning. While the delay would have significant impact at the start of the following season, it symbolised the dichotomy that the club found itself in.

Julie Welch feels that this was the point of no return for Scholar:

> Up until 1988, Scholar was a mysterious character to most Spurs fans. He heralded the future in many ways but there were two sides to him. Steve Perryman was instantly wary of him and the episode with Burkinshaw showed that he wanted to be hands on. As for the average fan, he clearly shared their passion for the club but he was also a businessman. In helping secure a better TV deal, he also raised ticket prices. Merchandising was great but providing a mail order catalogue with many matchday programmes and the exploitation of fans through Spursline showed a different side to him. What was his main priority – making Spurs great or making Scholar great?
>
> The removal of The Shelf was a seminal moment. Scholar should have been aware of the historical significance and his failure to properly consult supporters – and then his role in trying to push through the plans – was an indication of how out of touch he was with the ordinary fan.

Scholar would never recover his credibility among the fanbase, though his next action would also have a profound impact on the club's immediate future.

League position	13th
Average home league attendance	25,921
Most appearances	Fairclough (45)
Top goalscorer	Clive Allen (13)
League winners	Liverpool
FA Cup winners	Wimbledon
League Cup winners	Luton Town

88/89 – FOG ON THE THAMES

MIMMS

BUTTERS FENWICK MABBUTT M.THOMAS

P.ALLEN GASCOIGNE HOWELLS WADDLE

WALSH STEWART

THE 1987/88 campaign was the definition of a 'transitional' season. Venables had taken the job knowing that he'd have to sell players to generate funds to subsidise the cost of the new players he wanted to bring in to make Spurs title challengers. He'd already spent £1.5m on Fenwick, Walsh and Mimms but had big ideas for further incomings.

As a result, Spurs created something of a 'Supermarket Sweep' through the sales of Hodge, Allen, Claesen, Parks, Metgod and Ruddock, plus the release of Ardiles. Those departures generated around £2.75m.

There was already a good group of youngsters with first-team experience. Howells, Samways and right-back Brian Statham were regularly in and around first-team matchday squads throughout the back end of the previous season. Guy Butters was one of a dozen youth team graduates who had been awarded professional contracts. Among his year group was Andy Polston, younger brother of John. They initially joined the reserve squad.

By relative standards, Division One clubs were awash with cash after a significant deal was signed by the Football League that would see league games broadcast exclusively by ITV. The deal was worth £44m over a four-year period and Irving Scholar had played a leading role in negotiations. He and his fellow 'Big Five' club chairmen had persuaded a supporting cast of other Division One clubs (Aston Villa, Newcastle, Nottingham Forest, Sheffield Wednesday and West Ham) to rally together to strike a deal they felt more befitting of the value of English football.

Fledgling satellite broadcaster BSB had been the preferred choice for a majority of clubs in the lower divisions but the reconstitution of the league rules, led by Scholar in 1985, provided top-flight clubs with enough power to dictate the terms. As part of the deal with ITV, the 'Big Five' received an initial £600,000 each, with a guarantee of at least two televised home fixtures that would generate a further £145,000 per game. Scholar insisted that the potential audience and commercial partners were attracted to the 'Big Five' and, therefore, they could justify the financial chasm that was opening up to create divisions within the division.

Money was spent freely by English clubs through the summer of 1988. Mark Hughes rejoined Manchester United for a club record fee of £1.8m. Tony Cottee (West Ham to Everton £2.1m) and Ian Rush (Juventus back to Liverpool £2.7m) both broke the British transfer record. It was a staggering summer and the spending was deemed by many in the media and wider society to be reckless and vulgar.

Though Scholar had to watch the club's purse strings, he remained a football romantic and was still prepared to speculate to accumulate in an attempt to keep Spurs at the top table.

That Spurs needed a centre-forward was palpable. Allen and Claesen had scored 21 goals between them and Spurs only managed 38 goals all season in the league – their lowest tally in the club's history – and this was despite the creative talent of Chris Waddle.

With both Allen and Claesen leaving, a centre-forward was the first priority. With Cottee set to join either Everton or Arsenal, Spurs had to look elsewhere and their search took them beyond the top division entirely. The 23-year-old Manchester City striker Paul Stewart had made an impression on Venables several years earlier while playing for Blackpool. Venables had monitored a career that had seen him join Manchester City in

1987 shortly before they were relegated. In Division Two, he scored 24 goals, despite City failing to gain promotion.

Stewart had also attracted interest from Everton but they eventually put all their efforts and resources into signing Cottee, leaving the path clear for Spurs to agree a deal for £1.7m – a new club record. But Stewart was just the aperitif.

At the beginning of the summer, Venables and Scholar agreed that Paul Gascoigne was going to be their No.1 priority. Interest in the player was well known and Scholar had already made an offer to Newcastle the previous September while Pleat was still in charge but it had gone no further.

As revealed in *The Biography Of Tottenham Hotspur* by Julie Welch, Bill Nicholson, in his role as scout, had been to watch Gascoigne play for Newcastle at West Ham the previous season. Several years later, Nicholson's handwritten report card was found in his White Hart Lane office drawer. He'd commented:

> He has explosive pace off the mark, he seldom stands still and watches; in fact, he always wants the ball. But he is undisciplined and often goes where he pleases. He has great control and confidence on the ball and good vision. He virtually invites the tackle but always seems to be that little bit faster than his opponent. He screens the ball well and he turns so tightly with the ball with a full knowledge of what and who is around him. Some of his passing was exceptional, too, so that I can't think of anyone else with similar ability ... he was very reckless in the tackle that got him his caution ... but he is still very young and just has to be recommended.

Gascoigne was in high demand. Liverpool and Manchester United, who had finished the previous season as champions and runners-up respectively, were both very interested. For all his precocious talent, there were also doubts about Gascoigne's fitness; he had a liking for chocolate bars, which dented his ability to perform for 90 minutes. And, as highlighted in Nicholson's report, he could be positionally irresponsible.

Gascoigne was also vulnerable to lapses in concentration and his desire to hold on to the ball for too long could also frustrate team-mates. As had been the case with Hoddle, English football remained sceptical about creative central midfielders. They were invariably shifted into wide positions.

Gascoigne was a player Scholar felt had all the qualities to become a superstar at Spurs – a club that historically had always indulged maverick stars.

Manchester United were first to make an official approach. However, Scholar utilised his good relationship with the Newcastle chairman and requested to be become informed of any successful bids. He matched Manchester United's bid, offering £2m – an initial payment of £1m, with the balance to be paid over a 12-month period. No player had been transferred for £2m in England at this point.

After an anxious wait, the bid was accepted, with a condition added about a potential sell-on percentage. It was now up to the player and his advisers whether to choose Spurs or wait for Manchester United or Liverpool.

Spurs were a tough sell. Gascoigne had grown up in Newcastle and was surrounded by family and friends. From a football perspective, he was desperate to get into the England senior squad but Liverpool and Manchester United offered the more immediate opportunity to challenge for silverware.

The ace in Spurs' pack was the personal relationship between Gascoigne and fellow Geordie Chris Waddle, who was tasked with persuading Gascoigne to join him in north London. The two had briefly been part of the same Newcastle team in 1985 and had developed an instant rapport.

Gascoigne and his advisers met with Scholar in London to negotiate the deal. Initially, Gascoigne asked to have a clause inserted that would allow him to move to Liverpool if they came in for him at a later stage. While this sort of clause was commonplace on the continent, Scholar wouldn't entertain it and it created an anxious moment while player and agent considered their options. However, they returned to say that they were happy to sign without the stipulation.

Knowing that he held all the power, Gascoigne finalised personal terms only after he managed to add a car, a new house for his parents and a sunbed for his sister into the contract!

Scholar had pulled off a transfer coup and one that would go down as one of the best signings in the club's history, though it would be a few more days until the deal was announced. Gascoigne had also spoken with Alex Ferguson and the Manchester United manager thought he would be going to Old Trafford. Ferguson was furious to miss out.

Theo Delaney was delighted to learn of Gascoigne's arrival:

> There's no doubt that Gascoigne was a wonderkid and had a huge reputation, so it was a statement of intent that we got him over Liverpool and Manchester United. I'd grown up in love with the football mavericks of the 70s – Worthington, Marsh, Bowles etc and then Hoddle came along and he was better than all of them, so there was a real craving for a player like Gascoigne, but we had no idea how good he was actually going to be!

In the intervening days between the deal being agreed and announced, Gascoigne was put up in a local hotel, along with several friends. In a sign of things to come, Scholar was concerned to receive phone calls from the hotel manager explaining that Gascoigne and friends had been up late at night letting off fire extinguishers, making a lot of noise and generally being a nuisance. It would be quite the rollercoaster ride for player and club for the next four years.

For now, the problem Spurs had, apart from how to manage Gascoigne away from the pitch, was how they were going to pay for him. They had to find an initial £1m to pay Newcastle. Despite the pending outgoings, Spurs had poor cashflow, with expenditure already set aside for the East Stand rebuild. The club's bankers, Barclays, whom Spurs had held their account with since their formation, insisted on personal guarantees from directors to authorise an overdraft extension. Scholar claims that he and Tony Berry were willing to do so but that Bobroff refused.

With nowhere to go with Barclays, Bobroff decided to move the club accounts to Midland Bank, which offered a bigger overdraft facility.

Having spent more than £3.5m, Spurs were branded in the press as a 'moneybags' club, seemingly throwing cash around nonchalantly. The accusations of financial recklessness would be used as a stick to beat the club and manager with from opposing fans throughout the season.

There's no doubt that Gascoigne's signing provided some immediate returns, however. He was used as the model to promote the new yellow away kit manufactured by Hummel.

The riches that the Hummel acquisition were supposed to generate were becoming a burden. Earlier in 1988, Scholar was shocked when alerted to a huge overstock of Hummel merchandise in the warehouse. Many of the kits and items held were now out of date and had little chance of generating any sales. There was barely any space to purchase and hold anything new. This was a fundamental flaw in agreeing to stock and distribute other clubs' merchandise for Hummel. The clubs with Hummel deals – now Aston Villa, Coventry, and Southampton – only had relatively small supporter bases and/or minimal retail outlets. It made it very difficult to distribute stock at any speed.

It was the beginning of the end of the Hummel experiment and would continue to drain valuable resources for the next three years.

Gascoigne's first outing in a Spurs shirt came in a pre-season friendly at Dundee United. He and Stewart both started in a 1-1 draw in which Walsh scored Spurs' goal.

Pre-season also included an intriguing four-team tournament, sponsored by the tool firm Makita, at Wembley Stadium in mid-August. It featured Spurs and Arsenal alongside European heavyweights AC Milan and Bayern Munich and sought to provide the English clubs with experience against meaningful European opposition.

Spurs played Arsenal in the semi-final. Gascoigne started and showed signs of his incredible dribbling ability from central midfield but Spurs were overpowered in a 4-0 trouncing.

They put up a better showing the following day but lost 2-1 to AC Milan.

Having suffered so badly with an ultra-high defensive line in 87/88, Venables introduced a new sweeper system that incorporated Terry Fenwick behind two central defenders – initially Mabbutt and Fairclough.

Both on and off the field, Spurs were in a period of rebuild. However, it was the East Stand construction works that caused the most chaos as the new season approached.

The prolonged planning process caused a crucial delay of six weeks before any work could start and, unhelpfully, Spurs had been given a home game (against Coventry) on the opening day, 27 August.

Scholar wrote in *Behind Closed Doors* that he left the stadium at 6pm on the Friday evening and had received assurances that all work would be complete by the morning in time to gain the appropriate safety certificate from the local council.

It transpired that many of the labourers on site had complained of fatigue and had been sent home during the night. By morning, when the council officials arrived, they found large amounts of debris and concluded that the site was not safe. Red-faced, the club had no choice but to seek a postponement of the fixture with the Football League.

By lunchtime, the media was reporting that the game had been postponed. Scholar even appeared on BBC Radio London to give his account. He was alarmed by a previous incident in which Tranmere had postponed a game in similar circumstances and received a points deduction as punishment.

Alan Fisher was already on his way to the ground when he learned of the postponement:

This sorry episode seemed to perfectly sum up the incompetence that was engulfing the club at the time and we didn't know anything about the Hummel farce that was beginning to unravel at the same time. We were all football supporters first and foremost and had looked forward to the start of the new season, especially to see Gascoigne on his debut.

Anyone who'd been to the ground during the off-season knew there were real concerns that it wouldn't be ready in time but by the morning of the game, there was no official statement from the club, so I had no reason not to set off. Scholar seemed to be blaming everyone else, including the fans who'd protested against The Shelf redevelopment. His reputation with us was now irreparable.

Gascoigne had to wait a further week to make his competitive debut and fate dictated that it would come away at Newcastle. He received a predictably hostile welcome from the home crowd but they were quickly appeased by their team's fast start, which provided two first-half goals.

Spurs' second-half response was instant. Waddle scored within seven seconds of the restart and, midway through the second half, another Geordie-in-exile, Terry Fenwick, popped up to score an equaliser and secure a draw.

Spurs' home campaign got off to a belated start, with the East Stand partially reopened for the north London derby. After an absorbing first half, Spurs found themselves 3-2 behind at the break. Waddle had equalised an early Marwood goal but Mimms was helplessly out of position for two Arsenal goals. Gascoigne became an instant hero when he pulled a goal back, despite having lost a boot in the build-up. It proved no more than a consolation, though. Samways and Mabbutt both had late goals ruled out for offside, meaning Arsenal had won five games in a row at White Hart Lane.

Next up was an away game at Liverpool. The prospect of winning at Anfield no longer possessed the mental barrier it had before 1985 but Liverpool had run away with the title in 1988 and had started the season with three wins and a draw from their opening four games. Spurs caused several problems to Liverpool's high defensive line in the first half and Waddle and Walsh both squandered golden opportunities. It was possibly the best Spurs performance under Venables to date and, despite going behind to Beardsley's 80th-minute goal, Spurs equalised within two minutes through Fenwick.

Spurs ended the game with ten players after Fairclough was sent off for punching Liverpool forward John Aldridge in an off-the-ball incident.

Having played well in all three games but without securing a win, the first victory of the season came in the next game. Middlesbrough were the visitors to White Hart Lane and led twice late into the second half. It was an afternoon for the substitutes. Venables threw on David Howells and Paul Moran with just over ten minutes remaining. Howells scored the equaliser and then, minutes later, Moran's pace got him in behind the Middlesbrough defence, where he was fouled inside the penalty area. Fenwick, who had assumed penalty-taking duties, converted to score the winner.

Gascoigne had already made an impact but Paul Stewart had to wait for his debut. He had received a suspension while at Manchester City and this carried over into the new season. He replaced Moran on the bench for the following league game against Manchester United.

On a balmy early autumn afternoon, Waddle drew first blood. United equalised before half-time and then found themselves ahead with just five minutes to play. With Waddle and Gascoigne both substituted, it was left to Walsh to rescue Spurs with a smart finish following an intricate move between Samways and Howells.

Spurs then had the chance to win it. In the final minute, Stewart used his power to drive into the penalty area but was bundled over. Fenwick had scored the winner from the spot the week before but Stewart insisted on taking this penalty. The forward was desperate to make an immediate impact.

He stepped up to the ball confidently enough but his shot cannoned off the crossbar and away. Stewart would later become a cult hero following his 1991 FA Cup Final goal but the penalty miss set the tone for a difficult first season.

October was an abysmal month for Venables and Spurs. They drew at Charlton before successive defeats at Norwich, at home to Southampton and then at Aston Villa. The only note of joy was a narrow League Cup victory over second-tier Notts

Ossie, Crooks and Danny Thomas mark the club's flotation on the London Stock Exchange in October 83.

Ardiles, Roberts, Stevens and Hughton react to Parks' crucial penalty save

Tony Parks holds the UEFA Cup aloft after his penalty shoot-out heroics

Keith Burkinshaw waves goodbye to White Hart Lane ahead of his testimonial in May 1984.

Clive and Paul Allen with Peter Shreeve in new Hummel kits ahead of the 85/86 season

Keith Houchen and Coventry celebrate their second equaliser in the 1987 FA Cup Final. It was one of the greatest cup finals of all time but Spurs were on the wrong end of it.

Diego Maradona with Glenn Hoddle ahead of Ossie Ardiles' benefit match in May 1986

Clive Allen scored his 49th goal of the 86/87 season in the FA Cup Final.

Bill Nicholson tosses the coin to determine which corner Bruno and Joe Bugner will occupy for the upcoming heavyweight boxing bout at White Hart Lane

Irving Scholar welcomes Terry Venables as his new manager in November 1987

The Shelf in its full glory before the stand was rebuilt in 1988

Gascoigne and Waddle formed a great relationship on and off the pitch.

County. By now, the Football League had decided to deduct Spurs two points following the Coventry postponement and defeat at Villa Park sent Spurs to the bottom of Division One – a position they hadn't occupied since the relegation season of 76/77.

They remained rooted to the foot of the table after a dreadful home defeat to Derby on Bonfire Night. Paul Stewart scored his first goal and Spurs started brightly but they fell to three avoidable goals. Post-match, Venables remained calm in front of the media, highlighting the positive start to the game but lamenting the individual defensive errors. Venables felt his team would be fine in the long run but supporters looking at the league table were more concerned.

Venables had referenced the defensive mistakes that were costing the team. It was goalkeeper Bobby Mimms, now referred to as 'Booby' in the press, who came in for most criticism. Speculation increased about Venables seeking a new goalkeeper. As November arrived, it was now 12 months since Venables had taken over.

Tim Vickery assesses the first year under Venables:

Following the huge fanfare of his arrival, Venables looked completely lost. He had tried to implement some of his successful strategies from Barcelona – namely an ultra-high defensive line – that failed miserably in 87/88. You could count on us conceding because of it in every game. I know that he was really concerned by the quality that had been sold before he'd arrived – Roberts, Miller and then, of course, Hoddle and Gough, so he'd inherited a squad in transition that then lost Hodge and Clive Allen. His signings had failed to convince, too. Fenwick might have been an international defender but he didn't immediately win anyone over. Mimms was greeted like a hero but soon became a bag of nerves and never recovered and Walsh was a busted flush due to an ankle injury he'd picked up at Liverpool; he was a quick player who was no longer quick.

By this point, Gascoigne hadn't yet emerged as the world-class player that he would soon become and it was hard to see why we'd bought Paul Stewart.

Despite the perilous league position, Vinny Samways doesn't recall any nerves from within the squad:

Terry was excellent. He always had a positive vibe about him and showed us no signs of negativity. It was the sign of a top manager. We were always confident we'd pull through.

In a break from league action, Spurs' next game was a League Cup replay at Blackburn, who had drawn 0-0 at White Hart Lane a week earlier. Venables made just one change to the starting XI at Ewood Park. Walsh, who'd missed the last three games through illness, replaced Moran. Both Mabbutt and Fairclough had been struggling with injuries but were passed fit at lunchtime. To bolster defensive options, Guy Butters and Andy Polston were selected as subs.

Spurs had to withstand heavy pressure from a confident Blackburn team who were riding high at the top of Division Two. Spurs relied on Mimms, who made an excellent save early on. Shortly after half-time, Butters replaced Fairclough and this coincided with Gascoigne starting to get a grip on the game. Neither team scored, taking the game into extra time.

Two minutes into the second period, the tie finally saw its first goal. Gascoigne's free kick was glanced in by Mitchell Thomas to give Spurs the lead but it was short-lived. On a bittersweet night for Butters, his saw the ball deflected off him for an own goal just minutes into his senior debut.

It was far from a howler but Butters' blushes were spared within two minutes anyway when Stewart demonstrated his power, pace and composure in front of goal, driving through the Blackburn defence to slot home what proved to be the winner.

After the game, Venables spoke of his desire to put things right and stated that he, and the players, would take collective responsibility. It was a man-management mantra that served him well throughout his career.

Spurs' next opponents were Wimbledon, who were also receiving their share of criticism in the media. Having won the FA Cup the previous season, the Dons were also struggling at the bottom of the table but it was their continued rough approach that was creating headlines.

Two weeks earlier, in a League Cup tie with Manchester United, a brawl ensued, culminating in John Fashanu landing a punch on Viv Anderson in the tunnel. Sections of the press were incensed, feeling that it was time the authorities clamped down on the south London club's violent on-field behaviour. For Spurs, memories of their 1986 encounter with the Dons at White Hart Lane were still fresh.

Gascoigne had his own personal experience of Wimbledon's intimidatory tactics. A photographer had famously captured the moment when, while Gascoigne was playing for Newcastle, he had his 'crown jewels' squeezed by Vinnie Jones.

Spurs had plenty of players who could hold their own against such intimidation but it was 19-year-old Butters, yet to make his first start, who stoked the flames:

I'd been training with the first team the day before, as Fairclough was still 50-50, so I didn't know whether I'd be involved. I was approached by a reporter, who asked me a couple of questions about how I felt about playing against Wimbledon. I'd never had any media training, so I didn't think too much of it and responded that I was up to the physical challenge or something like that. I didn't think anything more about it, so was astonished the next morning when Dad called to tell me I needed to see the back page of the *Star*. The headline quoted me: 'I'll bash Fash!'

I can remember getting to the ground, still unsure whether I'd be involved or not, so was hanging around the changing room a bit sheepish when the Wimbledon team arrived. I hid away in the boot room until they'd all passed but when I came back into the tunnel, Bobby Gould was on his way through. He clocked me and looked me in the eye and said 'Watch your teeth, lad!'

Initially, a football match looked like it might break out. Fenwick put Spurs ahead but Wimbledon were quickly level when ex-Spurs striker Terry Gibson pounced on another Mimms error.

The temperature of the game was simmering when, midway through the first half, Gary Stevens challenged Fashanu on the touchline. The ball was stuck between the pair, seemingly about to roll out for a throw-in. Both were on the floor when Jones came flying in, touching a bit of the ball but crashing into Stevens's leg, which was planted into the ground. It was a completely unnecessary challenge. The impact on Stevens was significant.

Just as he had been in 1986, he was carried off on a stretcher under the eye of physio John Sheridan, who uncharacteristically lost his cool and berated Jones for the damage he'd done. Stevens was conscious this time but scans later revealed a ruptured cruciate ligament, which would rule him out for the season. The extent of the injury delayed the restart and Butters' arrival as substitute by nearly ten minutes.

Stewart looked to exact revenge when his challenge on Roger Joseph sent the Wimbledon full-back across the cinder track in front of the West Stand. A melee followed, involving up to 16 players.

While the rhetoric around Spurs continued to be about the money that they had spent, it was ironic that the two goals they scored within three second-half minutes came from youth team graduates. From a left-wing corner, Butters atoned for his own goal at Blackburn with a firm back-post header to put Spurs ahead. That lead quickly doubled as Moran, back in for Walsh, found room on the edge of the area and teed up Samways for his first league goal. Gibson pulled one back for Wimbledon but Spurs held on for a crucial win to lift them off the bottom.

The new TV deal agreed in the summer would see up to 20 games covered live by ITV. The first opportunity for the nation to see Gascoigne came the following week in a fixture at Sheffield Wednesday. Spurs, who had Butters starting for the first time, were unhappy with the state of the pitch. The snow had been swept off the centre circle and penalty areas but covered the rest of the playing surface.

It was not Gascoigne, but Stewart, who shone brightest, scoring twice late in the second half without reply to secure Spurs' first league away win of the season and first clean sheet in the league.

The TV cameras did get their Gascoigne fix, however. Having been substituted, he showed his playful side, munching through a bag of popcorn as he sat in the dugout and breaking into a huge grin when he realised the camera was focussed on him. Eagle-eyed TV viewers may also have glimpsed Gascoigne throwing snowballs at the Sheffield Wednesday furry owl mascot before the game!

Most of Gascoigne's impish behaviour was harmless enough. Guy Butters recalls a typical day at the training ground:

He just couldn't sit still and was always up to something. We all had to be on our guard at all times around him. I remember we had a lady called Sue, who used to run the canteen and cook the lunches. She could be a little neurotic at times but Gazza had no filters! She'd made a bolognaise sauce and, without anyone seeing, he crept up to it and tipped a bucket of salt in it! We were all spitting it out and Sue was going mad and couldn't understand what had happened. Meanwhile, he was in hysterics but he had such a look on his face that not even Sue could stay mad at him for long! I don't think anyone could have managed him better than Terry did. There's all this talk that he'd have been better with Fergie at United but, unless you literally locked him in a room, you couldn't control him. He was a great, bubbly character, though; very kind and generous to anyone that he met.

However, Gascoigne almost caused himself severe injury on a number of occasions. Chris Waddle spent a lot of time with him and recalled on *The Spurs Show* an occasion where Gascoigne had talked him into a fishing trip just a few hours before an evening home game with Notts County. Despite being a keen angler, Gascoigne managed to get a hook caught in the back of his neck and neither he nor Waddle could remove it.

In significant pain, Gascoigne demanded that Waddle call the club doctor and request to see him at the stadium immediately. They were able to meet and have the hook removed without Venables finding out. Gascoigne played that night and scored the winning goal!

In another well-documented incident, Gascoigne dragged Waddle to White Hart Lane one Friday after training. Speaking with one of the groundstaff, Gascoigne was intrigued to learn of a pigeon problem at the top of the East Stand. He promptly fetched a rifle from his car and proceeded to lead Waddle up to the top of the stand. He identified that his best vantage point would be from the old press box that hung off the roof. It hadn't been used in years and was one of the condemned sections of the stand. As he clambered along the rickety structure, the floorboards gave way and Gascoigne crashed through, falling 15ft into the upper tier seating.

He was incredibly fortunate to get away with just heavy bruising to his chest and ribs. Waddle revealed that Gascoigne could barely breathe but managed to hobble back down to pitchside and back to his car, wheezing and unable to speak. His primary concern seemed to be Venables finding out.

Like Butters and Waddle, everyone who played with or spent enough time around Gascoigne could recite a similarly crazy story.

The win in the snow at Hillsborough seemed to galvanise the team, who embarked on a run of just one loss in the next seven before the end of the year. Gascoigne, who earned his long-awaited call-up to the England senior squad, became the driving force in the Spurs team, producing several majestic performances. He was also a marked man. Having dominated the first half in Spurs' 2-0 win at West Ham just before Christmas, he was withdrawn at half-time due to an ankle injury that forced him to miss much of the next three weeks.

Venables added to the squad by signing Icelandic defender Guðni Bergsson. He made his debut in central defence against Luton on Boxing Day and went on to operate either in midfield or as part of a three-man defence throughout the rest of the season.

With Gascoigne out injured, the Icelandic international wore the No.8 shirt in the north London derby on 2 January, although he played in defence. Ahead of the game, televised live on ITV, Venables helped his counterpart, George Graham, unveil the new refurbished clock at the Clock End at Highbury.

Spurs played well and rightly felt aggrieved when Waddle was scythed down by John Lukic inside the area, only for the referee to wave play on. It was the worst penalty decision to go against Spurs since Kenny Hibbitt's dive in 1981. Arsenal went on to win 2-0 but had Spurs been awarded that penalty (and scored it) it would have deprived Arsenal of their eventual league title success, won by the smallest margin of a one-goal goal difference over Liverpool.

Bergsson was soon joined by Norwegian goalkeeper Erik Thorstvedt, who was brought in to replace the hapless Mimms. Standing 6ft 4in, Thorstvedt was an imposing size and had a good track record at Viking Stavanger, as well as having already been capped 46 times by Norway. He'd spent time at both Arsenal and Spurs on trial but Venables pushed through a deal that saw the Norwegian become the new No.1.

Spurs had been knocked out of the League Cup at Southampton in November, so the FA Cup offered an opportunity to keep the season alive. Having been humiliated at Port Vale the season before, another banana skin lay in store with a trip to Bradford and the match was one of three games featured on *Match of the Day's* highlights show that evening.

Bradford were a decent second-tier side but should have been no match for an improving Spurs side, even without Gascoigne. It proved to be one of those days where the ball just wouldn't roll for Spurs, who missed a hatful of chances either side of Bradford scoring what proved to be the only goal of the game. While not quite as humiliating as the Port Vale defeat, it was yet another cup disappointment and meant that the remainder of the season was just about the league.

Thorstvedt made his debut at home to Nottingham Forest in mid-January in another game televised live on ITV but he suffered the most inauspicious of starts to what would prove to be an otherwise distinguished career at White Hart Lane.

With Spurs already trailing 1-0, Thorstvedt allowed a weak shot from Nigel Clough to slip through his hands and bobble across the line. Although Waddle headed Spurs back into contention just before half-time, the game ended in a 2-1 defeat.

With Gascoigne returning, Spurs embarked on a great run throughout spring, losing just one of ten games before the end of March – and that was against Liverpool. Gascoigne and Waddle seemed to be in a personal goal of the season competition.

Waddle scored from 40 yards on a mudbath of a pitch at Southampton in February, chipped the goalkeeper at Coventry with an effort reminiscent of Hoddle and ran riot with two goals against Aston Villa.

Jill Lewis had enjoyed watching the evolution of Waddle throughout his Spurs career:

> Waddle evolved from a winger who overdid it when he first joined, when he'd beat a player but then go back and beat them again and again. He developed into an all-rounded attacker who played with real intelligence. He could pass the ball beautifully and, once Hoddle left, he was our star player.

Not to be outdone in the goal stakes, Gascoigne ran the length of the pitch, slaloming between three defenders, to score a winner at Luton.

Further creativity was added when Venables returned to Barcelona to sign Mohamed Ali Amar – better known as Nayim. Born in Spanish-governed Cueta in Morocco, the attacking midfielder, capped at Under-21 level by Spain, joined for the remainder of the season on loan. Owing to the league's ruling that only two foreign nationals could be named in a matchday squad (Spurs had already signed Thorstvedt and Bergsson), Nayim had to wait patiently in the reserves.

An injury to Bergsson provided Nayim with the opportunity to make his debut against Norwich. Mark Robson, signed by Pleat in 1986, made his full debut (he'd come on as a sub against West Ham in December). Both played well but Nayim was particularly impressive, assisting Gascoigne's first-half goal in a 2-1 win. Robson made eight more appearances for Spurs before enjoying a solid Football League career at West Ham, Charlton and Notts County.

Throughout spring, Nayim, Samways, Howells and Paul Allen provided the support act to the Gascoigne and Waddle pairing that headlined Spurs' attack. The dark days of the winter, when Spurs propped up the division, now seemed a long time ago and Guy Butters has his view on the turnaround in fortunes:

> I'd love to say it was all down to me getting in the first team! There were a number of factors, really. Terry had come in and had different ideas and ways of doing things that needed time to iron out. One little thing was the way that he wanted us to defend in one-v-one situations. We'd all been brought up to show attackers wide but, in Spain, Terry had learned to show players inside to crowded areas. It took a while to get used to. We would occasionally play three at the back, which required us taking up different positions, but Terry knew in the long run we'd benefit from having that tactical flexibility. It may have been connected but Gazza, Waddle and Stewart really found some form in the second half of the season but throughout the team there was competition for places, so we were all on our toes.

A 2-1 win at Wimbledon on 15 April 1989 saw Spurs move up into fifth but there was no mood for celebration as details of the horrific events at Hillsborough began to emerge throughout the afternoon and into the evening.

English football mourned the deaths of those Liverpool fans (and one Spurs fan who had attended with his Liverpool-supporting friends) who had travelled to watch their team play in an FA Cup semi-final but would never return home. The incident occurred at the Leppings Lane End where, eight years earlier, Spurs fans had endured overcrowding and narrowly avoided being involved in a similar disaster.

Spurs were one of a number of clubs who immediately pulled down perimeter fencing that had originally been erected to prevent hooligans entering the pitch area. A government inquiry, led by Lord Justice Taylor, was launched and would eventually result in a number of changes to laws governing the safety of football supporters. It condemned the state of football stadiums, the complacency of the authorities and highlighted that previous warnings hadn't been heeded.

Perhaps the most significant result was the recommendation that stadiums in the top two divisions should be all-seater by 1994 and the scrapping of the proposed football supporter ID card legislation.

As recently as March, Spurs were one of many clubs to provide a strongly worded matchday programme article spelling out the significant inconvenience that would be caused for every supporter wishing to enter a football stadium, regardless of age, gender or previous record of causing trouble (or not for the vast majority) and that supporters would all be liable for the cost and issuance of their card in the first place.

A list of local MPs, including none other than the Rt Hon Mrs Margaret Thatcher (Finchley), was provided to supporters, who were encouraged to write and express their indignation at the proposal.

Poignantly, Spurs' next opponents were Liverpool's Merseyside neighbours, Everton. In a show of solidarity, a wreath was presented to the Everton fans, who had made their way down to north London for a game in which the result seemed thoroughly inconsequential.

Spurs ended the season with two away London derbies. The first of those was at Millwall, who had enjoyed their first-ever top-flight season, finishing comfortably in mid-table after being tipped for relegation. They had actually topped the division briefly in autumn. Their ground, The Den, was a notorious place to go, with Lions fans often cited as being the most violent and intimidating in the country.

The stands contained a network of cages and fences that created an intimidating environment and the players' tunnel from the main stand had to be extended on to the pitch to mitigate the chances of players being attacked. Gascoigne was not one to be intimidated, though, and he responded to having coins and chocolate bars thrown at him by unwrapping a Mars bar, half eating it and then throwing the rest into the crowd. Fortunately, it was largely met in the spirit that was intended and some of the home crowd even showed signs of enjoying Spurs' masterclass of a performance in a 5-0 victory, the biggest league away win since 1951!

Tim Vickery was there and, in particular, remembers Gascoigne's performance:

It was the moment where I realised just how good he was. He didn't score that day but he ran the game. His range of passing, movement off the ball and strength and guile with it were all exceptional. We had an extraordinary talent and Waddle was also exceptional. Not just in this game but throughout 1989. It felt like the parts were coming together and that we had the making of an exciting team.

The season ended in a 1-0 defeat at QPR in which Mark Falco scored the only goal but it couldn't dampen the enthusiasm over what looked to be a young and talented team on the rise. Spurs finished in sixth place which, in the context of the early 80s, was a little underwhelming but, when considering the huge rebuild that had been required, there was room for optimism.

Gascoigne was a star in the making and looked likely to join the pantheon of world-class 80s Spurs' central midfielders that included Hoddle, Ardiles and Villa.

While Spurs' season ended, the league championship was reaching a dramatic finale. Arsenal had been top since Boxing Day but Liverpool got progressively closer. When Liverpool lost at Old Trafford on New Year's Day, they were fifth, nine points behind Arsenal, but they then embarked on an invincible run of 15 wins and two draws, taking them within touching distance of the summit.

The fateful FA Cup semi-final understandably took its toll. Manager Kenny Dalglish attended each funeral of those killed at Hillsborough, occasionally going to two or three on the same day. Other members of the playing squad were equally affected.

By the time Liverpool played again, on 3 May, fittingly against Everton at Goodison, Arsenal had opened up a six-point lead. Though the derby ended 0-0, Liverpool won their next four league games, which put them top again with one game to play … against Arsenal.

The only way that Arsenal could win the league would be to win by at least two clear goals at Anfield. In part because of the public outpouring of emotion post-Hillsborough, the game attracted huge interest and ITV were able to cover the crescendo to the season live on a Friday evening.

In one of the most dramatic finales in English sporting history, Arsenal won the title with virtually the final kick of the season. It was one of those 'where were you when' moments that transcended modern culture resulting in, among others, Nick Hornby's best-selling book *Fever Pitch*.

The relevance of the occasion to Spurs (beyond the bitter resentment at seeing their rivals win the league championship that Spurs had always seemed best-placed to bring back to London throughout the decade) and the wider football community was that TV had finally been vindicated in its decision to broadcast live football and proved that the game could become the marketable commodity that Irving Scholar had believed so passionately in.

Despite their closest rival's success, Spurs must surely now be able to capitalise on the commercial opportunities about to be realised?

League position	Sixth
Average home league attendance	24,467
Most appearances	Mabbutt, Waddle (44)
Top goalscorer	Waddle (14)
League winners	Arsenal
FA Cup winners	Liverpool
League Cup winners	Nottingham Forest

89/90 – AT WHAT COST?

THORSTVEDT

VAN DEN HAUWE   SEDGLEY   MABBUTT   M. THOMAS

P. ALLEN   GASCOIGNE   HOWELLS   SAMWAYS

LINEKER   STEWART

THE BASIC premise of the plc's diversification strategy was a sound one. The football club would be the main subsidiary, while the other businesses in the portfolio would make money that would pump funds back into the first team. The problem by 1989 was that the other businesses were not only failing to generate significant revenue but some were losing money at an alarming rate.

The situation with Hummel was continuing to go south but it was the acquisition of Synchro Systems in early 1989 that began the unravelling of Scholar's brave new era.

Shortly after Scholar had taken over the club, he had recognised the need to revolutionise the archaic ticketing system and Synchro Systems provided a solution. Scholar remained on good terms with the owners and, with the prospect of supporter identity cards seeming a very real possibility from the mid-80s onwards, Synchro seemed a good company to invest in.

As a 'broadly based leisure company', Tottenham Hotspur plc was obliged to explore further partnership opportunities and purchased 75 per cent of Synchro for £120,000 in early 1989. Projections presented to the club's board suggested that Synchro could expect to make £500,000 per year, especially if it was able to secure big contracts, like the following summer's World Cup tournament in Italy.

At face value, both the plc and the football club were performing well. The plc had made a profit of £501,000. At a board meeting in February, the board was dismissive of any teething problems associated with several of the subsidiary companies, believing that all would become profitable in the very near future.

In 1987, the company welcomed a new director on to the board. Tony Berry owned the recruitment company Blue Arrow and, like Scholar, was a Spurs fan going back to the double era. His company owned a West Stand box and, after several positive conversations, he purchased previously unissued shares and also secured a loan of around £3.5m for the East Stand rebuild, payable over seven years.

Initially, Berry's interventions positively affected the plc share price, which rose by almost three times to £2.50 per share. However, the company, like many on the Stock Exchange, suffered badly from the October 1987 stock market crash. By that point, the acquisition of two clothing-based companies (Stumps and Martex) at a cost of around £3m were well in the process of being completed. They ended up being two additional millstones around the company's neck.

In the summer of 1989, the plc elected a new chief executive, Bob Holt, and he was bullish in his view that the company needed to expand, via the merger of another major public company.

A number of options were discussed, including the suggestion of selling off Hummel. In the end, neither option materialised but what did remain was an overdraft of more than £1.5m, which it was hoped would be written off once the other subsidiaries turned profitable.

For some time, Venables had been told that he needed to offload players and Scholar revealed in *Behind Closed Doors* a list of the players the manager felt were expendable and the amount of money the club could expect to recoup. The list, as provided by Scholar, included Gary Mabbutt (£600,000), Chris Fairclough (£500,000) and Gary Stevens (£300,000), in addition to a number of the youth team graduates. There was an expectation that any sales would generate up to £2m before more money could be spent.

Perhaps buoyed by the mood of the plc board meeting, Scholar led on a marquee player acquisition. Venables told Scholar that he needed a new striker as a priority. Scholar wrote in *Behind Closed Doors* that he had always dreamed of a Spurs team with three genuine star players. He cited the Dutch triumvirate of Ruud Gullit, Frank Rijkaard and Marco van Basten at AC Milan. With Gascoigne and Waddle, he was one step away from creating his own magical trio at White Hart Lane.

The perfect opportunity arose when England's leading striker, Gary Lineker, became surplus to requirements in Barcelona. Since Venables departed, Lineker had become marginalised by Johan Cruyff. Lineker had a house in St John's Wood, so a move to the capital appealed.

Scholar has subsequently revealed that Lineker very nearly joined Spurs from Leicester in 1984/85. On that occasion, Scholar dug in his heels over an additional £100,000 and the move didn't happen. Perhaps his inertia cost Spurs the league title that season? Instead, Lineker moved to Everton, scoring 40 goals in his only season there, before joining Venables in Barcelona. At Mexico 86, he won the World Cup golden boot to confirm himself as a world-class goalscorer.

The deal was relatively straightforward. Barcelona were looking to sell and Lineker was keen to link up again with Venables and also play alongside Gascoigne and, in particular, Waddle, with whom he'd developed a good understanding and rapport on England duty.

Venables was still well connected with the senior executives at Barcelona but even he was astonished to learn that they would accept a deal of around £1.2m and would throw in the permanent transfer of Nayim, too!

Scholar had achieved his ambition of building a team made up of three stylish attackers and a press conference was held at White Hart Lane on 23 June to parade Lineker, who was wearing the new Hummel home shirt, alongside Venables on the terrace of Paxton Road.

The large media presence at White Hart Lane brimmed with optimism, not just for Spurs but for English football in general. The *Daily Mirror* reported that more than £100,000 had been generated already in season ticket sales. Spurs' title odds had been slashed to 8/1 and they were now third favourites behind Liverpool and Arsenal.

Lineker spoke positively about the challenge ahead and both he and Venables referenced the club's ambition to become league champions within the next couple of years. The article suggested that Lineker and Stewart were stylistically similar to the great 60s partnership of Jimmy Greaves and Bobby Smith, while Gascoigne, like Dave Mackay, was the engine room. Similar comparisons could also be made between the flair and creativity of Cliff Jones and Chris Waddle.

As the media swooned over Venables and Lineker, Scholar was unusually absent, having just taken a strange phone call in his office. He claims that, literally minutes before the Lineker press conference had started, he received a phone call from an agent he knew, who was operating in France. Scholar said the agent came straight to the point – Marseille wanted to buy Chris Waddle and were prepared to offer £3m.

There is a discrepancy in Scholar's and Venables's accounts of what happened next but both agree that there had never been any intention or thoughts of selling Waddle. Scholar suggests that Venables was more open to the idea than he was and that Waddle's resale value was now very high. The player had signed a seven-year contract the previous summer and that came with quite a financial burden to carry well into the next decade.

Venables, by contrast, suggests that it was Scholar's insistence on reducing the overdraft that led to a deal even being entertained.

Either way, a series of talks took place, eventually between the two clubs. Marseille were owned by Bernard Tapie, who was desperate to make his club the best in France and competitive in Europe – and would later receive a prison sentence for match-fixing. Much to the astonishment of Scholar and Venables, Tapie was prepared to pay more than £4.25m for Waddle and there had even been talk of Walsh going in a double deal worth £5m.

Speaking to *The Spurs Show*, Waddle explained that he had no knowledge of any interest from Marseille. He had gone to Wimbledon to watch tennis with Paul Walsh when he got a call, via Walsh's primitive mobile telephone, from his agent, demanding that he go to White Hart Lane the following morning because an offer had been accepted for him.

As instructed, he arrived at White Hart Lane on Saturday morning with his representatives to meet with Scholar and Venables, who told him that they had reluctantly agreed to sell him. It was now up to the player whether he wanted to go.

Waddle had no desire to leave, especially after having helped persuade Lineker to join him and Gascoigne at Spurs. However, he was offered a staggering financial package and welcomed the opportunity to test himself in what was becoming the most competitive league in Europe. There was also the prospect of playing in the European Cup at a time when English clubs were still banned.

The fee of £4.25m was a British transfer record but it was of little consolation to Spurs fans, who, like Scholar, believed that they were about to see the most exciting attack in the country. Theo Delaney still remembers how he found out:

> I'd spent the week with my mates in a state of bliss, writing down what our team was going to look like and dreaming of a front three of Gascoigne, Waddle and Lineker. I was on the bus on my way to Gunnersbury Station when I spotted the *Evening Standard* headlines outside the newspaper kiosk. '*WADDLE TO MARSEILLE*' – What?? I bought the paper and realised, to my horror, that it was a done deal. It just didn't make any sense – a week ago we'd signed Lineker. It made me question just what sort of a club were we? The one that had signed England's superstar striker or the one that had just sold its best player?

The sale of Waddle was as much a surprise to the players as it was to supporters, as Vinny Samways recalls:

I was shocked when Chris left. He was so far ahead of his time as a winger playing on his unnatural side and other teams couldn't live with him. They'd often have to double up on him because they didn't want to leave him one-v-one against anyone. That created space for others. It was so sad that we were denied the chance to play alongside him, Gazza and Lineker. We'd have scored so many goals.

If there was a positive to come from the Waddle sale, it was that it seemingly balanced the books and Venables expected to be able to spend most of the money on strengthening his team. Unbeknown to him, the state of the club's accounts was perilous. The Lineker deal required a downpayment of around £600,000 to Barcelona, with the remainder due the following year. However, having initially sanctioned the deal, Bobroff told Scholar and the board that the money wasn't there, resulting in Scholar personally underwriting the deal himself.

In the hours after agreeing the Waddle deal, Scholar and Venables had discussed offering a record fee to Liverpool for John Barnes but chose against it. Bobroff expected the funds to service the overdraft and, so, Venables was left with little over a half of the Waddle fee to reinvest.

He moved quickly to bring Steve Sedgley from Coventry. Sedgley should perhaps never have needed to cost a penny, as he was one that got away from the youth team as a teenager. Born and bred in nearby Enfield, Sedgley instead joined Coventry as an apprentice and then became a professional in 1986. During his first season, he played 30 games and was the Sky Blues' unused substitute for the infamous 1987 FA Cup Final.

Sedgley, who was versatile and could operate in defence or midfield, was signed for around £1m. He was effectively a replacement for Chris Fairclough, who was sold to Leeds for £750,000. The summer continued to create a chasm between Scholar and Bobroff. Venables still wanted to buy a defender and had identified Everton's tough-tackling full-back Pat Van Den Hauwe as having the experience and qualities Spurs needed. An initial deal was agreed with Everton but Bobroff refused to release the funds. The transfer was eventually completed but not before the season started.

Amid the boardroom disagreements, there was still genuine excitement at the arrival of Lineker.

Spurs' pre-season took them to Ireland, Norway and Scotland. Lineker scored six times, linking up well with Gascoigne, but it soon became apparent that he offered different qualities than Stewart or Walsh and that there would be a period of adaptation, as Guy Butters explains:

> 'Links' was the master finisher but he only really did any running when we had the ball and he thought he could score or create a goal. We'd got used to Stewy's tireless running off the ball and Walshy offered a bit more defensive work, too. However, you couldn't take it away from Links. I marked him in training and he'd lull you into a false sense of security. One moment he's standing there doing nothing and then, in a flash, especially if Gazza was on his team, he'd be gone and his finishing was lethal.

Over the summer, the second phase of the East Stand rebuild began. Throughout 1988/89, the back of The Shelf had been closed. In March 1989, the club had unveiled images of the proposed changes that would eventually see the roof of the North Stand raised to join the top of the East and West stands. The new structure would include seating in the top, with two tiers of terracing adjoining the East Stand.

Having learned the lessons of the previous season, the whole stand was closed to fans for the opening day fixture against Luton. Consequently, a crowd of just 17,668 were there to see Lineker's debut.

The matchday programme included an exclusive interview with Lineker, who reiterated his ambition to win the league championship with Spurs. The publication also included an open letter from the Chief Superintendent of the Tottenham division of the Metropolitan Police in which he highlighted the decline in hooligan behaviour but gave a warning that any threatening behaviour or obscene or offensive language would not be tolerated. Was English football emerging out of its darkest hours of the mid-80s? UEFA was making positive noises about English clubs returning to European competition for the start of the following season.

Darryl Telles hadn't been to White Hart Lane in nearly four years but felt that the battle against hooliganism and discrimination was on the turn:

> Society was changing and attitudes towards racism and homophobia had taken a turn. Don't get me wrong, there was a long way to go, but it was around this time that the Gay Football Supporters' Network (GFSN) was formed. They were recruiting members and each week would produce a league table that showed which clubs members supported. Spurs and Arsenal were top by a considerable margin! It provided a platform for us to build networks and start to feel more comfortable going to games! The GFSN was unimaginable at the start of the 80s and it was the genesis of the Proud Lilywhites that I helped to establish and became co-chair of when it was launched in 2014.

Darryl became a season ticket holder in 1991 and continued to be a trailblazer for gay football supporters. He became co-chair of the Proud Lilywhites, founded in 2014 to advocate the rights of LGBQ fans at Spurs, and, in 2017, his book *We're Queer and We Should Be Here* was published.

All eyes were on Lineker but it was his strike partner, Stewart, who scored Spurs' first goal of the season when he powered in a header from a Gascoigne free kick in the first half. Luton equalised within seconds of the restart but it was Spurs' afternoon when Paul Allen reacted first inside the Luton six-yard box to stab Spurs back ahead and score what proved to be the decisive goal.

Despite the opening day victory, Spurs repeated their poor start from the previous season. They drew one and lost three of the next four league games – the last of which was a chastening 4-1 home defeat to newly promoted Chelsea, whose team included both Roberts and Hazard. Venables described the performance against Chelsea as 'awful'. Spurs were second from bottom and Lineker was yet to score.

According to the Monday edition of the *Daily Mirror*, Venables was under real pressure and the bookies had slashed the odds on him being sacked before the end of the season. The correlation between results and the money spent on the team was front and centre of the criticism levelled against the manager and his under-performing team.

A narrow League Cup second-round first-leg win over Southend did little to ease the nerves. Lineker made it six games without a goal, with Spurs relying on Fenwick to score the only goal of the game.

Lineker's arrival had, at this stage of the season, created more problems than it had solved. Having ended the season in good form, Walsh was either a sub or redeployed out to the left wing and the balance just wasn't right. Sedgley, Samways, Allen and Howells were in and out of the team and not once in the opening six games of the season did Venables name an unchanged XI.

Pat Van Den Hauwe completed his long-drawn-out transfer from Everton and his arrival spelt the end of Guy Butters' run in the team. Butters had played the first four games of the season but was dropped for the Chelsea game. Venables explained to the press that 'he has done remarkably well but made an error at Everton and had a couple of bad games'.

If Venables was under pressure, then so was Scholar. In *Behind Closed Doors*, he detailed a conversation initiated by Bobroff in which he recommended that Scholar resign from the company and that Bobroff run both the plc and the football club. Scholar suggests that Bobroff had already sounded out other board members in an attempt to pull off a coup that would see Scholar forced to step down.

It transpired that Scholar had more allies in the boardroom than Bobroff and the coup failed. Instead, Bobroff was asked to step aside and sell his shares, allowing Scholar to lead both boards. After several heated discussions and knowing that he didn't have sufficient support, Bobroff did agree, in principle, to sell his shares and step aside but this created a problem. Now that the club were listed on the Stock Exchange and subject to strict City rules, Scholar, by owning in excess of 30 per cent of the company, was obliged to bid for the remaining shares in the company. He didn't possess the personal wealth to do so.

As it turned out, Bobroff, having sought legal advice, reneged on his initial agreement and the plc had to sheepishly publicly reinstate Bobroff as plc chairman days after announcing that he had resigned. It was a real mess but the situation had enabled Scholar to learn more about the state of the company accounts and the mounting overdraft. Contrary to what had been reported at the summer's board meeting, the subsidiary companies were haemorrhaging money.

While the friction in the boardroom continued, matters on the pitch started to improve.

Lineker scored in his sixth game, a 2-2 draw at Norwich and that sparked a run of four successive league wins in which the striker scored six goals. That run also included the much-awaited full opening of the East Stand for a midweek north London derby in mid-October. A crowd of 33,944 attended, creating an English record gate receipt of more than £300,000, which was aided by the executive boxes where The Shelf had previously been situated.

The opening of the stand was not even the highlight of the evening, as Spurs won 2-1 with goals from Samways and Walsh. It ended a run of five successive home defeats to Arsenal and was the first real landmark victory of the Venables era. It was a personal highlight for Samways:

> I didn't score that many goals, so this was particularly memorable. We'd taken a corner, which was half cleared, and it landed kindly for me on the edge of the area. I struck it well and it went through a crowd and ended up in the net. Having grown up as a Spurs fan and from a big Spurs family, that was an incredible moment but it was a really

special night for us. It was the first really significant win in a while against any of the top teams and even sweeter that it was against Arsenal. They were league champions and an exceptional team – very well organised – and you knew if they scored first against you, they'd be very hard to beat. Terry always wanted us to attack, as that's where our strengths lay. We caught them cold that night and the two-goal lead proved decisive.

As was so familiar a story for late 80s Spurs, though, every silver lining seemed to have a cloud. The East Stand may have been opened but the total cost of the rebuild exceeded £6m, almost double the anticipated cost. The additional costs were, in part, down to the London property boom that saw costs of materials and labour rise significantly. The agreed restructure was only ever really a compromise anyway; despite the facilities provided by the executive boxes, the structure of the new roof was supported by three large concrete pillars which obstructed the views of many in the upper and lower tiers. A cantilever roof was out of the club's price range.

As autumn gave way to winter, the team began to take a more settled shape but it was at the expense of Terry Fenwick, who unfortunately broke his leg, and Guy Butters, who found himself exiled to Southend in Division Four:

I wasn't getting the same level of support and guidance as I'd received in my first season. Maybe Terry thought I was now a senior player but I still needed lots of instructions. I found myself out of the team and wasn't happy with my situation. I just wanted to play football. They'd paid a lot for Sedgley and then Van Den Hauwe, too, so I guess it was easy to leave me out but Terry never really said anything to me, which was frustrating, having made a breakthrough. We'd played Southend in the cup and I know Terry really liked their full-back, Justin Edinburgh. Terry was great mates with their manager, David Webb, and I think they did a deal that saw Justin come to Spurs on loan, with me going the other way for the rest of the season. I was just desperate to play, having got a taste for first-team football, so I went down there. It didn't bother me what division they were in.

It proved to be the end of the road at White Hart Lane for Butters. Having spent the season with Southend, he was sold at the start of the following season to Portsmouth in Division Two and would go on to have a distinguished Football League career spanning 20 seasons and more than 650 appearances for Portsmouth, Oxford, Gillingham and Brighton. He is now employed by Brighton's club foundation, which serves the local community.

Having beaten Arsenal in the league, Spurs recorded an even more impressive result in the League Cup the following midweek. They'd scraped past Southend on away goals and then, rather unfortunately, been drawn away at Manchester United in round three. Alex Ferguson was under immense pressure. United had spent big in the summer, with the purchases of Paul Ince and Neil Webb, but were languishing in the bottom half and had recently suffered a humiliating 5-1 defeat at neighbours Manchester City. Like Spurs, they had dominated the back pages for non-football reasons.

At the start of the season, it appeared that the self-made 'millionaire' Michael Knighton was about to the buy the club as part of a £20m consortium. Before the opening home game of the season, Knighton had appeared on the pitch, wearing a full replica kit and juggling a football in front of the Stretford End. He was interviewed live on *Saint & Greavsie* and tried to prove his credentials as a genuine football fan, though his over-emphasis of the word 'soccer' was a red flag.

He purported to be both a highly successful businessman and a passionate United fan. With the takeover seemingly imminent, his consortium partners withdrew and, by September, the deal was off. The impasse and uncertainty possibly contributed to Ferguson's stay of execution.

Despite their difficult situation, Manchester United remained a test for any visiting club and Spurs looked to address a run of eight games without a win at Old Trafford since the League Cup victory in 1981. It wasn't anything like the Anfield hoodoo but it was the sort of place Spurs needed to go to and win. Victories at home were one thing but Spurs hadn't recorded any sort of statement win on the road since 1987.

They travelled to Old Trafford without the injured Gascoigne. It was an opportunity to prove that they could win games without him. Venables had already proved to be tactically flexible and picked a team with a midfield five of Paul Allen, Sedgley, Howells, Samways and Nayim, leaving Lineker alone in attack.

The system worked a treat. With the extra man in midfield, Spurs kept possession of the ball and were able to cut United apart. Lineker continued his hot streak with a first-half goal that unnerved the home crowd. Minutes into the second half, Samways added a second after a delightful move down Spurs' right.

Pressing for a goal to get them back into the game, United poured forward, which only created more space on the break and Nayim rounded off the scoring with a sweetly struck volley two minutes from time.

Right at the start of the decade, Spurs had won 1-0 at Old Trafford through Hoddle's heroics and Ardiles's goal and it was the precursor to the cup successes that followed. Would this win, in the closing weeks of the 80s, have the same impact?

Having failed so miserably in the cup competitions since 1987, Spurs seemed to have a team suited to a prolonged run this time around. The fourth-round draw sent Spurs back to the north-west, where Tranmere provided a far sterner test than Manchester United had but a 2-2 draw in Birkenhead was followed up with a comfortable 4-0 win in the replay. Next up in the competition would be Nottingham Forest, with the quarter-final tie scheduled for January.

In the league, the four-game winning streak in October failed to launch an assault on the title race. Spurs travelled to Anfield knowing that an unlikely 3-0 win would put them top of the league but Liverpool were in fine form and, with machine-like efficiency, beat Spurs 1-0.

From then onwards, Spurs were dogged by their old foe, inconsistency. Throughout November and early December, they won one, drew two and lost two of their next five, which meant they dropped back into mid-table. Stewart had been brought back into the team and Venables flitted between attacking formations. While Lineker continued to score at a healthy rate, Stewart struggled, scoring just twice in a run of 11 appearances.

As the Christmas decorations started to go up, so did Spurs' form. They won three on the spin against Everton, Millwall and at Old Trafford again to provide Spurs fans with some festive cheer. At the halfway point of the season, they now sat in fifth, eight points behind leaders Liverpool.

The final game of the calendar year was an absorbing, but ultimately fruitless, home game against Nottingham Forest. Brian Clough's team were worthy opponents for the final game of the 1980s, as the two sides had met on 20 previous occasions during the decade. They were arguably the two great entertainers of the era and whether it was under Burkinshaw, Shreeve, Pleat or Venables, Spurs and Clough's Forest always played the right way.

Fixture 21 of the 80s between the two sides was possibly the most entertaining of all but the away side came out 3-2 victors. Lineker scored both Spurs goals.

A game ending 3-2 was a fitting way to conclude the 80s – it was, of course, the same scoreline as the 1981 FA Cup Final replay and, infamously, the 1987 final. In total, Spurs had been involved in 26 3-2 games during the 80s, winning 15 and losing 11. By contrast, Arsenal participated in 19 3-2 scorelines (twice against Spurs), Everton 15 and Liverpool 11. It was a sign of a consistently entertaining team but not necessarily one that was destined to win a league championship. Steve Perryman had alluded to as much earlier in the decade.

The 90s began more inauspiciously with a 0-0 draw at Coventry – another team who had left an indelible mark on Spurs in the 80s!

If the new decade was going to see a change in fortunes in the FA Cup, it would have to wait another 12 months, as

Southampton pulled off a 3-1 victory at White Hart Lane at the first hurdle. At least Spurs hadn't been humbled by a lower-division opponent this time.

League form through the early months of 1990 provided a mixed bag of results. There was a narrow 1-0 defeat at Highbury but a 4-0 thumping of Norwich, in which Lineker scored a hat-trick, and the following week, when the world's attention was drawn to the release of Nelson Mandela from prison, Spurs recorded a last-minute victory at Chelsea. Stamford Bridge had been a happy hunting ground for Spurs during the 80s. This would be the last Spurs win there for 28 years!

The League Cup had been Spurs' best route to glory and the tie with Nottingham Forest proved to be another classic. The first game at the City Ground ended in a 2-2 draw, requiring a replay at White Hart Lane just 26 days after the 3-2 defeat in the league.

Nayim, deputising for the injured Gascoigne, scored inside the first minute but Clough's team turned around the tie with three goals inside an hour. Walsh pulled one back to set up a grandstand finish but to no avail. The first 3-2 of the 90s but it had gone against Spurs.

Forest went on to lift the League Cup for a second successive season but whoever had won that quarter-final would have been favourites to win the competition, as they were the only sides left from the top half of Division One.

Games between Spurs and Forest were often the most entertaining of the season, as Vinny Samways recalls:

Matches against them were always such pure football games. Terry's philosophy was very similar to Clough's, so they were always entertaining and I loved playing in them. The City Ground was always my favourite away ground – the pitch was always perfect. I had the chance to go there a couple of years later. It didn't happen in the end but their style was the most like ours. It would have been easy to transition from our midfield to theirs.

A return to European football for English clubs was now seemingly a certainty for the 1990/91 season. The five-year exile was due to end for all English clubs, with the exception of Liverpool, who would have to serve a further 12-month ban. In a phased approach, this was likely just to include one UEFA Cup spot, in addition to a European Cup Winners' Cup place. Going into March, Spurs were sixth, 13 points behind Aston Villa, who were the only threat to Liverpool. Only five points separated Arsenal, in third, and Coventry in tenth.

March began with three back-to-back London derbies; in fact, the 89/90 season saw a record eight London clubs participate in Division One – Arsenal, Charlton, Chelsea, Crystal Palace, Millwall, QPR, Spurs and Wimbledon – meaning nearly half the division was based in the capital. The north London derby was always the biggest game in Spurs' league campaign and, while there were localised rivalries across town, it always seemed that beating Spurs generated a little extra incentive.

That run of three games in March saw defeats against Crystal Palace and QPR, either side of a 3-0 victory over Charlton. The game against Palace was memorable for the Polston family when Andy made his debut as a second-half substitute, lining up alongside his older brother, John. It was the first time two siblings had appeared in the same Spurs team since 1910 when the three Steel brothers had lined up in lilywhite.

Andy became the 38th player (out of a total of 83) to appear in the first team since 1980 who had graduated through the youth system.

One of those graduates was Chris Hughton, who made his 406th and what turned out to be his final appearance for the club at QPR. He was the last survivor of the 1981 FA Cup-winning team and was the only player to have appeared in the first team in each calendar year of the 80s. Still only 31, Hughton had been affected by a number of injuries and found himself in a constant battle for places among a competitive revolving stable of full-backs.

He enjoyed a further four years as a player with West Ham and Brentford but it was no surprise to anyone who knew him that he soon went into coaching, returning in the mid-90s to Spurs, where he progressed up to the first team and supported a number of different managers before embarking on a managerial career of his own with Newcastle, Brighton and the Republic of Ireland national team among others.

Of Spurs' remaining league games, the one at home to Liverpool was the most high-profile and it was selected for live midweek coverage. Liverpool trailed Villa by three points but had two games in hand. They were on a 20-game unbeaten streak and had clicked into invincible mode in pursuit of another league championship.

Having beaten Arsenal and Manchester United earlier in the season, Kenny Dalglish's team remained the one big scalp that Spurs needed to prove to themselves that they could beat anyone. While results had been mixed, Venables was starting to gel a team that began to take on a familiar look. Sedgley was playing alongside Mabbutt in central defence and Howells and Paul Allen provided the balance for Gascoigne to link up with Lineker.

It was a night where Spurs played with the sort of pragmatism that was so often missing when it really mattered. In the first half, their performance was excellent for its organisation and determination rather than any prolonged spell of flair or beauty but, against such illustrious opposition, this was acceptable.

With eight minutes remaining, Spurs' forgotten man, Stewart, stole the headlines by converting Gascoigne's cross with a powerful header that arrowed into the bottom corner for what proved to be the winner.

The goal marked a turning point for both Stewart and Spurs, who went on to win the next five games in a row. Stewart scored in four successive games and finally appeared to be fulfilling his potential.

Stewart was scoring goals but there was no doubt that Gascoigne was the heartbeat of the team and he enjoyed a particularly fine run of form that saw him finally establish himself in Bobby Robson's England plans in the months leading up to the 1990 World Cup.

The England manager had been present at White Hart Lane to see Gascoigne put in a virtuoso performance against Manchester United in which he was directly up against England captain Bryan Robson. Gascoigne scored and assisted Lineker for a 2-1 win. That performance earned him a rare start for the midweek friendly international with Czechoslovakia at Wembley – the last game before Bobby Robson named his final tournament squad.

Gascoigne took his club form to the national team and dominated the game with a goal and two assists. As he scored what proved to be the clincher in a 4-2 win, the cameras panned to Bobby Robson, whose expression told of his delight at Gascoigne's display. His inclusion was now a certainty. Eventually, Robson decided to build a midfield around Gascoigne's mercurial talent, something he had failed to do with Hoddle. Spurs fans could feel vindicated in their appreciation of exciting and technically gifted central midfielders, while other clubs' fans preferred grit and determination. It was a constant thread throughout the 80s.

Spurs' excellent form came to an end at Wimbledon on 28 April. John Fashanu scored the only goal of the game but Spurs were still in a head-to-head battle with Arsenal to finish third. Since that fateful League Cup semi-final trilogy of 1987, it appeared that Arsenal were racing ahead of Spurs, having won a League Cup and finished well above Spurs in each of the past two seasons, lifting the championship trophy in 1989.

They had suffered a dip in 89/90 and fell well short of defending their title. Arsenal had uncharacteristically dropped points at home to Southampton in midweek but were still in the driving seat ahead of the final round of league games. They needed to win at Norwich to guarantee third place ahead of Spurs, who faced Southampton at White Hart Lane.

UEFA Cup qualification was not to extend beyond second place, which Aston Villa had long since secured, so there was no tangible reward beyond local bragging rights. Spurs had beaten Arsenal, Manchester United and now Liverpool, so finishing ahead of their north London rivals would be another statement of intent.

In a time before the internet and social media, fans at White Hart Lane had to rely on handheld transistor radios to learn what was happening at Carrow Road but that would only be relevant if Spurs could win themselves. They did, 2-1, with first-half goals from Allen and Stewart, providing a neat symmetry from the opening day of the season when Spurs beat Luton by the same score and with the same scorers.

Arsenal came from behind twice but couldn't score a winner, meaning Spurs were top dogs in north London for the first time in three years.

'Spooky' remembers the joy of becoming north London's 'finest':

> The way the 1987 season ended, losing Richard Gough after a single season, Hoddle leaving, Pleat gone. The decade ended unlike how it started and blossomed. A new era was often feeling like a new error. There would be more turmoil in the boardroom and off it to come but, now and again, Spurs would puncture the narrative with something tangible, something grand like this olde team (and fans) deserve. We finished third in 1990, above them lot down the road – all on the final day of the season. It felt like a bit of payback for that League Cup semi-final(s) debacle. Chest finally puffed out and that summer Gascoigne (who I idolised) along with Lineker would spark at the World Cup in the summer, one that would also ruin my emotions. Club or country, I can't escape heartbreak.

Just over 31,000 fans were in the ground to bid farewell to the team, unaware that Gascoigne would return in August as a national hero after his exploits in the summer's World Cup.

Beyond the assists, goals and points Gascoigne was winning for Spurs, it was the attention that he brought to the club that would leave an even more indelible mark. Just as Hoddle and Ardiles had attracted fans to the club a decade earlier,

Gascoigne, and Lineker, turned many football fans into lifelong Spurs supporters. One of those young, impressionable fans in 1990 was Chris Cowlin, now a prominent and well-known vlogger and podcaster in the Spurs community:

> My love for Tottenham Hotspur all started by watching Paul Gascoigne and Gary Lineker. As a young boy in the late 1980s, all my classmates just wanted to copy everything Gazza did. The guy was just incredible, he was an entertainer. My interest in Spurs then grew very strong during the 1990 World Cup because of this tremendous duo.
>
> Everyone was absolutely delighted in 1988 when he signed from Newcastle for a British record fee of over £2m, a lot of money back then, but this was a top, top talent, someone who could create and score goals, someone who could run with confidence and had so much ability, someone who could just turn a game, provide that killer pass, a quality delivery and someone who could put one in the top corner. He wasn't only creative but also very hard-working.
>
> Gazza was one of the most entertaining players I've ever seen – just sheer brilliance. He was a midfielder that could do everything, he was truly gifted. His link-up play with Lineker was outstanding, which, of course, worked well for Tottenham and for England.

How optimistic you were depended on whether you saw the glass being half full or half empty. Seen through the prism of anyone who'd lived through the thrilling period at the start of the decade, a third-place finish without the sniff of a Wembley visit was underwhelming. For younger fans and particularly those who would only have the traumatic 90s as a reference point, the third place of 1990 felt like something of an achievement. Not until 2016 did Spurs match that third-place finish.

Vinny Samways was confident that he was part of a team that was going places:

To finish third was an achievement. We'd finished above Arsenal and beaten them, Liverpool and Manchester United during the season. We had an excellent squad which included Gazza, who was by now a world-class talent, as he'd prove at the World Cup that summer. We had a brilliant manager and I really felt that we were going to kick on. I don't think any of us had any awareness whatsoever about what was happening between the owners and the club's financial position. It was never discussed but we were incredibly positive about the future.

The clouds continued to circle around the boardroom. Bobroff, according to Scholar, invited him to become chairman of both the club and the plc around the same time that the overdraft facility was initially raised from £5.8m to £6.5m. However, this was just to service other loans. Scholar and another director, Frank Sinclair, had to make personal payments of £350,000 each. All of these transactions had to be made public, owing to the plc status.

Scholar was actively seeking external investment and referenced a meeting with an Indonesian-based company which had expressed an interest in buying a stake in an English football club. It turned out to be a wild goose chase and the investment never materialised. The pending deadline on the horizon was the final payment to Barcelona due on 1 August for Lineker and Nayim. It wasn't clear where that income was going to come from and the prospect of having to sell the club's major assets – namely Gascoigne and Lineker – became an increasingly likely solution until Scholar took a fateful phone call from Derby owner and media magnate Robert Maxwell. That call would prove to be the beginning of the end for Scholar and his love affair with Spurs.

Before the summer's World Cup in Italy, which would go down as one of the most iconic, largely due to England's journey to the semi-final, the final action of the domestic season saw Spurs' youth team win their first FA Youth Cup since 1974. It was a double of sorts, as they'd also won a fifth successive South

East Counties title, but the junior version of the FA Cup was the yardstick that all youth teams' success was measured against.

Spurs beat their Middlesbrough counterparts over two legs, winning 2-1 at Ayresome Park with goals from Anthony Potts and Scott Houghton. Back at White Hart Lane, Ollie Morah scored in a 1-1 draw, meaning Spurs won 3-2 on aggregate.

The youth department at the club had been its most consistently high-performing department over the decade and credit must go, among others, to the likes of Keith Blunt, Keith Waldon, Peter Shreeve, John Pratt and head scout John Moncur, who did so much to produce a conveyor belt of talent that would serve the first team so well. Even those players who couldn't make a significant impact were often sold on, generating funds back into the club. Of that 1990 FA Youth Cup-winning team, only Ian Walker would enjoy a sustained career in the first team. However, from the year groups below them, Sol Campbell and Stephen Carr both captained the club and became full internationals.

Luck continues to play such a huge part in the making or breaking of a young player's career. Hughton, Samways, Howells and Falco all got their opportunities and served the club with distinction, winning trophies. But for every one of those, there is an Anthony Potts, regarded as one of the youth team's hottest prospects and who scored in that FA Youth Cup Final but suffered a series of horrific injuries, as detailed in his excellent book, *Losing My Spurs*, that cost him the brilliant career he seemed destined to achieve.

The 1990 World Cup finals played a considerable role in the revolution that engulfed English football in the decade that followed and Gascoigne's heroics and tears changed the trajectory of his career and life beyond that summer in Italy.

With the concept of the Premier League on the horizon, Spurs' immediate future, both on and off the pitch, was uncertain but you'll have to read my first book, *Is Gascoigne Going To Have a Crack?*, to learn what happened next!

League position	Third
Average home league attendance	26,465
Most appearances	Lineker (45)
Top goalscorer	Lineker (26)
League winners	Liverpool
FA Cup winners	Manchester United
League Cup winners	Nottingham Forest

HOT SHOT TOTTENHAM POSTSCRIPT (FEBRUARY 2025)

WHEN I wrote my first book, *Is Gascoigne Going To Have a Crack?*, I did so from a position of knowledge, having lived through the whole of the 90s avidly following Spurs. I've always been very anxious about writing about the 80s, as it's before my time (as a fan) and not my era. I hope that what you have read does justice to what must have been a truly remarkable decade in which to follow Spurs and *consume* football.

I was always aware of the top-level events that shaped the decade: the FA Cup wins, 'it's still Ricky Villa', Tony Parks's heroics, the 'fantastic disappointment' of the 86/87 season and then the Gascoigne and Waddle/Lineker partnerships. But writing this book allowed me to piece together a transformative decade and answer several questions that I'd had in the back of my mind, like why did such a great team never go on to capture the ultimate prize of a league championship? How should history remember Irving Scholar? And how truly horrifying was it to come to matches amid hooliganism? More than anything, I wanted to understand why the following decade was such a difficult period for the club.

In seeking to answer why the league championship never arrived in N17, there are some obvious conclusions: the might and brilliance of the Merseyside pair, successive managers' prioritisation of style over substance ... and a bit of bad luck along the way. But I'd now frame that question differently. Rather than attempt to work out what went wrong, it feels more appropriate to highlight what went so right.

After all, Spurs were a team in the wilderness as the 70s progressed and a club stuck in the past. As I worked my way through books, podcasts and footage of the 80/81 season and effectively lived through the emotions, I got goosebumps and cheered out loud when Crooks scored the equaliser in the replay. I can't imagine what it must have been like to be there for that and Ricky Villa's subsequent winner.

Irving Scholar is named in this book more than any other individual bar Glenn Hoddle. His book, *Behind Closed Doors*, was an incredibly insightful and helpful resource when putting this book together. He wrote this – with the help of esteemed sports writer Mihir Bose – in 1992, just 12 months after he'd left the club. His role as majority shareholder and chairman defined the 80s and set the scene for what the club became in the 90s. He (and Bobroff) sold the controlling stake to Alan Sugar and Terry Venables and Scholar was removed from the board in 1991. After a very brief return to football as a director at Nottingham Forest in the late 90s, Scholar has disappeared from the public eye, residing permanently in Monaco.

I spoke with Mihir about his relationship with Scholar and how he thinks he should be remembered. He told me:

Irving was undeniably a visionary and innovator. He had great dreams and genuinely wanted to see Spurs become the greatest team in the country again. He recognised the sorry state that English football found itself in and laid out a vision for the way it could improve. He had a difficult hand to play – stadiums were decrepit and many supporters had been turned off because of the facilities and the hooliganism that was rife.

Football generated minimal commercial revenue, so he had his hands tied behind his back and English football was falling further and further behind the Italian, German and French leagues. Irving was a pioneer who sought to address these challenges and provided many solutions which became the genesis of the inception of the Premier League. He knew football's worth and worked tirelessly to ensure that television understood the potential that the game provided.

On a club level, he successfully increased revenue. Merchandise income rose from £350,000 to £2.5m per year in 1991. He formed a great partnership with Edward Freedman, who ran the club's merchandising operations. The huge increase in club-commissioned products, including the VHS and clothing ranges, were way ahead of their time in the 80s.

I believe his legacy would have been very different had the great team of 84/85 gone on to win the league, as they should have done. I know for a fact that Peter Shreeve had wanted to bring Gary Lineker in towards the end of that season and his arrival might have made all the difference. Alas, Irving refused to meet their [Leicester City's] asking price.

He undoubtedly made mistakes. He instantly regretted going into partnership with Bobroff and, having made the beeline for Venables in 1987, never formed the strong working relationship that was required. In many ways, he was too far ahead of his time but just about everything about the way we consume football today can be dated back to Irving. The commercial opportunities, the global reach of English football and the far more family-friendly environment of a matchday experience are all his legacies.

I spent a lot of time writing *Behind Closed Doors* with Irving and I consider him a friend. I am sorry for the way that his time at the club ended.

In many ways Scholar, Bobroff and the plc symbolised the economic climate of the time and with that came a carefree and cavalier approach. Scholar, always more concerned with the fortunes of the football club, opened Pandora's box and set in motion, or at least accelerated, the revolution that came in the 90s. To watch Spurs in the 2020s involves games being scheduled at the behest of TV companies' demands. You can become fully immersed in the club through social media before, during and after a game. The matches are played by squads made up, in some cases entirely, by foreign players coached by managers from all four corners of the globe. The disparity between the top clubs and the also-rans is monumental.

The Premier League is one of the UK's greatest exports of the 21st century. All-new stadia provide extensive facilities for corporate guests and clubs seek revenue sources from a variety of commercial partnerships and opportunities. There is no better example than Tottenham Hotspur Stadium, opened in 2019. Whether you think these developments are for good or bad, the genesis will lead you back to Irving Scholar. Perhaps this revolution was always destined to happen and maybe we should be proud that our club were the pioneers? Better to be in the tent peeing out rather than … you get the point.

Scholar also hammered home the point that there was no substitute to actually being at a game. It is a mantra I live by, much to the despair of my wife, Ellie, but the comforts of Tottenham Hotspur Stadium I enjoy are completely different to the experiences I remember of White Hart Lane in the 90s and 2000s and of those of the 80s, as described by contributors to this book.

For all the affection so many people had for The Shelf, or even the other three sides of the old White Hart Lane, it was, at best, a safety hazard and, at worst, a death trap … and that's before you consider the hooliganism that occurred both inside and outside the stadium and on the way to and from games. Football, like society, was not as culturally aware and discrimination on the grounds of gender, colour and sexuality was rife. However, what is equally clear is the sense of community and belonging – among supporters but also a connection between fans, players and the club.

Gradually, the authorities and the clubs, with the support of fantastic organisations like Kick it Out and Proud Lilywhites, have endeavoured to make matchdays more accessible for everyone, though there is still work to do. The 70s and 80s were less progressive times. I shudder to think how many generations of would-be fans were turned off and made to feel unwelcome.

Apart from those prominent issues, I have uncovered some incredible stories about some of the players, matches and events I wasn't previously aware of. I'm sure you will have drawn comparisons between the way the game was played, officiated, consumed and governed then and now.

One unexpected gem that I have come to be incredibly proud of was the club's youth set-up (the term 'academy' didn't come into use until the latter part of the 90s). As a young kid, I often went with Dad when he refereed the Spurs youth team at Mill Hill on Sunday mornings; it really hit me as I researched and wrote this book the importance of the youth set-up. It was the one constant source of success and competence throughout the 80s. To speak with Guy Butters, Terry Gibson, Tony Parks and Vinny Samways gave me a sense of pride in the way Spurs developed footballers and human beings.

In my lifetime, I've enjoyed some magic moments amid the mediocrity of the 90s and early 2000s and was at Wembley for our cup wins in 91, 99 and 2008 and enjoyed the run to the Champions League Final in 2019 but there's just something about the early 80s team that leaves a mark on me, despite never seeing them play.

Thank you to everybody who helped bring this project to life. Firstly, to Paul and Jane Camillin and everyone at Pitch Publishing.

Speaking with all of the ex-players was a surreal experience. I have tried explaining to my son, Albie, the gravitas of speaking with Steve Perryman and I thoroughly enjoyed my conversations with him, Clive Allen, Tony Parks, Terry Gibson, Guy Butters and Vinny Samways.

Adam Powley, Alan Fisher, Chris Cowlin, Daniel Wynne, Danny Jarvis, Darryl Telles, David Harris, Jason McGovern, Jill Lewis, Julie Welch, Marlene Peirce, Mihir Bose, Mike Leigh, Paul Malshinger, Simon Shroot, 'Spooky', Steffan Chirazi, Stephen Peace, Theo Delaney, Tim Vickery and Willie Morgan were all very generous with their time and their memories and personal recollections add incredible context and colour.

Thanks also to Richard Thomas for proof-reading and his constructive feedback and to Daniel Wynne, Jill Lewis and Roy Beck for fact and sense checking.

Finally, thanks to my dad, Peter, who took me to White Hart Lane for the first time in May 1988 when he refereed a behind-closed-doors THFC staff game on the pitch. This was the genesis of my infatuation that has existed ever since.

BIBLIOGRAPHY

A People's History of Tottenham Hotspur Football Club – Alan Fisher and Martin Cloake

Behind Closed Doors – Irving Scholar (and Mihir Bose)

Born to Manage – Terry Venables

Fantastic Disappointment – Stephen Peace

Forever A Spur – Steve Perryman

Glory, Glory Gone – Samuel Rooke

Go To War – Football On the Brink in the '80s – Jon Spurling

Hell Razor – Neil Ruddock

My Dream – Ossie Ardiles

One More Goal – David Pleat

Playmaker – Glenn Hoddle

Spurs – A Complete Record 1882 – 1991 – Bob Goodwin

The Boys from White Hart Lane – Adam Powley and Martin Cloake

The Limping Physio – John Sheridan

Tottenham Hotspur Football Club. The Official Biography – Julie Welch

We're queer and we should be here: The perils and pleasures of being a gay football fan – Darryl Telles

PODCASTS:

The Spurs Show – David Pleat Special (Oct 2023)
The Spurs Show – When Steve went up to lift the FA Cup (May 2021)
The Spurs Show – Gary Mabbutt Special (April 2020)
The Spurs Show – In Conversation with Don McAllister (March 2020)
The Spurs Show – John Pratt Special – Feb 2020
The Spurs Show – Crooks and Archibald – Jan 2020
The Spurs Show – Kneeling at the feet of Ghod – Jan 2018
The Spurs show – Graham Roberts – Jan/Feb 2018
The Spurs Show – Paul Miller – March 2018
The Spurs Show – Micky Hazard – Sept 2018
The Spurs Show – Chris Waddle – Dec 2018
The Spurs Show – Clive and Paul Allen – Dec 2023
The Brazilian Shirt Name – Tottenham v Anderlecht – July 2023
OFF THE SHELF – ep 06 Gary Mabbutt
OFF THE SHELF – ep 21 Micky Hazard

WEBSITES:

enfa.co.uk
britishnewspaperarchive.co.uk
Superhotspur.com
thfcdb.com

SEASON RESULTS

1979/80

18 Aug	Div 1	Middlesbrough H	1-3	Hoddle
22 Aug	Div 1	Norwich A	0-4	
25 Aug	Div 1	Stoke A	1-3	Perryman
29 Aug	FL Cup 2	Manchester U H	2-1	Pratt, Hoddle
1 Sept	Div 1	Man City H	2-1	Jones, Hoddle
5 Sept	FL Cup 2	Manchester U A	1-3	Armstrong
8 Sept	Div 1	Brighton H	2-1	Armstrong, Hoddle
15 Sept	Div 1	Southampton A	2-5	Jones, Hoddle
22 Sept	Div 1	West Brom H	1-1	Hoddle
29 Sept	Div 1	Coventry A	1-1	Jones
6 Oct	Div 1	Crystal Palace A	1-1	Villa
10 Oct	Div 1	Norwich H	3-2	Hoddle 2, Villa
13 Oct	Div 1	Derby H	1-0	Armstrong
20 Oct	Div 1	Leeds A	2-1	Jones, Armstrong
27 Oct	Div 1	Nottingham F H	1-0	Hoddle
3 Nov	Div 1	Middlesbrough A	0-0	
10 Nov	Div 1	Bolton H	2-0	Yorath, Hoddle
17 Nov	Div 1	Liverpool A	1-2	Jones
24 Nov	Div 1	Everton A	1-1	Jones
1 Dec	Div 1	Manchester U H	1-2	Hoddle
8 Dec	Div 1	Bristol C A	3-1	Miller. Hoddle 2
15 Dec	Div 1	Aston Villa H	1-2	Ardiles
21 Dec	Div 1	Ipswich A	1-3	McAllister
26 Dec	Div 1	Arsenal A	0-1	
29 Dec	Div 1	Stoke H	1-0	Pratt
5 Jan	FA Cup 3	Manchester U H	1-1	Ardiles
9 Jan	FA Cup 3R	Manchester U A	1-0	Ardiles
12 Jan	Div 1	Man City A	1-1	Hoddle

19 Jan	Div 1	Brighton A	2-0	Hughton, Villa
26 Jan	FA Cup 4	Swindon A	0-0	
30 Jan	FA Cup 4R	Swindon H	2-1	Armstrong 2
2 Feb	Div 1	Southampton H	0-0	
9 Feb	Div 1	West Brom A	1-2	Hoddle
16 Feb	FA Cup 5	Birmingham H	3-1	Armstrong, Hoddle 2
23 Feb	Div 1	Derby A	1-2	Galvin
27 Feb	Div 1	Coventry H	4-3	Hoddle 3, Falco
1 Mar	Div 1	Leeds H	2-1	Hoddle, Falco
8 Mar	FA Cup QF	Liverpool H	0-1	
11 Mar	Div 1	Nottingham F A	0-4	
15 Mar	Div 1	Crystal Palace H	0-0	
22 Mar	Div 1	Bolton A	1-2	Jones
29 Mar	Div 1	Liverpool H	2-0	Pratt, Hoddle
2 Apr	Div 1	Ipswich H	0-2	
5 Apr	Div 1	Wolves A	2-1	Jones, Galvin
7 Apr	Div 1	Arsenal H	1-2	Jones
12 Apr	Div 1	Manchester U A	1-4	Ardiles
19 Apr	Div 1	Everton H	3-0	Miller, Ardiles, Galvin
23 Apr	Div 1	Wolves H	2-2	Armstrong, Galvin
26 Apr	Div 1	Aston Villa A	0-1	
3 May	Div 1	Bristol C H	0-0	

80/81

16 Aug	Div 1	Nottingham F H	2-0	Hoddle, Crooks
19 Aug	Div 1	Crystal Palace A	4-3	Crooks 2, Hoddle, Archibald
23 Aug	Div 1	Brighton H	2-2	Crooks, Hoddle
27 Aug	FL2 Cup 2	Orient A	1-0	Lacy
30 Aug	Div 1	Arsenal A	0-2	
3 Sept	FL Cup 2	Orient H	3-1	Archibald 2, Crooks
6 Sept	Div 1	Manchester U H	0-0	
13 Sept	Div 1	Leeds A	0-0	
20 Sept	Div 1	Sunderland H	0-0	
24 Sept	FL Cup 3	Crystal Palace H	0-0	
27 Sept	Div 1	Leicester A	1-2	Villa
30 Sept	FL Cup 3R	Crystal Palace A	3-1	Hoddle, Crooks, Villa

4 Oct	Div 1	Stoke A	3-2	Taylor, Archibald, Hughton
11 Oct	Div 1	Middlesbrough H	3-2	Villa, Crooks, Archibald
18 Oct	Div 1	Aston Villa A	0-3	
22 Oct	Div 1	Man City A	1-3	Hoddle
25 Oct	Div 1	Coventry H	4-1	Archibald 2, Hoddle 2
1 Nov	Div 1	Everton A	2-2	Archibald 2
4 Nov	FL Cup 4	Arsenal H	1-0	Ardiles
8 Nov	Div 1	Wolves H	2-2	Hoddle, Crooks
12 Nov	Div 1	Crystal Palace H	4-2	Crooks 3, Archibald
15 Nov	Div 1	Nottingham F A	3-0	Archibald 2, Ardiles
22 Nov	Div 1	Birmingham A	1-2	Ardiles
29 Nov	Div 1	West Brom H	2-3	Lacy, Perryman
2 Dec	FL Cup 5	West Ham A	0-1	
6 Dec	Div 1	Liverpool A	1-2	Archibald
13 Dec	Div 1	Man City H	2-1	Archibald, Hoddle
17 Dec	Div 1	Ipswich H	5-3	Crooks, Hoddle, Perryman, Archibald, Ardiles
20 Dec	Div 1	Middlesbrough A	1-4	Lacy
26 Dec	Div 1	Southampton H	4-4	Archibald, Brooke 2, Crooks
27 Dec	Div 1	Norwich A	2-2	Archibald, Hoddle
3 Jan	FA Cup 3	QPR A	0-0	
7 Jan	FA Cup 3R	QPR H	3-1	Crooks, Galvin, Hoddle
10 Jan	Div 1	Birmingham H	1-0	Crooks
17 Jan	Div 1	Arsenal H	2-0	Archibald 2
24 Jan	FA Cup 4	Hull H	2-0	Archibald, Brooke
31 Jan	Div 1	Brighton A	2-0	Ardiles, Crooks
7 Feb	Div 1	Leeds H	1-1	Archibald
14 Feb	FA Cup 5	Coventry H	3-1	Ardiles, Archibald, Hughton
17 Feb	Div 1	Manchester U A	0-0	
21 Feb	Div 1	Leicester H	1-2	Archibald
28 Feb	Div 1	Sunderland A	1-1	Crooks
7 Mar	FA Cup QF	Exeter H	2-0	Miller, Roberts
11 Mar	Div 1	Stoke H	2-2	Ardiles, Brooke
14 Mar	Div 1	Ipswich A	0-3	
21 Mar	Div 1	Aston Villa H	2-0	Archibald, Crooks
28 Mar	Div 1	Coventry A	1-0	O.G.
4 Apr	Div 1	Everton H	2-2	Galvin, Crooks
11 Apr	FA Cup SF	Wolves	2-2	Archibald, Hoddle

15 Apr	FA Cup SFR	Wolves	3-0	Crooks 2, Villa
18 Apr	Div 1	Norwich H	2-3	Miller, Hoddle
20 Apr	Div 1	Southampton A	1-1	Miller
25 Apr	Div 1	Liverpool H	1-1	Hoddle
30 Apr	Div 1	Wolves A	0-1	
2 May	Div 1	West Brom A	2-4	Smith, Falco
9 May	FA Cup F	Man City	1-1	O.G.
14 May	FA Cup F R	Man City	3-2	Villa 2, Crooks

81/82

22 Aug	Charity Shield	Aston Villa	2-2	Falco 2
29 Aug	Div 1	Middlesbrough A	3-1	Villa, Hoddle, Falco
2 Sept	Div 1	West Ham H	0-4	
5 Sept	Div 1	Aston Villa H	1-3	Villa
12 Sept	Div 1	Wolves A	1-0	Galvin
16 Sept	ECWC 1	Ajax A	3-1	Falco 2, Villa
19 Sept	Div 1	Everton H	3-0	Roberts, Hughton, Hoddle
22 Sept	Div 1	Swansea A	1-2	Hoddle
26 Sept	Div 1	Man City A	1-0	Falco
29 Sept	ECWC 1	Ajax H	3-0	Galvin, Falco, Ardiles
3 Oct	Div 1	Nottingham F H	3-0	Falco 2, Hazard
7 Oct	FL Cup 2	Manchester U H	1-0	Archibald
10 Oct	Div 1	Stoke H	2-0	Ardiles, Crooks
17 Oct	Div 1	Sunderland A	2-0	Archibald, Hazard
21 Oct	ECWC 2	Dundalk A	1-1	Crooks
24 Oct	Div 1	Brighton H	0-1	
28 Oct	FL Cup 2	Manchester U A	1-0	Hazard
31 Oct	Div 1	Southampton A	2-1	Roberts, Corbett
4 Nov	ECWC 2	Dundalk H	1-0	Crooks
7 Nov	Div 1	West Brom H	1-2	Crooks
11 Nov	FL Cup 3	Wrexham H	2-0	Hughton, Hoddle
21 Nov	Div 1	Manchester U H	3-1	Roberts, Hazard, Archibald
28 Nov	Div 1	Notts County A	2-2	Crooks 2
2 Dec	FL Cup 4	Fulham H	1-0	Hazard
5 Dec	Div 1	Coventry H	1-2	Hazard
12 Dec	Div 1	Leeds A	0-0	

2 Jan	FA Cup 3	Arsenal H	1-0	Crooks
18 Jan	FL Cup 5	Nottingham F H	1-0	Ardiles
23 Jan	FA Cup 4	Leeds H	1-0	Crooks
27 Jan	Div 1	Middlesbrough H	1-0	Crooks
30 Jan	Div 1	Everton A	1-1	Villa
3 Feb	FL Cup SF	West Brom A	0-0	
6 Feb	Div 1	Wolves H	6-1	Hoddle, Villa 3, Crooks, Falco
10 Feb	FL Cup SF	West Brom H	1-0	Hazard
13 Feb	FA Cup 5	Aston Villa H	1-0	Falco
17 Feb	Div 1	Aston Villa A	1-1	Crooks
20 Feb	Div 1	Man City H	2-0	Hoddle 2
27 Feb	Div 1	Stoke A	2-0	Crooks 2
3 Mar	ECWC QF	E Frankfurt H	2-0	Miller, Hazard
6 Mar	FA Cup QF	Chelsea A	3-2	Archibald, Hoddle, Hazard
9 Mar	Div 1	Brighton A	3-1	Ardiles, Crooks, Archibald
13 Mar	FL Cup Final	Liverpool	1-3	Archibald
17 Mar	ECWC QF	E Frankfurt A	1-2	Hoddle
20 Mar	Div 1	Southampton H	3-2	Roberts
23 Mar	Div 1	Birmingham A	0-0	
27 Mar	Div 1	West Brom A	0-1	
29 Mar	Div 1	Arsenal H	2-2	Archibald, Hughton
3 Apr	FA Cup SF	Leicester	2-0	Crooks, O.G.
7 Apr	ECWC SF	Barcelona H	1-1	Roberts
10 Apr	Div 1	Ipswich H	1-0	Hoddle
12 Apr	Div 1	Arsenal A	3-1	Hazard, Crooks 2
14 Apr	Div 1	Sunderland H	2-2	Galvin, Hoddle
17 Apr	Div 1	Manchester U A	0-2	
21 Apr	ECWC SF	Barcelona A	0-1	
24 Apr	Div 1	Notts County H	3-1	Galvin, Villa, Archibald
28 Apr	Div 1	Birmingham H	1-1	Villa
1 May	Div 1	Coventry A	0-0	
3 May	Div 1	Liverpool H	2-2	Perryman, Archibald
5 May	Div 1	Swansea H	2-1	Brooke 2
8 May	Div 1	Leeds H	2-1	Brooke, O.G.
10 May	Div 1	West Ham A	2-2	Hoddle, Brooke
12 May	Div 1	Nottingham F A	0-2	
15 May	Div 1	Liverpool A	1-3	Hoddle

17 May	Div 1	Ipswich A	1-2	Crooks
22 May	FA Cup F	QPR	1-1	Hoddle
27 May	FA Cup F R	QPR	1-0	Hoddle

82/83

21 Aug	Charity Shield	Liverpool	0-1	
28 Aug	Div 1	Luton H	2-2	Mabbutt, Hazard
31 Aug	Div 1	Ipswich A	2-1	Archibald, Crooks
4 Sept	Div 1	Everton A	1-3	Archibald
8 Sept	Div 1	Southampton H	6-0	Galvin 2, Villa, Perryman, Crooks, Brooke
11 Sept	Div 1	Man City H	1-2	Mabbutt
15 Sept	ECWC 1	Coleraine A	3-0	Archibald, Crooks 2
18 Sept	Div 1	Sunderland A	1-0	Brooke
25 Sept	Div 1	Nottingham F H	4-1	Crooks 2, Mabbutt 2
28 Sept	ECWC 1	Coleraine H	4-0	Crooks, Mabbutt, Brooke, Gibson
2 Oct	Div 1	Swansea A	0-2	
6 Oct	FL Cup 2	Brighton H	1-1	Brooke
9 Oct	Div 1	Coventry H	4-0	Crooks, Brooke 3
16 Oct	Div 1	Norwich A	0-0	
20 Oct	ECWC 2	Bayern Munich H	1-1	Archibald
23 Oct	Div 1	Notts County H	4-2	Mabbutt, Crooks 2, Brooke
26 Oct	FL Cup 2	Brighton A	1-0	Crooks
30 Oct	Div 1	Aston Villa A	0-4	
3 Nov	ECWC 2	Bayern Munich A	1-4	Hughton
6 Nov	Div 1	Watford H	0-1	
9 Nov	FL Cup 3	Gillingham A	4-2	Archibald 2, Crooks 2
13 Nov	Div 1	Manchester U A	0-1	
20 Nov	Div 1	West Ham H	2-1	Archibald 2
27 Nov	Div 1	Liverpool A	0-3	
1 Dec	FL Cup 4	Luton H	1-0	Villa
4 Dec	Div 1	West Brom H	1-1	O.G.
11 Dec	Div 1	Stoke A	0-2	
18 Dec	Div 1	Birmingham H	2-1	Mabbutt 2
27 Dec	Div 1	Arsenal A	0-2	
28 Dec	Div 1	Brighton H	2-0	Villa, Hughton

1 Jan	Div 1	West Ham A	0-3	
3 Jan	Div 1	Everton H	2-1	Gibson 2
8 Jan	FA Cup 3	Southampton H	1-0	Hazard
15 Jan	Div 1	Luton A	1-1	Hoddle
19 Jan	FL Cup 5	Burnley H	1-4	Gibson
22 Jan	Div 1	Sunderland H	1-1	Gibson
29 Jan	FA Cup 4	West Brom H	2-1	Gibson, Crooks
5 Feb	Div 1	Man City A	2-2	Gibson, Brooke
12 Feb	Div 1	Swansea H	1-0	Crooks
19 Feb	FA Cup 5	Everton A	0-2	
26 Feb	Div 1	Norwich H	0-0	
5 Mar	Div 1	Notts County A	0-3	
12 Mar	Div 1	Coventry A	1-1	Miller
19 Mar	Div 1	Watford A	1-0	Falco
23 Mar	Div 1	Aston Villa H	2-0	Falco 2
2 Apr	Div 1	Brighton A	1-2	Roberts
4 Apr	Div 1	Arsenal H	5-0	Hughton 2, Falco 2, Brazil
9 Apr	Div 1	Nottingham F A	2-2	Brazil, Mabbutt
16 Apr	Div 1	Ipswich H	3-1	Brazil 2, Mabbutt
23 Apr	Div 1	West Brom A	1-0	Archibald
30 Apr	Div 1	Liverpool H	2-0	Archibald 2
3 May	Div 1	Southampton A	2-1	Brazil, Mabbutt
7 May	Div 1	Birmingham A	0-2	
11 May	Div 1	Manchester U H	2-0	Roberts, Archibald
14 May	Div 1	Stoke H	4-1	Brazil, Archibald 3

83/84

27 Aug	Div 1	Ipswich A	1-3	Archibald
29 Aug	Div 1	Coventry H	1-1	Hoddle
3 Sept	Div 1	West Ham H	0-2	
7 Sept	Div 1	West Brom A	1-1	Roberts
10 Sept	Div 1	Leicester A	3-0	Crooks, Mabbutt, Stevens
14 Sept	UEFA 1	Drogheda A	6-0	Falco 2, Crooks, Galvin, Mabbutt 2
17 Sept	Div 1	Everton H	1-2	Falco
24 Sept	Div 1	Watford A	3-2	Hoddle, Archibald, Hughton

28 Sept	UEFA 1	Drogheda H	8-0	Falco 2, Roberts 2, Brazil 2, Archibald, Hughton
2 Oct	Div 1	Nottingham F H	2-1	Stevens, Archibald
5 Oct	FL Cup 2	Lincoln H	3-1	Archibald, O.G., Galvin
15 Oct	Div 1	Wolves A	3-2	Archibald 2, Falco
19 Oct	UEFA 2	Feyenoord H	4-2	Archibald 2, Galvin 2
22 Oct	Div 1	Birmingham A	1-0	Archibald
26 Oct	FL Cup 2	Lincoln A	1-2	Falco
29 Oct	Div 1	Notts County H	1-0	Archibald
2 Nov	UEFA 2	Feyenoord A	2-0	Hughton, Galvin
5 Nov	Div 1	Stoke A	1-1	Falco
9 Nov	FL Cup 3	Arsenal H	1-2	Hoddle
12 Nov	Div 1	Liverpool H	2-2	Archibald, Hoddle
19 Nov	Div 1	Luton A	4-2	Cooke, Archibald 2, Dick
23 Nov	UEFA 3	Bayern Munich A	0-1	
26 Nov	Div 1	QPR H	3-2	Falco 2, Archibald
3 Dec	Div 1	Norwich A	1-2	Dick
7 Dec	UEFA 3	Bayern Munich H	2-0	Archibald, Falco
10 Dec	Div 1	Southampton H	0-0	
16 Dec	Div 1	Manchester U A	2-4	Brazil, Falco
26 Dec	Div 1	Arsenal H	2-4	Roberts, Archibald
27 Dec	Div 1	Aston Villa A	0-0	
31 Dec	Div 1	West Ham A	1-4	Stevens
2 Jan	Div 1	Watford H	2-3	Hughton, Hoddle
7 Jan	FA Cup 3	Fulham A	0-0	
11 Jan	FA Cup 3R	Fulham H	2-0	Roberts, Archibald
14 Jan	Div 1	Ipswich H	2-0	Roberts, Falco
21 Jan	Div 1	Everton A	1-2	Archibald
28 Jan	FA Cup 4	Norwich H	0-0	
1 Feb	FA Cup 4R	Norwich A	1-2	Falco
4 Feb	Div 1	Nottingham F A	2-2	Falco, Hughton
8 Feb	Div 1	Sunderland H	3-0	Archibald 2, Perryman
11 Feb	Div 1	Leicester H	3-2	Falco, Galvin, Archibald
21 Feb	Div 1	Notts County A	0-0	
25 Feb	Div 1	Birmingham H	0-1	
3 Mar	Div 1	Stoke H	1-0	Falco
7 Mar	UEFA QF	Austria Vienna H	2-0	Archibald, Brazil

10 Mar	Div 1	Liverpool A	1-3	Stevens
17 Mar	Div 1	West Brom H	0-1	
21 Mar	UEFA QF	Austria Vienna A	2-2	Brazil, Ardiles
24 Mar	Div 1	Coventry A	4-2	Brazil 2, Roberts, Hazard
31 Mar	Div 1	Wolves H	1-0	Hazard
7 Apr	Div 1	Sunderland A	1-1	Falco
11 Apr	UEFA SF	Hajduk Split A	1-2	Falco
14 Apr	Div 1	Luton H	2-1	Roberts, Falco
18 Apr	Div 1	Aston Villa H	2-1	Mabbutt, Roberts
21 Apr	Div 1	Arsenal A	2-3	Archibald 2
25 Apr	UEFA SF	Hajduk Split H	1-0	Hazard
28 Apr	Div 1	QPR A	1-2	Archibald
5 May	Div 1	Norwich H	2-0	Falco, Archibald
7 May	Div 1	Southampton A	0-5	
9 May	UEFA F	Anderlecht A	1-1	Miller
12 May	Div 1	Manchester U H	1-1	Archibald
23 May	UEFA F	Anderlecht H	1-1	Roberts (won 4-3 pens)

84/85

25 Aug	Div 1	Everton A	4-1	Falco, C Allen 2, Chiedozie
27 Aug	Div 1	Leicester H	2-2	Roberts 2
1 Sept	Div 1	Norwich H	3-1	Galvin, Chiedozie, Falco
4 Sept	Div 1	Sunderland A	0-1	
8 Sept	Div 1	Sheffield W A	1-2	Falco
15 Sept	Div 1	QPR H	5-0	Falco 2, C Allen 2, Hazard
19 Sept	UEFA 1	Sporting Braga A	3-0	Falco 2, Galvin
22 Sept	Div 1	Aston Villa A	1-0	Chiedozie
26 Sept	FL Cup 2	Halifax A	5-1	Falco 2, Crooks 3
29 Sept	Div 1	Luton H	4-2	Hazard, Perryman, Falco, Roberts
3 Oct	UEFA 1	Sporting Braga H	6-0	Stevens, Hughton, Crooks 3, Falco
6 Oct	Div 1	Southampton A	0-1	
9 Oct	FL Cup 2	Halifax H	4-0	Hazard 2, Hughton, Crooks
12 Oct	Div 1	Liverpool H	1-0	Crooks
20 Oct	Div 1	Manchester U A	0-1	
24 Oct	UEFA 2	Club Brugge A	1-2	C Allen

27 Oct	Div 1	Stoke H	4-0	C Allen 2, Chiedozie, Roberts
31 Oct	FL Cup 3	Liverpool H	1-0	C Allen
3 Nov	Div 1	West Brom H	2-3	Hazard, Chiedozie
7 Nov	UEFA 2	Club Brugge H	3-0	Hazard, C Allen, Roberts
10 Nov	Div 1	Nottingham F A	2-1	Hazard, Galvin
17 Nov	Div 1	Ipswich A	3-0	Mabbutt, Hoddle, C Allen
21 Nov	FL Cup 4	Sunderland A	0-0	
24 Nov	Div 1	Chelsea H	1-1	Falco
28 Nov	UEFA 3	Bohemians H	2-0	O.G., Stevens
1 Dec	Div 1	Coventry A	1-1	Falco
5 Dec	FL CUP4 R	Sunderland H	1-2	Roberts
8 Dec	Div 1	Newcastle H	3-1	Roberts, Falco 2
12 Dec	UEFA 3	Bohemians A	1-1	Falco
15 Dec	Div 1	Watford A	2-1	Falco, Crooks
22 Dec	Div 1	Norwich A	2-1	Crooks, Galvin
26 Dec	Div 1	West Ham H	2-2	Mabbutt, Crooks
29 Dec	Div 1	Sunderland H	2-0	Hoddle, Crooks
1 Jan	Div 1	Arsenal A	2-1	Falco, Crooks
5 Jan	FA Cup 3	Charlton H	1-1	Crooks
12 Jan	Div 1	QPR A	2-2	Crooks, Falco
23 Jan	FA Cup 3R	Charlton A	2-1	Falco, Galvin
27 Jan	FA Cup 4	Liverpool A	0-1	
2 Feb	Div 1	Luton A	2-2	Falco, Roberts
23 Feb	Div 1	West Brom A	1-0	Falco
2 Mar	Div 1	Stoke A	1-0	Crooks
6 Mar	UEFA QF	Real Madrid H	0-1	
12 Mar	Div 1	Manchester U H	1-2	Falco
16 Mar	Div 1	Liverpool A	1-0	Crooks
20 Mar	UEFA QF	Real Madrid A	0-0	
23 Mar	Div 1	Southampton H	5-1	Ardiles, Hoddle, Falco, Crooks, Brooke
30 Mar	Div 1	Aston Villa H	0-2	
3 Apr	Div 1	Everton H	1-2	Roberts
6 Apr	Div 1	West Ham A	1-1	Ardiles
13 Apr	Div 1	Leicester A	2-1	Hoddle, Falco
17 Apr	Div 1	Arsenal H	0-2	
20 Apr	Div 1	Ipswich H	2-3	Leworthy 2

27 Apr	Div 1	Chelsea A	1-1	Galvin
4 May	Div 1	Coventry H	4-2	Falco 2, Hoddle, Hughton
6 May	Div 1	Newcastle A	3-2	Leworthy, Hoddle, Crook
11 May	Div 1	Watford H	1-5	Hoddle
14 May	Div 1	Sheffield W H	2-0	Falco, Hoddle
17 May	Div 1	Nottingham F H	1-0	Falco

85/86

17 Aug	Div 1	Watford H	4-0	Waddle 2, P Allen, Falco
21 Aug	Div 1	Oxford A	1-1	D Thomas
24 Aug	Div 1	Ipswich A	0-1	
26 Aug	Div 1	Everton H	0-1	
31 Aug	Div 1	Man City A	1-2	Miller
4 Sept	Div 1	Chelsea H	4-1	Roberts, Miller, Chiedozie, Falco
7 Sept	Div 1	Newcastle H	5-1	Falco, Chiedozie 2, Hoddle, Hazard
14 Sept	Div 1	Nottingham F A	1-0	Hughton
21 Sept	Div 1	Sheffield W H	5-1	Waddle 2, Falco 2, Hoddle
23 Sept	FL Cup 2	Orient A	0-2	
28 Sept	Div 1	Liverpool A	1-4	Chiedozie
2 Oct	Super Cup	Southampton H	2-1	Falco 2
5 Oct	Div 1	West Brom A	1-1	Waddle
20 Oct	Div 1	Coventry A	3-2	Hoddle, Falco, Chiedozie
26 Oct	Div 1	Leicester H	1-3	Falco
30 Oct	FL Cup 2	Orient H	4-0	Roberts 2, Galvin, Waddle
2 Nov	Div 1	Southampton A	0-1	
6 Nov	FL Cup 3	Wimbledon H	2-0	Mabbutt, Leworthy
9 Nov	Div 1	Luton H	1-3	Cooke
16 Nov	Div 1	Manchester U A	0-0	
20 Nov	FL Cup 4	Portsmouth H	0-0	
23 Nov	Div 1	QPR H	1-1	Mabbutt
27 Nov	FL Cup 4R	Portsmouth A	0-0	
30 Nov	Div 1	Aston Villa A	2-1	Mabbutt, Falco
3 Dec	Super Cup	Liverpool A	0-2	
7 Dec	Div 1	Oxford H	5-1	C Allen 2, Falco, Hoddle, Waddle
10 Dec	FL Cup 4R2	Portsmouth A	0-1	
14 Dec	Div 1	Watford A	0-1	

17 Dec	Super Cup	Southampton A	3-1	Falco, C Allen, Leworthy
21 Dec	Div 1	Ipswich H	2-0	C Allen, Hoddle
26 Dec	Div 1	West Ham H	1-0	Perryman
28 Dec	Div 1	Chelsea A	0-2	
1 Jan	Div 1	Arsenal A	0-0	
4 Jan	FA Cup 3	Oxford A	1-1	Chiedozie
8 Jan	FA Cup 3R	Oxford H	2-1	Waddle, C Allen
11 Jan	Div 1	Nottingham F H	0-3	
14 Jan	Super Cup	Liverpool H	0-3	
18 Jan	Div 1	Man City H	0-2	
25 Jan	FA Cup 4	Notts County A	1-1	C Allen
29 Jan	FA Cup 4R	Notts County H	5-0	Chiedozie, C Allen, Falco, Waddle, Hoddle
1 Feb	Div 1	Everton A	0-1	
5 Feb	Super Cup SF	Everton H	0-0	
8 Feb	Div 1	Coventry H	0-1	
22 Feb	Div 1	Sheffield W A	2-1	Chiedozie, Howells
2 Mar	Div 1	Liverpool H	1-2	Waddle
4 Mar	FA Cup 5	Everton H	1-2	Falco
8 Mar	Div 1	West Brom H	5-0	Mabbutt, Falco 2, Galvin, Waddle
15 Mar	Div 1	Birmingham A	2-1	Stevens, Waddle
19 Mar	Super Cup SF	Everton A	1-3	Falco
22 Mar	Div 1	Newcastle A	2-2	Hoddle, Waddle
29 Mar	Div 1	Arsenal H	1-0	Stevens
31 Mar	Div 1	West Ham A	1-2	Ardiles
5 Apr	Div 1	Leicester A	4-1	Falco 3, Bowen
12 Apr	Div 1	Luton A	1-1	C Allen
16 Apr	Div 1	Birmingham H	2-0	Falco, Chiedozie
19 Apr	Div 1	Manchester U H	0-0	
26 Apr	Div 1	QPR A	5-2	C Allen 2, Falco 2, Hoddle
3 May	Div 1	Aston Villa H	4-2	Falco 2, C Allen 2
5 May	Div 1	Southampton H	5-3	Waddle, Galvin 3, C Allen

86/87

23 Aug	Div 1	Aston Villa A	3-0	C Allen 3
25 Aug	Div 1	Newcastle H	1-1	C Allen
30 Aug	Div 1	Man City H	1-0	Roberts
2 Sept	Div 1	Southampton A	0-2	
6 Sept	Div 1	Arsenal A	0-0	
13 Sept	Div 1	Chelsea H	1-3	C Allen
20 Sept	Div 1	Leicester A	2-1	C Allen 2
23 Sept	FL Cup 2	Barnsley A	3-2	Waddle, Roberts, C Allen
27 Sept	Div 1	Everton H	2-0	C Allen 2
4 Oct	Div 1	Luton H	0-0	
8 Oct	FL Cup 2	Barnsley H	5-3	Close, Hoddle 2, Galvin, C Allen
11 Oct	Div 1	Liverpool A	1-0	C Allen
18 Oct	Div 1	Sheffield W H	1-1	C Allen
25 Oct	Div 1	QPR A	0-2	
29 Oct	FL Cup 3	Birmingham H	5-0	Waddle, C Allen 2, Roberts, Hoddle
1 Nov	Div 1	Wimbledon H	1-2	M Thomas
8 Nov	Div 1	Norwich A	1-2	Claesen
15 Nov	Div 1	Coventry H	1-0	C Allen
22 Nov	Div 1	Oxford A	4-2	C Allen 2, Waddle 2
26 Nov	FL Cup 4	Cambridge A	3-1	C Allen, Close, Waddle
29 Nov	Div 1	Nottingham F H	2-3	C Allen 2
7 Dec	Div 1	Manchester U A	3-3	Mabbutt, O.G., C Allen
13 Dec	Div 1	Watford H	2-1	Hoddle, Gough
20 Dec	Div 1	Chelsea A	2-0	C Allen 2
26 Dec	Div 1	West Ham H	4-0	C Allen 2, Hodge, Waddle
27 Dec	Div 1	Coventry A	3-4	C Allen 2, Claesen
1 Jan	Div 1	Charlton A	2-0	Claesen, Galvin
4 Jan	Div 1	Arsenal H	1-2	M Thomas
10 Jan	FA Cup 3	Scunthorpe H	3-2	Mabbutt, Claesen, Waddle
24 Jan	Div 1	Aston Villa H	3-0	Hodge 2, Claesen
27 Jan	FL Cup 5	West Ham A	1-1	C Allen
31 Jan	FA Cup 4	Crystal Palace H	4-0	Mabbutt, O.G., C Allen, Claesen
2 Feb	FL Cup 5R	West Ham H	5-0	Claesen, Hoddle, C Allen 3
8 Feb	FL Cup SF1	Arsenal A	1-0	C Allen
14 Feb	Div 1	Southampton H	2-0	Gough, Hodge
21 Feb	FA Cup 5	Newcastle H	1-0	C Allen

25 Feb	Div 1	Leicester H	5-0	Claesen 2, C Allen 2, P Allen
1 Mar	FL Cup SF2	Arsenal H	1-2	C Allen
4 Mar	FL Cup SFR	Arsenal H	1-2	C Allen
7 Mar	Div 1	QPR H	1-0	C Allen
15 Mar	FA Cup QF	Wimbledon A	2-0	Waddle, Hoddle
22 Mar	Div 1	Liverpool H	1-0	Waddle
25 Mar	Div 1	Newcastle A	1-1	Hoddle
28 Mar	Div 1	Luton A	1-3	Waddle
4 Apr	Div 1	Norwich H	3-0	C Allen 3
7 Apr	Div 1	Sheffield W A	1-0	C Allen
11 Apr	FA Cup SF	Watford	4-1	Hodge 2, C Allen, P Allen
15 Apr	Div 1	Man City A	1-1	Claesen
18 Apr	Div 1	Charlton H	1-0	C Allen
20 Apr	Div 1	West Ham A	1-2	C Allen
22 Apr	Div 1	Wimbledon A	2-2	Claesen, Bowen
25 Apr	Div 1	Oxford H	3-1	Waddle, P Allen, Hoddle
2 May	Div 1	Nottingham F A	0-2	
4 May	Div 1	Manchester U H	4-0	M Thomas 2, C Allen, P Allen
9 May	Div 1	Watford A	0-1	
11 May	Div 1	Everton A	0-1	
16 May	FA Cup F	Coventry	2-3	C Allen, Mabbutt

87/88

15 Aug	Div 1	Coventry A	1-2	Mabbutt
19 Aug	Div 1	Newcastle H	3-1	C Allen, Waddle, Hodge
22 Aug	Div 1	Chelsea H	1-0	Claesen
29 Aug	Div 1	Watford A	1-1	C Allen
1 Sept	Div 1	Oxford H	3-0	Claesen 2, C Allen
5 Sept	Div 1	Everton A	0-0	
12 Sept	Div 1	Southampton H	2-1	Claesen, C Allen
19 Sept	Div 1	West Ham A	1-0	Fairclough
23 Sept	FL Cup 2	Torquay A	0-1	
26 Sept	Div 1	Manchester U A	0-1	
3 Oct	Div 1	Sheffield W H	2-0	P Allen, Claesen
7 Oct	FL Cup 2	Torquay H	3-0	Claesen 2, O.G.
10 Oct	Div 1	Norwich A	1-2	Claesen
18 Oct	Div 1	Arsenal H	1-2	Claesen

24 Oct	Div 1	Nottingham F A	0-3	
28 Oct	FL Cup 3	Aston Villa A	1-2	Ardiles
31 Oct	Div 1	Wimbledon H	0-3	
4 Nov	Div 1	Portsmouth A	0-0	
14 Nov	Div 1	QPR H	1-1	P Allen
21 Nov	Div 1	Luton A	0-2	
28 Nov	Div 1	Liverpool H	0-2	
13 Dec	Div 1	Charlton H	0-1	
20 Dec	Div 1	Derby A	2-1	Claesen, C Allen
26 Dec	Div 1	Southampton A	1-2	Fairclough
28 Dec	Div 1	West Ham H	2-1	Waddle, Fairclough
1 Jan	Div 1	Watford H	2-1	C Allen, Moran
2 Jan	Div 1	Chelsea A	0-0	
9 Jan	FA Cup 3	Oldham A	4-2	C Allen 2, M Thomas, Waddle
16 Jan	Div 1	Coventry H	2-2	C Allen 2
23 Jan	Div 1	Newcastle A	0-2	
30 Jan	FA Cup 4	Port Vale A	1-2	Ruddock
13 Feb	Div 1	Oxford A	0-0	
23 Feb	Div 1	Manchester U H	1-1	C Allen
27 Feb	Div 1	Sheffield W A	3-0	C Allen, Claesen, P Allen
1 Mar	Div 1	Derby H	0-0	
6 Mar	Div 1	Arsenal A	1-2	C Allen
9 Mar	Div 1	Everton H	2-1	Fairclough, Walsh
12 Mar	Div 1	Norwich A	1-3	Claesen
19 Mar	Div 1	Wimbledon A	0-3	
26 Mar	Div 1	Nottingham F H	1-1	O.G.
2 Apr	Div 1	Portsmouth H	0-1	
4 Apr	Div 1	QPR A	0-2	
23 Apr	Div 1	Liverpool A	0-1	
2 May	Div 1	Charlton A	1-1	Hodge
4 May	Div 1	Luton H	2-1	Hodge, Mabbutt

88/89

3 Sept	Div 1	Newcastle A	2-2	Waddle, Fenwick
10 Sept	Div 1	Arsenal H	2-3	Waddle, Gascoigne
17 Sept	Div 1	Liverpool A	1-1	Fenwick
24 Sept	Div 1	Middlesbrough A	3-2	Waddle, Howells, Fenwick
27 Sept	FL Cup 2	Notts County A	1-1	Samways
1 Oct	Div 1	Manchester U H	2-2	Waddle, Walsh
8 Oct	Div 1	Charlton A	2-2	Fenwick, P Allen
11 Oct	FL Cup 2	Notts County H	2-1	Fenwick, Gascoigne
22 Oct	Div 1	Norwich A	1-3	Fairclough
25 Oct	Div 1	Southampton H	1-2	O.G.
29 Oct	Div 1	Aston Villa A	1-2	Fenwick
1 Nov	FL Cup 3	Blackburn H	0-0	
5 Nov	Div 1	Derby H	1-3	Stewart
9 Nov	FL Cup 3R	Blackburn A	2-1	M Thomas, Stewart
12 Nov	Div 1	Wimbledon H	3-2	Fenwick, Butters, Samways
20 Nov	Div 1	Sheffield W A	2-0	Stewart 2
23 Nov	Div 1	Coventry H	1-1	Stewart
26 Nov	Div 1	QPR H	2-2	Gascoigne, Waddle
29 Nov	FL Cup 4	Southampton A	1-2	O.G.
3 Dec	Div 1	Everton A	0-1	
10 Dec	Div 1	Millwall H	2-0	Waddle, Gascoigne
17 Dec	Div 1	West Ham A	2-0	Mabbutt, M Thomas
26 Dec	Div 1	Luton H	0-0	
31 Dec	Div 1	Newcastle H	2-0	Waddle, Walsh
2 Jan	Div 1	Arsenal A	0-2	
7 Jan	FA Cup 3	Bradford A	0-1	
15 Jan	Div 1	Nottingham F H	1-2	Waddle
21 Jan	Div 1	Middlesbrough A	2-2	Stewart 2
5 Feb	Div 1	Manchester U A	0-1	
11 Feb	Div 1	Charlton H	1-1	Stewart
21 Feb	Div 1	Norwich H	2-1	Gascoigne, Waddle
25 Feb	Div 1	Southampton A	2-0	Waddle, Nayim
1 Mar	Div 1	Aston Villa H	2-0	Waddle 2
11 Mar	Div 1	Derby A	1-1	Gascoigne
18 Mar	Div 1	Coventry A	1-1	Waddle
22 Mar	Div 1	Nottingham F A	2-1	Howells, Samways

26 Mar	Div 1	Liverpool H	1-2	Fenwick
28 Mar	Div 1	Luton A	3-1	Howells, Walsh, Gascoigne
1 Apr	Div 1	West Ham H	3-0	Nayim, Fenwick, Stewart
12 Apr	Div 1	Sheffield W H	0-0	
15 Apr	Div 1	Wimbledon A	2-1	Stewart, Waddle
22 Apr	Div 1	Everton H	2-1	Walsh 2
29 Apr	Div 1	Millwall A	5-0	Walsh, Stewart 3, Samways
13 May	Div 1	QPR A	0-1	

89/90

19 Aug	Div 1	Luton H	2-1	Stewart, P Allen
22 Aug	Div 1	Everton A	1-2	P Allen
26 Aug	Div 1	Manchester C A	1-1	Gascoigne
9 Sept	Div 1	Aston Villa A	0-2	
16 Sept	Div 1	Chelsea H	1-4	Gascoigne
20 Sept	FL Cup 2	Southend H	1-0	Fenwick
23 Sept	Div 1	Norwich A	2-2	Gascoigne, Lineker
30 Sept	Div 1	QPR H	3-2	Lineker 3
4 Oct	FL Cup 2	Southend A	2-3	P Allen, Nayim
14 Oct	Div 1	Charlton A	3-1	M Thomas, Lineker, Gascoigne
18 Oct	Div 1	Arsenal H	2-1	Samways, Walsh
21 Oct	Div 1	Sheffield W H	3-0	Lineker 2, Moran
25 Oct	FL Cup 3	Manchester U A	3-0	Lineker, Samways, Nayim
29 Oct	Div 1	Liverpool A	0-1	
4 Nov	Div 1	Southampton A	1-1	Gascoigne
11 Nov	Div 1	Wimbledon H	0-1	
18 Nov	Div 1	Crystal Palace A	3-2	Howells, Lineker, Samways
22 Nov	FL Cup 4	Tranmere A	2-2	Gascoigne, O.G.
25 Nov	Div 1	Derby H	1-2	Stewart
29 Nov	FL Cup 4R	Tranmere H	4-0	Howells, Stewart, Mabbutt, P Allen
2 Dec	Div 1	Luton A	0-0	
9 Dec	Div 1	Everton H	2-1	Lineker, Stewart
16 Dec	Div 1	Manchester U A	1-0	Lineker
26 Dec	Div 1	Millwall H	3-1	Samways, O.G., Lineker
30 Dec	Div 1	Nottingham F H	2-3	Lineker 2
1 Jan	Div 1	Coventry A	0-0	
6 Jan	FA Cup 3	Southampton H	1-3	Howells

13 Jan	Div 1	Manchester C H	1-1	Howells
17 Jan	FL Cup 5	Nottingham F A	2-2	Lineker, Sedgley
20 Jan	Div 1	Arsenal A	0-1	
24 Jan	FL Cup 5R	Nottingham F H	2-3	Nayim, Walsh
4 Feb	Div 1	Norwich H	4-0	Lineker 3, Howells
10 Feb	Div 1	Chelsea A	2-1	Howells, Lineker
21 Feb	Div 1	Aston Villa H	0-2	
24 Feb	Div 1	Derby A	1-2	Moncur
3 Mar	Div 1	Crystal Palace H	0-1	
10 Mar	Div 1	Charlton H	3-0	J Polston, Lineker, Howells
17 Mar	Div 1	QPR A	1-3	Walsh
21 Mar	Div 1	Liverpool H	1-0	Stewart
31 Mar	Div 1	Sheffield W A	4-2	P Allen, Lineker 2, Stewart
7 Apr	Div 1	Nottingham F A	3-1	Stewart, P Allen 2
14 Apr	Div 1	Coventry H	3-2	Lineker 2, Stewart
16 Apr	Div 1	Millwall A	1-0	Lineker
21 Apr	Div 1	Manchester U H	2-1	Gascoigne, Lineker
28 Apr	Div 1	Wimbledon A	0-1	
5 May	Div 1	Southampton H	2-1	Stewart, P Allen